BROUGHT TO YOU
SUPERKID ACADEMY
A SIMPLE GUIDE FOR HOME USE

THE SUPERKID CREED

BIBLE STUDY FOR KIDS!

Ordinary kids doing extraordinary things through the power of God's Word!

ISBN 978-1-60463-328-3   30-1070

Superkid Academy Home Bible Study for Kids—The Superkid Creed

© 2011, 2016 Eagle Mountain International Church Inc. aka Kenneth Copeland Ministries

Kenneth Copeland Publications
Fort Worth, TX 76192-0001

For more information about Kenneth Copeland Ministries, call 1-800-600-7395 (U.S. only) or +1-817-852-6000 or visit kcm.org.

SuperkidAcademy.com • 1-800-606-4190

TABLE OF CONTENTS

WELCOME!

Dear Parent/Teacher,

I believe you will experience great and exciting things as you begin the faith adventure of *Superkid Academy Home Bible Study for Kids—The Superkid Creed.*

As you launch into this faith-building time with your family or small group, take the opportunity to seek the Lord's direction about how to minister these lessons for maximum impact. God's Word does not return to Him void, and He will see to it that your children are BLESSED and grow strong in faith as you step out in His Anointing to teach them about Him.

Please keep in mind that we are praying for you. We believe and release our faith for a powerful anointing on you as you teach and impart His wisdom, and that your Superkids are strong in the Lord and mighty for Him.

Remember, we here at Academy Headquarters want to be a resource for you. Make sure you are in our contact base so we can keep in touch. And, let us know how we can better serve you and your Superkids.

We love you and look forward to hearing from you!

Love,

Commander Kellie

Commander Kellie

We are excited that you have brought Superkid Academy into your living room with the Home Bible Study for Kids! This powerful, Bible-based curriculum will guide your children into building a strong, personal relationship with the Lord and inspire them to live an extraordinary, faith-filled life.

Each of the 13 weeks included in this study provide five days of lessons, including a:

- **Lesson Introduction From Commander Kellie:** As the creator of Superkid Academy with more than 20 years' experience ministering to children, Kellie Copeland has a unique anointing and perspective for reaching children with the uncompromised Word of God. She passes on her wisdom through these timeless segments.
- **Lesson Outline:** Each lesson contains three main points, subpoints and supporting scriptures to empower you to clearly communicate the truth to your children.
- **Memory Verse:** Throughout the week, your kids will have the opportunity to memorize and understand a scripture. More than that, they'll learn how to apply it directly to their lives.
- **Bible Lesson:** Each Bible Lesson reinforces the memory verse and the principle behind it. Discussion questions will help you lead your children through not only comprehending the passage of Scripture, but also giving it meaning in their lives.
- **Giving Lesson:** Each week, you will have the opportunity to teach your children about the importance of tithing and giving so they can be "blessed to be a blessing" in the Body of Christ.
- **Game Time:** Reinforces the message and gives families an occasion to celebrate what they've learned in a fun way.
- **Activity Page:** Reinforces the lesson through acrostics, word searches, mazes and other activities.
- **Supplements:** Support the memory verse and lesson—two will be provided each week, including:
  - ° **Object Lesson:** Illustrates the focus of the lesson and provides visual and hands-on elements to the teaching.
  - ° **Real Deal:** Highlights a historical person, place or event that illustrates the current lesson's theme.
  - ° **Storybook Theater and You-Solve-It Myserties:** Reinforces the message with creative, read-aloud stories.
  - ° **Food Fun:** Takes you and your children into the kitchen where you will discuss, illustrate and experience God's truth, using everyday items.
  - ° **Academy Lab:** Brings the lesson and science together.

And, don't forget the enclosed Praise and Worship CD! These original, upbeat, kid-friendly songs put the Word in your children's minds and hearts. The CD can be listened to around the house or in the car, and the karaoke, sing-along tracks allow your kids to sing their favorite songs.

Making the Curriculum Work for Your Family

Superkid Academy's Home Bible Study for Kids gives you the flexibility to teach your children in a way that works for you. Each week's lesson is divided into five days of teaching. However, we understand that no two families—or their schedules—are the same, so feel free to adjust the lessons to meet your needs. Use all five days of lessons or select only a few to cover each week. Whether you're using the curriculum as part of your home school, as a boost to your family devotions or in a weekly small group, you have the flexibility to make it work for you.

A Homeschool Bible Curriculum

Superkid Academy's Home Bible Study for Kids is easy to use, flexible and interactive—no dry Bible lessons here! It is ideal for a variety of learning styles. Each of the 13 weeks contains five days of lessons—one Bible Lesson, one Giving Lesson, one Game Time and two other lessons or stories to support the week's message. You may choose to use all five days of lessons or pick and choose the ones that work best for your educational structure. Optional variations for several of the lessons have been included to meet a variety of needs.

Each week's Snapshot provides the type lessons and a list of supplies needed for that week, allowing you to easily prepare and customize each week's lessons. Here are just a few additional ideas for customizing for your home school:

- Re-read the Bible passage each day throughout the week to give your children—and you—time to meditate on the highlighted scripture
- Use one or more of the discussion questions as a journaling exercise
- Begin a weekly, family Game Night
- Use the Storybook Theater in your nighttime read-aloud routine

Family Devotions

Superkid Academy's Home Bible Study for Kids empowers you to disciple your children and teach them the Word of God in an easy, fun way. You may choose to use all five days' worth of lessons, or select only a few. Each lesson takes less than 15 minutes, so the curriculum fits easily into your busy life.

Lessons are numbered 1-5, giving you the flexibility to include whichever lesson fits your daily schedule for that week. This allows you freedom to plan around work schedules, church commitments and extracurricular activities. Here are two sample schedules:

5-Day Schedule

Sunday—Church (no lesson)

Monday—Bible Lesson

Tuesday—Object Lesson

Wednesday—Midweek services (no lesson)

Thursday—Giving Lesson

Friday—Storybook Theater

Saturday—Game Time

3-Day Schedule

Sunday—Church (no lesson)

Monday— Bible Lesson

Tuesday—Soccer practice (no lesson)

Wednesday—Giving Lesson

Thursday—Soccer practice (no lesson)

Friday—Object Lesson

Saturday—Family time (no lesson)

A Weekly Small Group

Superkid Academy's Home Bible Study for Kids is designed for use over several days, but a week's worth of lessons can easily be consolidated for a small group. Simply choose the lessons that work best for your location and schedule and allow additional time for discussion and prayer.

Sample Small Group Schedule

6 p.m.	Bible Lesson with discussion time
6:30 p.m.	Giving Lesson
6:45 p.m.	Object Lesson and prayer time
7:15 p.m.	Game Time
7:45 p.m.	Refreshments
8 p.m.	Closing

Thank you again for implementing Superkid Academy's Home Bible Study for Kids. We stand with you in faith as you disciple your children in the things that matter to Him. Proverbs 22:6 *(KJV)* says, "Train up a child in the way he should go: and when he is old, he will not depart from it." At Superkid Academy, we are confident that God will bless your efforts, and that you and your children will see the reality of THE BLESSING in all you do (Numbers 6:24-26).

Love,

Commander Kellie

Commander Kellie

HEALTH & SAFETY DISCLAIMER FOR "SUPERKID ACADEMY CURRICULUM"

Superkid Academy is a ministry of Eagle Mountain International Church, aka Kenneth Copeland Ministries (hereafter "EMIC"). The "Superkid Academy Curriculum" (hereafter "SKA Curriculum") provides age-appropriate teaching material to be used in the religious instruction of children. The SKA Curriculum includes physical activities in which children and leaders may participate. Before engaging in any of the physical activities, participants should be in good physical condition as determined by their health care provider. EMIC is not responsible for injuries resulting from the implementation of activities suggested within the SKA Curriculum. Prior to implementing the SKA Curriculum, carefully review your organization's safety and health policies, and determine whether the SKA Curriculum is appropriate for your organization's intended use.

By purchasing the SKA Curriculum, I, individually and/or as authorized representative for my organization, hereby agree to release, defend, hold harmless, and covenant not to sue EMIC, its officers, deacons, ministers, directors, employees, volunteers, contractors, staff, affiliates, agents and attorneys (collectively, the "EMIC Parties"), and the property of EMIC for any claim, including claims for negligence and gross negligence of any one or more of the EMIC Parties, arising out of my use or organization's use of and participation in the SKA Curriculum, participation in the suggested activities contained within the SKA Curriculum, or resulting from first-aid treatment or services rendered as a result of or in connection with the activities or participation in the activities.

WEEK 1: THE SUPERKID CREED

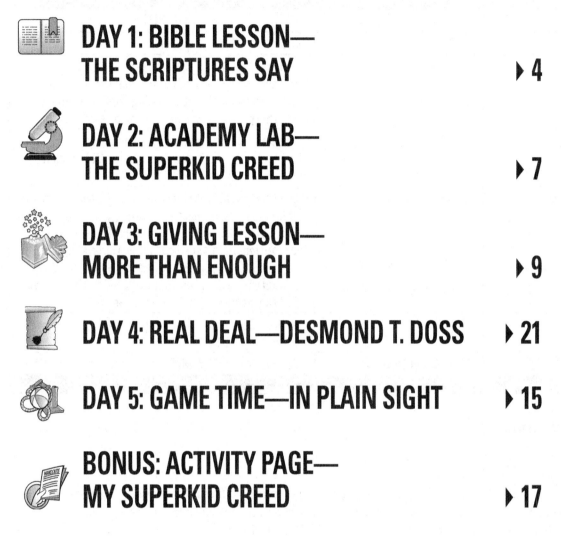
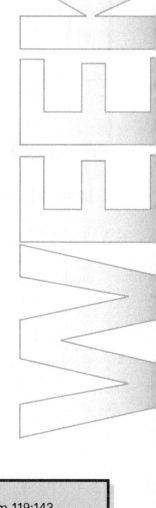

 Memory Verse: As pressure and stress bear down on me, I find joy in your commands.—Psalm 119:143

WEEK 1: SNAPSHOT — THE SUPERKID CREED

DAY	TYPE OF LESSON	LESSON TITLE	SUPPLIES
Day 1	Bible Lesson	The Scriptures Say	Dictionary, Bible, pen, paper
Day 2	Academy Lab	The Superkid Creed	1 Tall (at least 1 liter) clear plastic water bottle, Picture/drawing to tape to the back of the water bottle, Pen cap with a pocket clip, Paper clip, Poster tack, Thin plastic army man (not too heavy), Tape
Day 3	Giving Lesson	More Than Enough	Picnic basket, Loaf of bread, 2 Cans of tuna, Mayonnaise, Bowl, Spoon, Can opener, Butter knife, Plate
Day 4	Real Deal	Desmond T. Doss	U.S. Army Medal of Honor (replica or picture), Pictures of Desmond T. Doss' military company, Map of Okinawa, Picture of Hacksaw Ridge, Desmond T. Doss comic book (optional), Optional costume: United States Army outfit (Army-green slacks and shirt), White armband with a red cross (sign of a medic) and a green U.S. Army helmet with a medic cross on it
Day 5	Game Time	In Plain Sight	Blindfold, Soccer ball, Duct tape, Small prizes for participants (optional)
Bonus	Activity Page	My Superkid Creed	1 Copy for each child, Bibles

Lesson Introduction:

Today's lesson could change your Superkids' lives forever!

Wow, that's a BIG statement—but true. The way we <u>think</u> is the determining factor for everything. If we can teach our kids to put aside the way they think and begin to think like God, they will live the life God planned for them—THE BLESSING. At Superkid Academy we call it THE SWEET LIFE!

For the next few weeks, we will focus on showing your Superkids what a creed is and why they need one. The Superkid Creed is straight from the Word of God. It's a mission statement that works as a reminder about how every Superkid should choose to live his or her everyday life. There is a lot of pressure on kids today, but when the Creed—God's Word—is in their hearts, it will help them do what's right. The result? The Sweet Life!

Love,

Commander Kellie

Commander Kellie

Lesson Outline:

This week, your children will learn about their Superkid Creed. It's important to show your Superkids that having a creed will help make their lives *good*—and much LESS COMPLICATED. That's why the Psalmist said, "I find joy in your commands" (Psalm 119:143). This is because when we know what God's Word says, we can always make the best decisions and avoid the enemy's evil traps.

It's important that you understand how the Creed can help your Superkids, not as a tool for condemnation, but as a guide to living the best life possible (Ephesians 3:19-21).

I. GOD WANTS US TO DO THINGS HIS WAY, NOT OUR OWN WAY
Proverbs 3:5-6

  a. *Way*—how you think and react, how you do things.

  b. If you obey the Lord, you'll be blessed! Deuteronomy 28:1-14

  c. When we do things God's way, The Sweet Life is the result! Proverbs 3:1-8

II. WHAT IS A CREED?

  a. *Creed*—a system or formula of belief.

  b. We believe in God's way of doing things.

  c. The Superkid Creed is a list of decisions we make that come from God's Word.

III. THE WORD OF GOD IS JESUS' CREED

  a. Jesus had already decided to be led by God and do things His way. Matthew 3:15, 4:1

  b. When Jesus was under pressure to do things Satan's (or the world's) way, the Word came out of His mouth. Matthew 4:1-11

  c. When you are under pressure, the Word of God in your heart will help you. Psalm 119:143

  d. When you say the Superkid Creed, you are declaring your decision to do things God's way, no matter what the circumstances are. Hey, you're just like Jesus!

Notes: _____

_____

_____

_____

_____

_____

DAY 1: BIBLE LESSON **THE SCRIPTURES SAY**

 Memory Verse: As pressure and stress bear down on me, I find joy in your commands. —Psalm 119:143

Supplies: ■ Dictionary, ■ Bible, ■ Pen and paper or chalkboard

"The Scriptures say…" is how Jesus began every reply to Satan when He was being tempted in the wilderness. Jesus knew the right responses when He was older because He began putting God's Word into His heart at an early age. When tempted by Satan, Jesus spoke the Word of God from His heart and defeated Satan's attempt to make him sin. As you read this passage with your children, it's important to emphasize that if Jesus needed to start studying the Word at an early age, it's important for us to do the same.

Read Luke 2:41-49
Young Jesus Studies the Word

Every year, Jesus' parents went to Jerusalem for the Passover festival. When Jesus was twelve years old, they attended the festival, as usual. After the celebration was over, they started home to Nazareth, but Jesus stayed behind in Jerusalem. His parents didn't miss him at first, because they assumed he was among the other travelers. But when he didn't show up that evening, they started looking for him among their relatives and friends. When they couldn't find him, they went back to Jerusalem to search for him there. Three days later they finally discovered him in the Temple, sitting among the religious teachers, listening to them and asking questions. All who heard him were amazed at His understanding and His answers. His parents didn't know what to think. "Son," his mother said to him, "why have you done this to us? Your father and I have been frantic, searching for you everywhere."

"But why did you need to search?" he asked. "Didn't you know that I must be in my Father's house?"

Read Matthew 4:1-11:
Jesus Is Tempted

Then Jesus was led by the Spirit into the wilderness to be tempted there by the devil. For forty days and forty nights, he fasted and became very hungry. During that time the devil came and said to him, "If you are the Son of God, tell these stones to become loaves of bread." But Jesus told him, "No! The Scriptures say, 'People do not live by bread alone, but by every word that comes from the mouth of God.'"

Then the devil took him to the holy city, Jerusalem, to the highest point of the Temple, and said, "If you are the Son of God, jump off! For the Scriptures say, 'He will order his angels to protect you. And they will hold you up with their hands so you won't even hurt your foot on a stone.'" Jesus responded, "The Scriptures also say, 'You must not test the Lord your God.'"

Next the devil took him to the peak of a very high mountain and showed him all the kingdoms of the world and their glory. "I will give it all to you," he said, "if you will kneel down and worship me."

"Get out of here, Satan," Jesus told him. "For the Scriptures say, 'You must worship the Lord your God and serve only him.'" Then the devil went away, and angels came and took care of Jesus.

Discussion Questions:

1. **How did Jesus' knowledge of God's Word help Him when Satan was tempting Him?**

    Jesus always responded to Satan's lies with the Word of God, saying, "The Scriptures say.…"

2. **How old was Jesus when His parents searched all over for Him? Where did they find Him?**

    Jesus was 12 years old. They found Him in the Temple.

3. **What was Jesus doing in the Temple when they found Him?**

    He was sitting among the religious teachers, listening to them and asking questions.

4. **How did Jesus' knowledge of God's Word help Him when Satan was tempting Him?**

    Jesus always responded to Satan's lies and offers with the Word of God.

5. **Do you see a direct connection between studying God's Word and overcoming the temptation to sin?**

    Yes. If we don't know what God's Word says, then we can't always know right from wrong. We have to know when to say yes and when to say no.

6. **What is so important about knowing right from wrong and not walking in sin?**

    When we sin, we go against God's plan for our lives—even when we sin "by accident." God wants us to know right from wrong, and His grace is always available to us. But the more we know, the more we can receive from God and live His good plan for our lives.

7. **Dictionary Discussion:** Have your Superkids look up the following words in the dictionary (I recommend the *American Dictionary of the English Language,* Noah Webster, 1828 Edition, available online.[1]) There are a few definitions for each word, but it's good to find the ones that really apply to the Superkid Creed. If you have a pen and paper, or chalkboard, write down the ones that apply. Discuss each definition, and make sure your Superkids understand it before moving on.

    a. **Creed:** *noun* 2. That which is believed; any system of principles which are believed or professed; as a political *creed.*

    b. **Way:** *noun* (I chose definitions 10-13).

        10. Manner of thinking or behavior; particular turn of opinion; determination or humor. Let him have his *way* when that will not injure him, or any other person. But multitudes of children are ruined by being permitted to have their *way.*

        11. Manner; mode. In no *way* does this matter belong to me. We admire a person's *way* of expressing his ideas.

        12. Method; manner of practice. Find, if you can, the easiest *way* to live. Having lost the *way* of nobleness.

---

1 http://www.webstersdictionary1828.com/Dictionary.

13. Method or plan of life and conduct. Instruct your children in the right *way.* Her *ways* are ways of pleasantness, and all her paths are peace. Proverbs 3:17.

8. Read Proverbs 3:1-8

My child, never forget the things I have taught you. Store my commands in your heart. If you do this, you will live many years, and your life will be satisfying. Never let loyalty and kindness leave you! Tie them around your neck as a reminder. Write them deep within your heart. Then you will find favor with both God and people, and you will earn a good reputation. Trust in the Lord with all your heart; do not depend on your own understanding. Seek his will in all you do, and he will show you which path to take. Don't be impressed with your own wisdom. Instead, fear the Lord and turn away from evil. Then you will have healing for your body and strength for your bones.

9. Jesus is God—so why did He still need a creed (like God's Word) to live by?

Jesus needed to renew His mind with the Word of God in the same way we have to because He had a soul—a CHOOSER—just like us. He had to know what the right choices were so that He could make them and live a sinless life. Without the right to choose, Jesus would not have been able to overcome temptation and be the "spotless Lamb" whose death was able to save us from our sins.

10. In your own words, explain why you think *you* need a creed?

Answers may vary. Make sure Superkids understand the importance of needing a creed to live by. If Jesus needed one, so do we.

Notes: _____

_____

_____

_____

_____

_____

_____

_____

_____

_____

_____

_____

_____

_____

_____

_____

_____

_____

_____

DAY 2: ACADEMY LAB | THE SUPERKID CREED

 Suggested Time: 10 minutes

 Memory Verse: As pressure and stress bear down on me, I find joy in your commands.—Psalm 119:143

 Teacher Tip: Cut out a picture or create a drawing of a scene your Cadets are in every day, or use a photo from an online site, etc., to tape to the bottle. Test the experiment beforehand. Does your army man fit in the bottle? Is he too light/heavy? Is your bottle too small or plastic too thin? Learn the best way to carefully insert the army man and pen cap into the bottle. Also, if you have extra supplies, this is a great lesson to have your Superkids do the experiment along with you.

Supplies: ■ 1 Tall (at least 1 liter) clear plastic water bottle, ■ Picture/drawing to tape to the back of the water bottle, ■ Pen cap with a pocket clip, ■ Paper clip, ■ Poster tack, ■ Thin plastic army man (not too heavy), ■ Tape

Prior to Lesson:

1. Prepare one, clear plastic water bottle. Since the bottle will represent each Superkid's "world," it's most fun if you draw or cut out pictures of a schoolroom, home, playground or a place where each Superkid spends a lot of time. You can also have your Superkids draw the picture for you. Tape the pictures to the outside of the bottle, so the bottle represents a day in the life of a Superkid. Fill the water bottle, leaving a little room at the top.

2. Find a pen cap with a pocket clip, and block the opening with poster tack (reusable putty adhesive), if necessary, so water can't seep through.

3. Attach a paper clip to the pen-cap pocket clip.

4. Attach the army man to the paper clip using the poster tack.

5. Check to make sure the cap and plastic army man will float near the surface by trying it first in a glass of water. If it sinks, try removing some of the poster tack.

Lesson Instructions:

1. Carefully lower the pen cap, paper clip and army man into the bottle, and screw the lid on. The army man, connected to the paper clip and pen cap (with poster tack), is like the Superkid who is connected to the Creed—God's Word.

2. Squeeze (very hard) the sides of the bottle. You will see the army man sink because of the pressure placed on the bottle. Then let go, and watch how the air-filled pen cap draws him back up to the surface.

3. This is how our world operates. Our world is a structure. Just as there are water and air in the bottle, there are good and bad decisions we can make while we're here on earth. When pressure squeezes the outside of the

bottle (our world), the water and air move around and can put pressure on the army man to push him down.

4. Our Creed is like the pen cap. It provides a bubble of air for our lives. Even when pressure comes, if we'll stay connected to our Creed—just as the army man is connected to the pen cap—we will always rise to the top to live that Sweet Life God has called us to. But without the pen cap (Creed), the army man would have no air bubble to take him back up when the pressure tries to push him down.

Notes: _____

_____

_____

_____

_____

_____

_____

_____

_____

_____

_____

_____

_____

_____

_____

_____

_____

_____

_____

_____

_____

_____

_____

_____

_____

_____

_____

_____

_____

DAY 3: GIVING LESSON | MORE THAN ENOUGH

Suggested Time: 10 minutes

Offering Scripture: Jesus soon saw a huge crowd of people coming to look for him. Turning to Philip, he asked, "Where can we buy bread to feed all these people?" He was testing Philip, for he already knew what he was going to do.

Philip replied, "Even if we worked for months, we wouldn't have enough money to feed them!" Then Andrew, Simon Peter's brother, spoke up. "There's a young boy here with five barley loaves and two fish. But what good is that with this huge crowd?"

"Tell everyone to sit down," Jesus said. So they all sat down on the grassy slopes. (The men alone numbered about 5,000.) Then Jesus took the loaves, gave thanks to God, and distributed them to the people. Afterward he did the same with the fish. And they all ate as much as they wanted. After everyone was full, Jesus told his disciples, "Now gather the leftovers, so that nothing is wasted." So they picked up the pieces and filled twelve baskets with scraps left by the people who had eaten from the five barley loaves. —John 6:5-13

Supplies: ☐ Picnic basket, ☐ Loaf of bread, ☐ 2 Cans of tuna, ☐ Mayonnaise, ☐ Bowl, ☐ Spoon, ☐ Can opener, ☐ Butter knife, ☐ Plate

Lesson Instructions:

Do you want to have a picnic? What's one thing you must have in order to enjoy a great picnic? It's food, isn't it? Let me show you what I have in my picnic basket. *(Pull out each item. Look out at your children/group and count—looking back and forth at your small amount of bread and two cans of tuna. Adjust the amounts to be clearly **less** than needed for your group. Then with a defeated look on your face, open up the cans of tuna and put it in bowl.)*

Do you think there's any possibility I could feed everyone in our family/group today with what I have here? I don't think so!

This reminds me of a time in the Bible when Jesus wanted to feed 5,000 people. Let's read John 6:5-13. Can you imagine having a picnic with 5,000 people and only this amount of food? *(Point to your food.)*

Why do you think Jesus was able to feed all those people? Well, the boy gave Jesus an offering of food, and Jesus used the boy's offering. He blessed it, and God multiplied it and fed 5,000 people! How cool is that? Not only was the boy taken care of, but also Jesus personally blessed him and gave him back 12 full baskets of food!

I'm sure sometimes it seems like because you can't give much, your offering won't make a difference. I know you don't have a full-time job that makes tons of money, or the ability to give your life to doing charity or missions work just yet. But that's not what God expects of you right now.

Remember: Giving isn't just what you do with spare change on Sunday. It's how you live your life.

Let's brainstorm together and think of a few ways you can give to Jesus this week! *(Try to help your children schedule a time to do/give it, as well.)* Here are some ways you can do that:

- Serve and give to Him by helping with chores.

- Help cook dinner.

- Pray for a teacher or friend.

- Give money to your church or to the poor.

- Make a gift for someone.

- Give someone an encouraging note.

Just like the boy in the story, give your all to Jesus. Don't hold anything back, and watch how He'll use it to do big things—not only in your life, but also in the lives of others!

Variation No. 1: Picnic

Bring the story to life by taking your children on a real picnic. Fill your basket with a few extra snacks or a meal so it's not just the tuna. Your Superkids may appreciate a picnic in the backyard or even at a park, while you explain the miracle of Jesus feeding the 5,000.

Notes: _____

_____

_____

_____

_____

_____

_____

_____

_____

_____

_____

_____

_____

_____

_____

_____

_____

DAY 4: REAL DEAL   DESMOND T. DOSS

 Memory Verse: As pressure and stress bear down on me, I find joy in your commands. —Psalm 119:143

 Concept: Highlighting an interesting historical place, figure or event that illustrates the theme of the day. The theme of the day is: What is the Superkid Creed?

 Teacher Tip: Show a DVD, comics, etc.[2] This segment has many possible variations. Choose the best that fits your family/group, and have fun! We suggest getting as familiar as possible with the script prior to teaching this lesson.

Supplies: ☐ U.S. Army Medal of Honor (replica or picture), ☐ Pictures of Desmond T. Doss' military company, ☐ Map of Okinawa, ☐ Picture of Hacksaw Ridge, ☐ Desmond T. Doss comic book (optional)

Optional Costume: ☐ United States Army outfit (army-green slacks and shirt), ☐ White armband with a red cross (sign of a medic) and a green U.S. Army helmet with a medic cross on it

Intro:

Today, we're going to learn about Desmond T. Doss, who was the FIRST *conscientious objector* to receive a Medal of Honor from the United States government.

Does anyone know what a conscientious objector is? It's someone who refuses to perform military service on the grounds of freedom of thought, conscience or religion.

Most conscientious objectors are simply anti-war and/or often anti-government, but Desmond believed that the Lord had commanded him to never kill and never carry a gun. But, he believed that the Lord had called him to duty for his country, and he wanted to serve God and country as a medic to help save lives instead of taking them.

Lesson Instructions:
What Was Desmond's Creed?

Desmond was born February 7, 1919, in Lynchburg, Virginia, to Tom and Bertha Doss.

His mother had a large picture on the wall of the Ten Commandments that Desmond would stare at and even stand on a chair to touch as a young boy. The commandment, "Thou shalt not kill," was illustrated with a picture of Cain killing his brother, Abel. Desmond could not understand how someone could kill his own brother. Staring at that drawing, he felt like the Lord said to him, "Desmond, if you love Me, you won't kill."

Desmond's father had alcohol problems, but his mother was very compassionate. One night, his father and uncle were very drunk and got into a fight. Desmond watched, horrified, as his dad pulled a gun on his very own brother (Desmond's uncle). Desmond was relieved as his compassionate mother stepped in between the men, demanding that Desmond's father hand over the gun, which saved both men's lives. After Desmond's father handed the bullets, and then the gun, to Desmond's mother, she gave it to Desmond and told him to hide

2 Watch a documentary about Desmond T. Doss called *The Conscientious Objector* on YouTube.com: https://www.youtube.com/watch?v=4mk-pX4LIyU. Also available on Amazon.com: http://www.amazon.com/Conscientious-Objector-The-documentary/dp/B000VDZ8Z8 (3/14/16).

it. Desmond obeyed and vowed that it would be the last time he would ever carry a gun. Desmond was a young boy when he chose to stick to a creed!

Desmond Doss Wanted to Serve His Country:

When World War II started, Desmond did not feel his convictions should excuse him from his duty to his country. Even though the U.S. Army draft officer offered him a way out, he refused. He wanted to serve his country as a medic.

But the Army didn't ask where he wanted to be assigned. They sent him to a conscientious objectors' camp. Most of the people at this camp were anti-war soldiers who didn't want to do their duties, wear uniforms and carry their flag. Desmond insisted that he was not an objector, but a "conscientious cooperator" because he still wanted to serve his country.

In response, the U.S. Army assigned him to a rifle division with the 77th Division—the hardest place to be for a conscientious objector. While in training, the officers ridiculed him and gave him extra toilet-cleaning duties. His fellow soldiers threw boots at him and made fun of him as he prayed every night at bedtime. He was called a pest and a nuisance, but he carried a little Bible with him everywhere he went.

Two of the officers even tried to get him court-martialed for not carrying a gun! They took away his rights to see his family. He was not even allowed to see his brother before the young man was shipped overseas with the U.S. Navy. But, even when they took away his rights, Desmond refused to compromise. He said, "I knew if I once compromised, I was going to be in trouble. Because if you can compromise once, you can compromise again."

Desmond's Creed Changed Things:

Desmond was not only devoted to not taking lives, but also to saving them. While in training, he was finally transferred to being a medic, and began looking after his men in the 77th Division.

When the men were sent into battle in Guam, Desmond began gaining their respect by his attitude of hard work and devotion to caring for the sick and wounded. He disregarded the danger of gunfire, crawling from foxhole to foxhole to tend the wounded in his division.

Next, the 77th Division was sent to Okinawa for one of the most difficult tasks. They were assigned to take a 400-foot ridge that was the most well-defended spot on the island.

April 30, 1945: Desmond asked if he could pray for his company of men—the B-company—before they went into battle. Both the A and B companies were being sent to accomplish a nearly impossible task. Desmond's request was granted, and the officers allowed him to pray for the B-company before going into battle. The A-company returned with very few soldiers, while NOT ONE of the B-company was killed or injured!

May 2, 1945: Desmond's unit was not given time to pray, and it was a tough day for his company. During the battle, a third of the men retreated back down the ridge while two-thirds were left wounded at the top. Desmond refused to go back down even though others retreated. Desmond faced and ran through heavy machine-gun and mortar fire, continuing to work 12 long hours through the battle, single-handedly carrying 75 wounded men to the edge of the ridge, and then lowering them down the cliff with a rope. He was never hit by a single bullet during that time. There was even a Japanese soldier, who after the war, reported that he'd gotten Desmond in his sights several times, but every time he tried to pull the trigger, his gun would jam. God was protecting Desmond as he obeyed!

Making History:

May 5, 1945: The entire division, with permission from the company commander, waited patiently for Desmond to finish his devotions before they went into battle. They were faced with another nearly impossible and deadly task, but each soldier agreed they were willing and able, as long as Desmond was there to care for them.

May 21, 1945: As Desmond's unit went into battle, they ran into a company of Japanese soldiers unexpectedly, and Desmond was caught in the middle of hand-to-hand combat. But, despite the heavy fighting going on all around him, Desmond continued caring for the wounded. When a grenade was thrown near him, Desmond covered it with his feet. When it exploded, he was thrown through the air and landed with serious injuries to his legs and backside. Instead of calling for aid and endangering the other medics' lives, he treated his own wounds and waited to be picked up. But even when he was picked up after waiting five hours, he gave up his stretcher to a soldier who had been shot in the head. While waiting for aid to return, his arm was hit by a sniper's bullet and broken. Determined to get back, he made a splint for his arm out of a broken rifle stock, and with all the strength he had left, crawled back to the medical area.

According to records, "Doss saved the lives of many soldiers. His name became a symbol throughout the 77th Infantry Division for outstanding gallantry far above and beyond the call of duty."[3] He even ended up saving the lives of the two officers who had tried to court-martial him.

On November 1, 1945, Desmond Doss became the first conscientious objector to ever receive the Medal of Honor. As President Truman awarded him the medal he said to Desmond, "You really deserve this. I consider this a greater honor than being president of the United States."

Outro:

Desmond was impressed by God that he was never to kill anyone. His trust in God and unwillingness to compromise produced miracles in the hardest circumstances. He depended on God's Word for his strength, not the friends around him. His determination to not kill, made him strong enough to make it through countless battles without compromising and gave him the endurance to save 75 men in one day, showing more kindness and fortitude on the battlefield than every other officer willing to carry a gun.

The Medal of Honor is the HIGHEST military decoration awarded by the United States government and is only given to the most undisputedly courageous individual serving in the armed services of the United States.

Variation No. 1: Dress Up

Entering in costume is an attention grabber for the Superkids. Feel free to present the information as if you were Desmond T. Doss himself!

Variation No. 2: Interview

If you are in a co-op and have teens or other adults involved, consider having another person play Desmond T. Doss and you can be the interviewer.

---

3 United States Congressional Medal of Honor official citation: www.history.army.mil/html/moh/wwII-a-f.html, listed under "Doss, Desmond T."

Variation No. 3: Biography

There are comics that have been made about Desmond's work in the U.S. Army. Feel free to find the comic pictures online and print them out to read like a book as you go along. You can even have reference cards on the back of your photos! Also, look up Desmond T. Doss online at the Congressional Medal of Honor Society and Home of Heroes.com.

Notes: _____

_____

_____

_____

_____

_____

_____

_____

_____

_____

_____

_____

_____

_____

_____

_____

_____

_____

_____

_____

_____

_____

_____

_____

DAY 5: GAME TIME

IN PLAIN SIGHT

 Suggested Time: 15 minutes

 Memory Verse: As pressure and stress bear down on me, I find joy in your commands. —Psalm 119:143

 Teacher Tip: If you are limited in numbers or space, adapt the game to your situation. Your "field" does not have to be large. You can rotate your players or use the same ones for each round.

Supplies: ■ Blindfold, ■ Soccer ball, ■ Duct tape, ■ Small prizes for participants (optional)

Prior to Game:

Use the duct tape to create a start and finish line about 15-20 feet apart, or less, if your space is limited.

Game Goal:

Players successfully and quickly get themselves and their soccer balls across the finish line.

This game teaches that boundaries are in place to help us quickly and easily get to the destination God has for us.

Relay 1:

- Choose 1 player to blindfold.

- Apply blindfold, then have player spin 3 times.

- After spinning, player attempts to move the soccer ball, and himself/herself, across the finish line.

- Player may not use a "power-house" kick to move the ball across the room; only gentle punts to get the ball across the finish line.

Relay 2:

- Choose a player to blindfold.

- Choose up to 2 contestants to be "boundaries" (they will serve as "bumpers," coaching the player to help him/her find the way to the finish line). If you're limited in numbers, you can play the "boundary" role yourself and guide the player.

- "Boundaries" will stand 6 feet apart, directly across from each other.

- Apply blindfold, then have player spin 3 times.

- After spinning, player attempts to move the soccer ball, and himself/herself, across the finish line, using gentle punts.

- "Boundaries" should keep the player and the ball moving forward by coaching him/her toward the finish line, keeping player and ball inside the boundaries.

- It should be much easier for player to find his/her way to the finish line with the boundaries in place.

Relay 3:

- Choose a player to blindfold.

- Choose up to 2 more players to add to your existing "boundaries" (or add another parent).

- "Boundaries" will stand 5 feet across from each other.

- Apply blindfold, then have player spin 3 times.

- After spinning, player attempts to get the soccer ball, and himself/herself, across the finish line, using gentle punts.

- "Boundaries" should keep the contestant and the ball moving forward by coaching him/her toward the finish line, keeping the player and the ball inside the boundaries.

- With less room, more bumpers and coaching, it should be much easier for player to find the way to the finish line.

Relay 4:

- Choose another player to find his/her way to the finish line.

- Choose enough contestants to make a solid "boundary" from start to finish line.

- DO NOT blindfold the player.

- Place the "boundaries" 3 feet across from each other; players should be able to touch the hands of the person standing across from them, with just enough room for the player to walk between.

- Have the player spin 3 times.

- After spinning, player must kick the soccer ball across the finish line, using gentle punts.

- Boundaries should be so close, the only way the player can move is forward. No coaching will be needed, since the boundaries are so close together.

Optional: Give every game participant a small prize.

Final Word:

As the boundaries moved closer, it was easier to get to the finish line, wasn't it? You did a great job! As we learn about the Superkid Creed today, it becomes easier and easier to follow the guided path God has already planned for us. Just like that last relay, God's plans are always easy to follow, and His boundaries are never hidden from us!

ACTIVITY PAGE

MY SUPERKID CREED

 Memory Verse: As pressure and stress bear down on me, I find joy in your commands. —Psalm 119:143

 Teacher Tip: For younger Superkids, feel free to help them find the answers in their Bibles by reading the scriptures to them.

ANSWER KEY:

MY SUPERKID CREED

Crossword answers:
- 2 Across: WORD
- 5 Across: FATHER
- 6 Across: SCRIPTURES
- 9 Across: JUMP
- 11 Across: TWELVE
- 12 Across: JOY
- 1 Down: BREED
- 3 Down: BLESS
- 4 Down: CHOOSE
- 7 Down: TREE
- 8 Down: FOR
- 10 Down: TREED

Name: _____

MY SUPERKID CREED

ACROSS

2. MATTHEW 4:4: JESUS SAID PEOPLE LIVE BY EVERY _____ THAT COMES OUT OF THE MOUTH OF GOD.

5. LUKE 2:49: JESUS SAID TO HIS PARENTS: "WHY DID YOU NEED TO SEARCH? DIDN'T YOU KNOW I'D BE IN MY _____'S HOUSE?"

6. MATTHEW 4:1-11: JESUS ALWAYS BEGAN HIS RESPONSE TO SATAN BY SAYING, "THE _____ SAY...."

9. LUKE 4:6: SATAN TOLD JESUS TO _____ OFF A CLIFF.

11. LUKE 2:41: HOW OLD WAS JESUS WHEN HIS PARENTS FOUND OUT HE WAS MISSING?

12. PSALM 119:143: "WHEN PRESSURE AND STRESS BEAR DOWN ON ME, I FIND _____ IN YOUR COMMANDS."

DOWN

1. MATTHEW 4:4: WHEN TEMPTED WITH FOOD, JESUS SAID, "PEOPLE DO NOT LIVE BY _____ ALONE."

3. DEUTERONOMY 28:1-14: OBEY THE LORD, AND HE WILL _____ YOU.

4. DEUTERONOMY 30:19: GOD WANTS US TO _____ LIFE (NOT DEATH).

7. LUKE 2:46: WHEN JESUS' PARENTS FOUND OUT HE WAS MISSING, WHERE DID THEY END UP FINDING HIM?

8. MATTHEW 4:2: JESUS WENT WITHOUT EATING FOR _____ DAYS AND NIGHTS.

10. WAY OF LIVING, SET SYSTEM OF BELIEFS.

WEEK 2: WHO NEEDS A CREED?

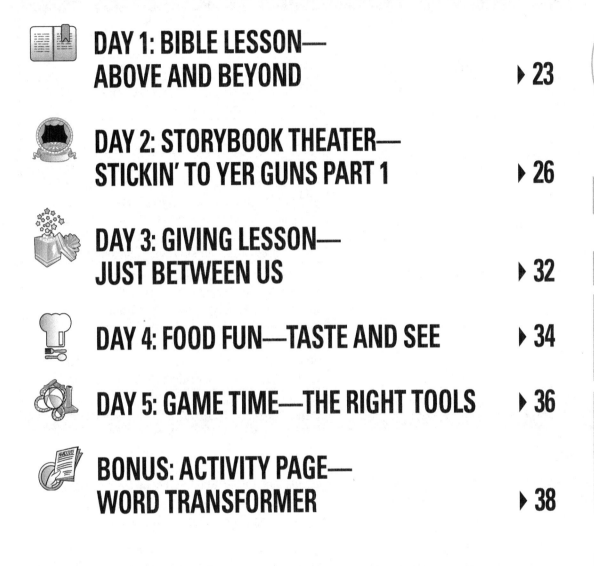

Memory Verse: Don't copy the behavior and customs of this world, but let God transform you into a new person by changing the way you think. Then you will learn to know God's will for you, which is good and pleasing and perfect. —Romans 12:2

WEEK 2: SNAPSHOT — WHO NEEDS A CREED?

DAY	TYPE OF LESSON	LESSON TITLE	SUPPLIES
Day 1	Bible Lesson	Above and Beyond	None
Day 2	Storybook Theater	Stickin' to Yer Guns Part 1	Optional Costumes/Props, Art supplies
Day 3	Giving Lesson	Just Between Us	Gift, Gift-wrapping, Scissors, Gifts for everyone else, if the group is small (optional)
Day 4	Food Fun	Taste and See	1 Glass (or microwaveable) pie plate, Microwave oven, Spatula, Mixer, Large bowl, Mixing spoons, Measuring cups, Recipe card with instructions, 1 Cup sugar, ½ Cup butter (softened), Extra butter and sugar to coat bottom of pie plate, 2 Eggs, 1 Teaspoon vanilla, ½ Cup flour, ½ Cup cocoa, ½ Cup milk-chocolate chips or chunks, Chocolate bar (to melt on top of brownies), Other ingredients your kids enjoy (optional)
Day 5	Game Time	The Right Tools	Lunchmeat (still in container), Sandwich bread, Mayonnaise/condiments, 2 Individually wrapped slices of cheese, 2 Spoons, 2 Dental floss, 2 New paintbrushes, 2 Ponchos/big coats, Bananas, Latex gloves (for both competitors), 2 Pair of swimming flippers or large shoes, Plates, 2 Napkins, 2 Place mats, 2 Cups, Table, 2 Folding chairs, Tablecloth
Bonus	Activity Page	Word Transformer	1 Copy for each child

Lesson Introduction:

After researching Jeremiah and Daniel in the *Holman Bible Handbook*[4] and the ArtScroll Series on Daniel,[5] I am convinced that the four Hebrew children heard and took to heart Jeremiah's warnings to Israel. Because they had God's ways in their hearts, they didn't allow themselves to be pressured to do things any other way.

Kids are under a tremendous amount of pressure in today's society. But when they let God tell them how to think, and do things His way, He works out the details (Romans 8:28)! Pastor Bill Winston of Living Word Christian Center in the Chicago, Ill., area said, "If you don't know who you are, the first thing you can be is manipulated."

Not our kids! They have the Creed in their hearts, telling them who they are. As they say the Creed, they are telling themselves who they are. Then, their lives will change and their lives will tell others who God is (Romans 12:2)! A Superkid with the Creed in his/her heart STANDS OUT!

Love,

Commander Kellie

Commander Kellie

Lesson Outline:

This week your children will learn: Who needs a creed? The answer is simple: *everyone.* Just as a good doctor needs a creed to bring help and not harm to his or her patients, Superkids also need a creed to live by. When you want to achieve a goal, you have to have a plan or a guide. One of the greatest examples is Jesus—His goal was to live His life without sin, and His creed was "LOVE GOD and LOVE OTHERS." However, in your Superkids' lives, YOU are the best flesh-and-blood example of living a creed. You can show them your creed and remind them that even though you make mistakes, you have set goals to be the mom or dad that God has called you to be!

I. GOD SENT JEREMIAH TO WARN ISRAEL THAT THEY WOULD BE TAKEN CAPTIVE IF THEY DIDN'T CHANGE THEIR WAYS
Jeremiah 1:1-3

a. God's people didn't want His wisdom. Jeremiah 10:21

b. They wouldn't obey Him. Jeremiah 6:16, 9:13-14, 18:12

c. Israel's finest young people were taken captive by Babylon. Daniel 1:1-4

d. Babylon represents a system of thinking, acting and doing without God. Genesis 11:1-4

II. DANIEL, HANANIAH, MISHAEL AND AZARIAH WERE TAKEN CAPTIVE
Daniel 1:6-7

a. They would have heard Jeremiah's warnings.

b. Daniel determined in his heart to honor God and His ways. Verse 8

c. Daniel was young, but God helped him lead Hananiah, Mishael and Azariah. Jeremiah 3:15

d. Even though all the others did things the king's (Babylon's) way, these four young men followed God's Word.

III. REMEMBER WHO YOU ARE! Daniel 1:7-20

a. Their captor wanted the boys to forget God's ways and who they were in Him, so he changed their names. Verses 7-14

b. It didn't work! They stuck with God, and He made them 10 times better! Verses 15-20

c. Satan wants you to forget God and His ways in your daily life.

d. But when you have God's Word (Creed) in your heart, God will make you into all He's called you to be! Romans 12:2

---

4 Holman Bible Handbook (Nashville: Holman Bible Publishers, 1992).

5 *Daniel: A new translation with a commentary anthologized from talmudic, midrashic, and rabbinic sources* (Artscroll Tanach Series), Rabbi Nosson Scherman (NewYork: Mesorah Publications Ltd., 2000).

Notes: _____

_____

_____

_____

_____

_____

_____

_____

_____

_____

_____

_____

_____

_____

_____

_____

_____

_____

_____

_____

_____

_____

_____

_____

_____

_____

_____

_____

_____

_____

_____

_____

_____

_____

_____

_____

_____

_____

_____

DAY 1: BIBLE LESSON   ABOVE AND BEYOND

Memory Verse: Don't copy the behavior and customs of this world, but let God transform you into a new person by changing the way you think. Then you will learn to know God's will for you, which is good and pleasing and perfect. —Romans 12:2

Daniel, Hananiah, Mishael and Azariah were captured by a foreign king and told to eat and drink in a way that went against God's commands. Instead of going with the flow, they obeyed God's Word and only drank water and ate vegetables. They ended up being healthier and wiser than all the others!

Read Daniel 1:1-20:
Daniel, Hananiah, Mishael, and Azariah set themselves apart from the crowd.

During the third year of King Jehoiakim's reign in Judah, King Nebuchadnezzar of Babylon came to Jerusalem and besieged it. The Lord gave him victory over King Jehoiakim of Judah and permitted him to take some of the sacred objects from the Temple of God. So, Nebuchadnezzar took them back to the land of Babylonia and placed them in the treasure-house of his god.

The king ordered Ashpenaz, his chief of staff, to bring to the palace some of the young men of Judah's royal family and other noble families, who had been brought to Babylon as captives. "Select only strong, healthy, and good-looking young men," he said. "Make sure they are well versed in every branch of learning, are gifted with knowledge and good judgment, and are suited to serve in the royal palace. Train these young men in the language and literature of Babylon." The king assigned them a daily ration of food and wine from his own kitchens. They were to be trained for three years, and then they would enter the royal service.

Daniel, Hananiah, Mishael, and Azariah were four of the young men chosen, all from the tribe of Judah. The chief of staff renamed them with these Babylonian names:

Daniel was called Belteshazzar. Hananiah was called Shadrach. Mishael was called Meshach. Azariah was called Abednego.

But Daniel was determined not to defile himself by eating the food and wine given to them by the king. He asked the chief of staff for permission not to eat these unacceptable foods. Now God had given the chief of staff both respect and affection for Daniel. But he responded, "I am afraid of my lord the king, who has ordered that you eat this food and drink his wine. If you become pale and thin compared to the other youths your age, I am afraid the king will have me beheaded."

Daniel spoke with the attendant who had been appointed by the chief of staff to look after Daniel, Hananiah, Mishael, and Azariah. "Please test us for ten days on a diet of vegetables and water," Daniel said. "At the end of the ten days, see how we look compared to the other young men who are eating the king's food. Then make your decision in light of what you see." The attendant agreed to Daniel's suggestion and tested them for ten days.

At the end of the ten days, Daniel and his three friends looked healthier and better nourished than the young men who had been eating the food assigned by the king. So after that, the attendant fed them only vegetables instead of the food and wine provided for the others.

God gave these four young men an unusual aptitude for understanding every aspect of literature and wisdom. And God gave Daniel the special ability to interpret the meanings of visions and dreams.

When the training period ordered by the king was completed, the chief of staff brought all the young men to King Nebuchadnezzar. The king talked with them, and no one impressed him as much as Daniel, Hananiah, Mishael, and Azariah. So, they entered the royal service. Whenever the king consulted them in any matter requiring wisdom and balanced judgment, he found them ten times more capable than any of the magicians and enchanters in his entire kingdom.

Discussion Questions:

1. **What are three things that happened in this passage?**

   Answers will vary, but make sure your children understand the passage.

2. **Do you think that Daniel, Hananiah, Mishael and Azariah experienced peer pressure from the others to just go with the flow and eat what everyone else ate?**

   Yes! There was even more pressure because their people were put into captivity, and their orders came from the king himself. Telling the king no could make the difference between life and death! Not only that, but the king's food and drink probably looked tastier than vegetables and water.

3. **What are some excuses Daniel, Hananiah, Mishael and Azariah could have made to be like everyone else?**

   • Everybody's doing it.

   • I have to because the king said. I could go to prison for disobeying!

   • I have to because my teacher/overseer made me.

   • It would just be for a few years—what's the big deal?

4. **It's important to obey and respect authority as God says in His Word, but how do you think Daniel, Hananiah, Mishael and Azariah felt when their overseer put pressure on them to go against the Scripture by eating the king's food? That would be like a teacher or authority figure putting pressure on you to do the wrong thing!**

   Often pressure comes from our peers—people our own age—but when your authority puts pressure on you to do something AGAINST the Word of God, it can mean more pressure or fear coming against you. I'm sure it was a difficult decision to make, going against a king's command. Daniel, Hananiah, Mishael and Azariah weren't even full adults, so they really had to know what God's Word said so they could make the right decision. Remember last week's verse: "When pressure and stress bear down on me, I find joy in Your commands" Psalm 119:143.

5. **What does "Don't copy the behavior and customs of this world" look like for you today? What are some things that you see happening with friends or neighbors that you can be pressured into? Do you think it was similar to what Daniel, Hananiah, Mishael and Azariah felt?**

   Answers will vary, but encourage everyone to participate in discussing personal experiences or what they've seen others do.

6. **Fill in the blank: Daniel, Hananiah, Mishael and Azariah were successful because they put more trust in _____'s commands than in the _____'s commands.**

   They put more trust in GOD's commands than in the KING's commands.

7. **What will make the difference for YOU when it comes to pressure or fear to do the wrong thing? Hint: It's what helped Daniel, Hananiah, Mishael and Azariah.**

   Your Superkid Creed! Putting God's Word into your heart! Daniel, Hananiah, Mishael and Azariah knew God's promises—that HE would take care of them, if they followed Him. Their trust in God and knowledge of His Word helped them to go against the king's command and not be like everyone else.

8. **How can a strong relationship with God help you overcome fear and pressure from the world? Hint: See second part of memory verse:**

   "…but let God transform you into a new person by changing the way you think. Then you will learn to know God's will for you, which is good and pleasing and perfect."

9. **What was the result of Daniel, Hananiah, Mishael and Azariah sticking to their Creed and not defiling themselves by eating the king's food?**

   Daniel, Hananiah, Mishael and Azariah were found to be more excellent than all the others. Plus God blessed them and made them WISER than all the rest of the men.

Notes: _____

_____

_____

_____

_____

_____

_____

_____

_____

_____

_____

_____

_____

_____

_____

_____

_____

_____

_____

_____

_____

DAY 2: STORYBOOK THEATER

STICKIN' TO YER GUNS PART 1

Concept: A two-week series about Daniel, Hananiah, Azariah and Mishael from Daniel 1, but set in the wild, wild West! A memorable way to tell a wonderful Bible story.

Teacher Tip:
- Select some Western-style music from a good, old-fashioned Western-movie soundtrack. Ennio Morricone (Italian composer and conductor) is brilliant for this. Play the music while the narrator talks, to give it a little more excitement and flow.
- Try to read with the Western accent that it's written in.

List of Characters/Optional Costumes & Props
- Narrator: Good reader, country-Western accent
- Buck: Big presence, very tough and intimidating, ranger badge
- Cookie: Craggy, old chuck-wagon cook, apron
- Daniel: Natural leader, FAKE shotgun, ranger badge
- Hananiah: Brainiac, maybe wears old-fashioned eyeglasses/smaller FAKE gun—Colt .45, ranger badge
- Mishael: The funny guy/rope, ranger badge
- Azariah: A bit of a follower; looks up to Daniel/FAKE knives, ranger badge

Costumes: Jeans (cowboy-style preferred), button-down flannel or country-style shirts. (Always better if they've been rolled in dirt to look more Western era.) Cowboy boots, cowboy hats, spurs, chaps
Daniel, Hananiah, Mishael, Azariah: get stuffing for muscles (polyester fiberfill or partially inflated swim floaties) after the return from eating cactus

Supplies: ■ Whiteboard, chalkboard or easel with paper, ■ Dry-erase markers if using whiteboard, colored chalks if using a chalkboard, or pencil (art pencils work best) and eraser, black marker and rags (to blend chalks) if using paper, ■ Art smock (to keep your artist's clothes clean)

Variation No. 1:

Read the story as part of your read-aloud time.

Variation No. 2:

Read this like a campfire story. Because it's a Western, this is a fun story to read in front of a fire. You can even have the option of making your own dinner as you talk about how Daniel, Mishael, Azariah and Hananiah refused to eat the king's food.

Variation No. 3:

Read the story as an old-time radio skit, complete with different actors for each part. If you are limited on participants, assign more than one part per person, and change the voice. Make copies of the skit and have each actor highlight his/her lines. This is great for a community Bible study or co-op.

Variation No. 4:

Act out the story as a fun skit. Perhaps your children can practice during the day (even creating costumes from everyday items) and then perform it in the evening before the whole family or community. Before beginning your skit, remember to introduce your cast! This is great for a community Bible study or co-op.

Production Tips and Supplies:

- **DO NOT USE REAL GUNS!** Purchase toy guns at toy stores or costume shops.

- You can make this drama as big or little a production as you want. Don't feel overwhelmed about props or costumes—it's only to equip you to create a big family/neighborhood production, if you choose, over the read-aloud variation.

- If you don't have enough boys, have girls read boys' roles.

- Try to narrate with a country-Western accent along with all the other actors.

- Costumes made EASY—use flannel shirts or even pajamas! Add jeans and boots, and you're set. Try to get your cast to supply costume items to add to what you have: hats, spurs, etc. Major costume and toy shops are great places to find fake guns, knives, ropes, etc.

- Really commit to playing the character with attitude, accent and costume, and the kids will LOVE it! You are part of helping them to really REMEMBER their Bible stories!

Set/Props: ☐ Cooking pot and spoon, ☐ Bowls, ☐ FAKE campfire: easy to make with wooden logs resting on top of an upturned fan with red and yellow tissue paper taped to the top of the fan and threaded between the logs. Turn fan to lowest setting. Paper will flutter upward between logs, simulating flames.

Variation No. 5:

Create a storybook theater where one person sketches the story on a whiteboard, chalkboard or artist's easel as another reads the story. Initially, there will be a few supplies to purchase, but don't let this be a deterrent from using the illustrated story option! Once the supplies have been purchased, they'll be long-lasting and reusable.

To make your presentation easier, lightly sketch the drawing with a pencil prior to presentation. Time may not allow the picture to be completely drawn and colored at the time of the lesson. Erase pencil lines, so light lines are visible to the artist but not visible to your children. Review the story ahead of time to determine the amount of time needed to complete the illustration while telling the story. When the story begins, use black markers to "draw" the picture, following the sketched pencil lines. Next, apply color using the pastel chalk. Then, blend the color with the rags. Finally, cut the illustration from the board, roll it up, secure it with rubber bands, and share it with one of your children!

Story:

[PLAY WESTERN MUSIC]

It was a ferocious time, livin' in the West. Hard 'nough for a cowboy. But for a young gun, there was nothing like the tale of Daniel, Mishael, Azariah and Hananiah.

Yes sir, them was some fine boys. Though not for the fault of their upbringin'. Their own Pa done lost 'em in a game of cards to a real nasty lawman named Buck, head of the Texas Rangers. Although them boys was just teens, Buck was plannin' on makin' 'em the youngest guns to ever enter the Texas Rangers. Yup, Buck was trainin' them rangers perty hard. And he had the best o' the West trainin' in his troop. So when them boys joined, they had to catch up real fast—'specially seein' as they'd never done much fightin' before.

But this one afternoon, the boys stood suited up on the Western front: spurs, boots, hats and jeans. Yes siree, they looked like real cowboys. Daniel with his shotgun held close, Mishael with his rope, Az with his set of throwin' knives, and Hananiah with his smaller Colt .45. But lookin' like a cowboy sure ain't bein' one. And, big ol' BUCK was tryin' his best to train the new boys how to use their weaponry in front of the big campfire that Cookie had lit on the prairie.

Cookie was the old chuck-wagon cook who'd followed Buck's troop to make sure they was always well-fed. As Cookie brought a new pot of grub to the fire, Buck was reminded of his new trainin' tactic: a big ol' diet!

"All right, boys," Buck began, "I only got three months to train ya to fight like men." Spitting on the ground, he looked over at Cookie: "So I'm puttin' y'all on a diet of pork 'n beans and poison water."

The boys' eyes got as big as a desert lizard! Daniel, Mishael, Az and Hananiah looked at each other with the same thought: *NOOOOOOOOOOOOO!*

Cookie stirred the pot and sniffed. "Mmmm.... Supper's almost done, Boss."

"All right," Buck agreed. "Let's break for dinner. Then you can get back to yer trainin.'"

As Buck pulled Cookie aside to further discuss the food preparations, Az spoke what all them boys was thinkin': "What're we gonna do?"

Always the leader of the pack, Daniel said with conviction: "We cain't drink that poison water!"

Mishael added, "And Momma'd be spinnin' in her grave if we ate that pork."

Still unsure, Az scratched his head with the blunt side of his knife. "I don't think we have a choice...."

But Daniel knew there was *always* a choice. "Did ya forget that Pa got us into this mess 'cause he was drinkin' that stuff?"

Brainiac brother, Hananiah, agreed. "Yeah. Remember how Pastor Jeremiah done warned Pa that he was gonna lose his land from drinkin' that poison water, and he didn't listen...?"

In unison, the boys took off their hats and shook their heads.

"So, what we gonna do?" Az asked.

"We gotta make a stand!" answered Daniel.

Before Mishael finished rolling his eyes, Cookie came with bowls to spoon up the grub.

Daniel approached Cookie. "Hey, Cookie."

Cookie nodded without lookin' up from his stew.

Daniel continued, "So, me and my brothers is Jewish…."

Cookie's not really sure what that's supposed to mean to him. "Yup," he said without lookin' up.

"What I mean is…" Daniel said, "we don't eat pork."

Cookie'd never heard such a thing! "Don't eat pork?!" he retorted.

"Yes," Daniel continued, "and we cain't drink no poison water, neither." The other boys stared at the ground, all embarrassed.

At this, Cookie started sloppin' the pork and beans into the bowl as if he was reslaughterin' that pig. "Listen here, strapper," he said intensely, "I been cookin' ranger meals for 15 years, and I ain't about to start caterin' to you just 'cause you got lily-livered stomachs."

Daniel knew he'd have to explain further. "Please, sir, it ain't 'cause we got weak stomachs. We cain't 'cause of religious reasons. Our Torah says…."

Cookie cut Daniel off before he could finish his fine speech. "I got 50 men to feed, an' I ain't got time to pick pork outa yer bowls just 'cause yer on some sorta diet. An', I ain't got time to spy out some creek for y'all to drink outa ever' day, neither."

Daniel prayed for favor with the old chuck-wagon cook under his breath, as Hananiah moved toward Cookie and implored, "Please, sir, if yer a God-fearin' man, you gotta understand…."

Cookie crossed himself and sized up the boys. He shook his head. "You boys don't git it…. Buck'll have my hide…."

"Buck don't have to find out," Mishael said quickly.

Cookie shook his head once more. "No, Buck'll see if you boys get thinner than you already are."

"We ain't gonna get thin, sir," Daniel replied.

"But what y'all gonna eat? All I got is pork 'n beans."

Daniel suddenly had a great idea. "We'll eat cactus!" Mishael, Azariah and Hananiah groaned as Daniel continued. "We ate it before, we can eat it again. 'Sides, it'll give us plenty to drink, too."

Cookie was shocked again. "Yer gonna live on cactus?"

"We done it before," Daniel replied.

Still not happy 'bout it, Mishael chimed in: "Yeah, when we was starvin'!"

Cookie began servin' up dinner again. Daniel threw Mishael a look. He was serious about not breaking any commandments, but he knew he was about to lose his chance with Cookie. "How 'bout you let us try it out for 10 days?" he suggested.

Cookie looked up. "Ten days, huh?"

Hananiah chimed in, "A probation kinda like...."

"Pro... what?" Clearly, this was too big a word for Cookie.

Daniel nodded, "Like a trial period. Let us try it out for 10 days, an' if we ain't stronger than the rest of them rangers, well...we'll eat whatever you put in front of us...."

Cookie scratched his chin with the skinny end of his spoon. "Ten days, huh?"

The boys felt real tense. Daniel gulped, "Yes, sir."

"And if you runts get any skinnier, you'll eat my food without cryin' about it?"

"Not a single tear, sir," Daniel replied.

"All right." Cookie stood up, spat in his hand and gestured it to Daniel. "You got yerself a deal, kid."

Daniel graciously shook Cookie's hand as Hananiah wondered about the last time Cookie'd had a good bath.

"Thank you, sir!" Daniel was overjoyed! "You won't regret it."

"Don't mention it." Cookie began to crouch over his pork 'n beans again, but quickly turned back to the boys. "But really, kids, don't mention it. I don't wanna lose my job. It's the only one I got."

Daniel tipped his hat, locked his mouth, and flicked the imaginary key to the dust. And Mishael, Azariah and Hananiah tipped their hats as well before mounting their horses to wrestle up a cactus for dinner.

[PLAY WESTERN MUSIC AGAIN]

Daniel, Mishael, Az and Hananiah collected prickly pears and all sorts of cacti and vegetation they found 'long the trail as they trained to become rangers. And, one other important thing.... Daniel made sure they prayed every day over their food—that it'd make 'em grow real strong so they could keep their covenant with God. And what do ya know...

Them boys sprouted muscles like weeds from eatin' that cactus fruit. Plus, they weren't drinkin' none o' that poison water, so they was able to keep their wits about 'em.... As Buck taught them boys to shoot and rope, they picked up on his teachin' 10 times faster than the rest of his outfit.

And when them 10 days was up, Cookie could see the boys was obviously lookin' a whole lot healthier than the rest of the lot, so he decided to let 'em keep fendin' fer themselves fer their food.

Finally, when their rangers' trainin' days were up, Buck brought the boys out 'cause they'd done outshined all the other rangers, even though they was the youngest in the camp.

Buck was mighty proud of them boys, and on graduation day, he gave a fine speech to all the graduates. He said, "Today is a special day 'cause yer all gradgeatin' into bein' bona fide rangers." The group of ranger trainees cheered as Buck continued: "From this day fo'ward, yer all rangers, and it's yer duty to defend and protect our state like she were yer own momma. Now, before ya get to yer duties, Hananiah, Azariah, Mishael and Daniel, you get up here."

As he called the boys forward, they got real nervous-like. *Are we in trouble?* they wondered. *Did Buck find out about our cactus dinners and wanna kick us out?*

The boys stepped forward, unsure, as Buck pulled out some badges. "I know some people might say I'm partial since yer sorta my boys," Buck began. "But I beg any of ya to challenge me on it. I'm appointin' you boys as sergeants over the rest of this outfit."

Well, them boys breathed a sigh of relief as Buck began speakin' to 'em one by one, pinning 'em with new shiny badges as he went. "Hananiah," Buck said proudly, "ya got a real mind for battle strategy, son."

"Thank you, sir."

Next Buck moved to Mishael. "Mishael, you could rope a movin' avalanche, boy."

Mishael grinned as he looked down at that new shiny badge of his. "Thank you, sir."

"Azariah," Buck pinned a badge on Az, "you could pin a fly with those knives you got there."

Az teared up a little. "Thanks, sir."

"And Daniel." Daniel stepped forward as Buck pinned him proudly. "Well, if I were ready to retire, I'd just hand ya the outfit. Yer a real leader, son."

Daniel smiled. "Thank you, sir."

Buck clapped him on the shoulder and added, "Not to mention the sharpest shooter in the West." Everyone hooted and hollered in agreement until Buck addressed the crowd. "Now, the rest of ya give it up for yer sergeants."

The crowd hollered again and good ol' Cookie even tossed his hat in the air with a resounding, "Yahoo!"

[PLAY WESTERN MUSIC]

And, there ya have it. Even though them boys was the youngest of the bunch, no one ever disputed their authority. They were clearly 10 times better and brighter than the whole lot. And lemme tell ya, 10 times better is quite a difference, 'specially if you cain't count that high. But, that there's the story of how four of the youngest cowboys ever, stuck to their guns and ruled the unruly West!

[FADE MUSIC]

Notes: _____

_____

_____

_____

_____

_____

_____

DAY 3: GIVING LESSON   JUST BETWEEN US

Suggested Time: 10 minutes

Offering Scripture: Watch out! Don't do your good deeds publicly, to be admired by others, for you will lose the reward from your Father in heaven. When you give to someone in need, don't do as the hypocrites do—blowing trumpets in the synagogues and streets to call attention to their acts of charity! I tell you the truth, they have received all the reward they will ever get. But when you give to someone in need, don't let your left hand know what your right hand is doing. Give your gifts in private, and your Father, who sees everything, will reward you. —Matthew 6:1-4

Supplies: ☐ Gift, ☐ Gift wrap, ☐ Scissors, ☐ Gifts for everyone else if the group is small (optional)

Prior to Lesson:

- Wrap a gift. It can be anything that you would consider to be a nice gift for your Superkid: candy, toy, notebook or apparel. It doesn't matter what it is, as long as it's a fun gift, and you remember what you put inside!

- The nicer the wrapping and the more complicated it is to unwrap, the better your joke will work.

- Try to make your gift next to impossible to unwrap. Wrapping many times with curling ribbon is a great way to accomplish this, or using lots of packing tape. Just try to make it look nice on the outside and impossible to open on the inside.

- Have scissors on hand to assist at the end.

Lesson Instructions:

- Single out one person to receive the gift.

- As your Superkid is opening his/her gift, blurt out what's in the package. Say something like, "I got you a _____."

- Bug your Superkid to the point he or she is unable to concentrate on opening the gift. (This is why making the gift more complicated to unwrap will help.) Ask questions and tell very specifically what's inside the gift, as your Superkid struggles to open it. Example: If you gave the Superkid a T-shirt, bug him/her with questions like: "Do you wear T-shirts, or are you more of a sleeveless guy/girl? Do you like cotton? I hope yellow is your color. I really like yellow, so I figured you would. My room at home is yellow. It's the best color, I think. Did I mention your T-shirt is yellow? It's from a really expensive store because that's where I shop. I'm so cool...."

- Annoy the Superkid as he/she tries to open the gift to the point where he/she doesn't even want to open it any longer. The Superkid already knows what's inside, anyway. Make this gift all about YOU!

- After a little of this madness, say, "You know what, I'll just open it for you." Using the scissors, cut open the package, and sure enough, the gift is exactly what you said it was!

It's fun to get gifts, isn't it? But, not this way! You didn't have much fun opening your gift, did you? When I kept bugging you, it took all the fun out of it. Did you know that's how we treat God sometimes in our giving? We take all the joy out of it. Let's read Matthew 6:1-4.

It's always annoying to open gifts on your birthday and have someone else trying to get all the attention because they brought a cool gift. That's not how friends act. Good friends don't announce their gifts loudly and try to make someone else's birthday party all about them, right?

Have you ever had a party someone ruined just because *they* wanted all the attention? Giving an offering is something personal that should just be between you and God. It's much more important than a birthday gift. Jesus is such a good Friend to us, we should be that to Him, as well. Whether you're giving a money offering or a toy away to someone, or maybe even singing in the praise band—whatever offering you give to God, don't make a big deal of yourself just for attention. Jesus said God can't bless that attitude, and you don't want to be the annoying party-ruiner when it comes time to bring your offerings to God!

If you'd like to, and your group is small enough, feel free to give gifts to the rest of the kids, but let them enjoy opening them.

Notes: _____

_____

_____

_____

_____

_____

_____

_____

_____

_____

_____

_____

_____

_____

_____

_____

_____

_____

_____

_____

_____

DAY 4: FOOD FUN

TASTE AND SEE

 Suggested Time: 10-15 minutes

 Memory Verse: Don't copy the behavior and customs of this world, but let God transform you into a new person by changing the way you think. Then you will learn to know God's will for you, which is good and pleasing and perfect. —Romans 12:2

 Ingredients: ☐ 1 Cup sugar, ☐ ½ Cup butter (softened) plus extra butter and sugar to coat bottom of pie plate, ☐ 2 Eggs, ☐ 1 Teaspoon vanilla, ☐ ½ Cup flour, ☐ ½ Cup cocoa, ☐ ½ Cup milk-chocolate chips or chunks, ☐ Chocolate bar (to melt on top of brownies), ☐ Other ingredients your kids enjoy (optional)

Recipe:

1. Cream the softened butter and sugar together in a bowl.
2. Add the eggs, 1 at a time, and the vanilla, into the creamed mixture; mix well.
3. Stir cocoa and flour together, separately, then add into egg mixture.
4. Mix well. Batter will be thick.
5. Butter the sides and bottom of pie plate, and coat with sugar.
6. Spread brownie mixture into pie pan. (Add optional ingredients.)
7. Microwave for 5 minutes. Depending on wattage of microwave, additional cooking at 1-minute intervals may be necessary.
8. Let brownies sit for 1 minute to cool, then serve.

Supplies: ■ 1 Glass (microwaveable) pie plate, ■ Microwave oven, ■ Spatula, ■ Mixer, ■ Large bowl, ■ Mixing spoons, ■ Measuring cups, ■ Recipe card with instructions

Lesson Instructions:

Today we're making CHOCOLATE brownies!

Who likes CHOCOLATE?

(Choose 1 helper; have them read the recipe card to you, so you can follow it with precision.)

After you've followed all the directions, tell the kids since you're making the brownies for THEM, you're going to add some of their favorite "optional" ingredients.

Add optional ingredients that you know your kids enjoy (nuts/candies/marshmallows, etc.), and place in microwave to cook. *(The brownies will be cooking while you're talking.)*

Why do you think we need a recipe?

Yes, we need to know how to make our yummy treat. If we don't follow or obey the instructions, it won't come out right, and we'll probably just have a mess!

Recipes for baking are kind of like the Creed we follow as we live our lives.

When we follow the brownie recipe exactly, the end result of our baking is ALWAYS perfect. When we follow God's recipe for us, which is our Creed, we'll always have His perfect plan for us! His plan is always good, pleasing and perfect.

Your brownies should be done by now! They sure smell good, don't they? Mmmm, I can almost taste them now. *(Talk more about how good they smell and how yummy they'll taste because you followed the recipe.)*

As soon as you remove the brownies from the microwave, immediately place the broken chocolate bar pieces on top. Let the chocolate melt and spread evenly across the top.

Final Word:

(Taste your brownies.) These are *so* yummy and they turned out just like they were supposed to *because we followed the recipe!*

I'm so glad I decided to add some of your favorite ingredients, too. Just like I made these brownies special just the way you like them, God's plans for us are always uniquely and specially made for each of us!

When you follow God's recipe for your life, you'll taste and see that God is good, and all His plans are good, pleasing and perfect *(take another bite),* just like these yummy brownies! Mmmm!

Notes: _____

_____

_____

_____

_____

_____

_____

_____

_____

_____

_____

_____

_____

_____

_____

DAY 5: GAME TIME   ## THE RIGHT TOOLS

 Suggested Time: 10 minutes

 Memory Verse: Don't copy the behavior and customs of this world, but let God transform you into a new person by changing the way you think. Then you will learn to know God's will for you, which is good and pleasing and perfect. —Romans 12:2

 Teacher Tip: Feel free to do this as a lunch game. Choose a lunchmeat and condiment that your kids enjoy. The suggestion is for 2 players, but if it's just your family, you can adjust the game to your number of kids.

Feel free to adjust this game to your needs. You don't have to go shopping for flippers if you don't have them; use oversized shoes (maybe yours). Feel free to use a big coat if you don't have ponchos.

Supplies: ☐ Lunchmeat (still in container), ☐ Sandwich bread, ☐ Mayonnaise/condiment, ☐ 2 Individually wrapped slices of cheese, ☐ 2 Spoons, ☐ 2 Dental floss, ☐ 2 New paintbrushes, ☐ 2 Ponchos/big coats, ☐ Bananas, ☐ Latex gloves (for both competitors), ☐ 2 Pair of swimming flippers or large shoes, ☐ 2 Plates, ☐ 2 Napkins, ☐ 2 Place mats, ☐ 2 Cups, ☐ Table, ☐ 2 Folding chairs, ☐ Tablecloth

Prior to Game:

Set up the "kitchen" and "dining room" opposite each other. They can be anywhere in the house or even outside.

Kitchen:

Set up a table for this station. Have the mayonnaise or condiment, bread, lunchmeat, cheese, bananas, spoons, dental floss and paintbrushes at this station. This will be the area where the competitors will prepare food. Have the table-setting supplies at this station, also.

Dining Room:

Set up a table and 2 chairs at this station.

Game Instructions:

Explain each step to the "chefs" before they begin, and let them know they may ask for your guidance throughout the game if they need a refresher on task instructions.

Each competitor will have 4 tasks to complete.

First Task:

Dress in "chef attire": poncho (big coat), flippers (oversized shoes) and gloves.

Second Task:

Set table: place mat, plate and napkin.

Third Task:

Go to "kitchen" and prepare meal.

1. Lay 2 pieces of bread on the table.

2. Using the paintbrush, cover each piece of bread with mayonnaise or condiment. The bread must be evenly covered before the chef can move on.

3. Unwrap the cheese and place it on 1 of the pieces of bread.

4. Open the container of lunchmeat, and place 2 pieces on the other piece of bread.

5. Place both pieces of bread together, forming a sandwich, and set aside.

6. Using the spoon, cut the sandwich in quarters.

7. After the sandwich is complete and has been cut in quarters, take each piece to the dining room and place the sandwich on the plate at the "dining room" table.

Fourth Task:

8. Peel the banana.

9. Use the dental floss to cut the peeled banana into 6 individual pieces.

10. Pick up the banana pieces, and take them to the plate at the "dining room" table.

11. All 6 pieces must make it to the table, or the chef must return to the kitchen, cut more banana pieces, and make the trip again.

Feel free to let your chefs eat the meal they've prepared as you give your final words.

Game Goal:

Whoever finishes preparing and serving his/her meal first, wins.

Final Word:

Ask your children if they've ever seen a chef wear swimming flippers and a poncho. Would they think that working in the kitchen would have been easier if they had the right tools?

As you learn the Superkid Creed and put God's Word into your heart, you'll be able to take on any task in life. God wants you to have victory, and you can always win if you use the right tools!

ACTIVITY PAGE | **WORD TRANSFORMER**

Memory Verse: Don't copy the behavior and customs of this world, but let God transform you into a new person by changing the way you think. Then you will learn to know God's will for you, which is good and pleasing and perfect. —Romans 12:2

ANSWER KEY:

WORD TRANSFORMER

1. DON'T COPY THE BEHAVIOR AND CUSTOMS OF THIS **WORLD.**

2. BUT LET GOD TRANSFORM YOU INTO A NEW PERSON BY CHANGING THE WAY YOU **THINK.**

3. THEN YOU WILL LEARN TO KNOW GOD'S WILL FOR YOU, WHICH IS **GOOD** AND **PLEASING** AND **PERFECT.**

4. GOD SENT JEREMIAH TO WARN ISRAEL THAT THEY WOULD BE TAKEN CAPTIVE IF THEY DIDN'T **CHANGE** THEIR WAYS.

5. ISRAEL'S FINEST **YOUNG** PEOPLE WERE TAKEN CAPTIVE BY BABYLON BECAUSE THEY REFUSED TO REPENT.

6. DANIEL WAS DETERMINED NOT TO DEFILE HIMSELF BY **EATING** THE FOOD AND WINE GIVEN TO THEM BY THE KING.

7. "PLEASE TEST US FOR TEN DAYS ON A **DIET** OF VEGETABLES AND WATER," DANIEL SAID.

8. (DANIEL CONTINUED,) "AT THE END OF THE TEN DAYS, SEE HOW WE LOOK COMPARED TO THE OTHER YOUNG MEN WHO ARE EATING THE **KING'S** FOOD. THEN MAKE YOUR DECISION IN **LIGHT** OF WHAT YOU SEE."

9. AT THE END OF THE TEN DAYS, DANIEL AND HIS THREE FRIENDS LOOKED **HEALTHIER** AND **BETTER** NOURISHED THAN THE YOUNG MEN WHO HAD BEEN EATING THE FOOD ASSIGNED BY THE KING.

10. GOD GAVE THESE FOUR YOUNG MEN AN UNUSUAL APTITUDE FOR UNDERSTANDING EVERY ASPECT OF LITERATURE AND **WISDOM.**

Name:_____

So often, the devil tries to scramble things in our minds. Another way of saying something is evil, is to say it's "twisted." Thankfully, God is the Great Unscrambler. When we think God's thoughts, we realize how to live in THE BLESSING, not in the curse.

WORD
TRANSFORMER

UNSCRAMBLE THE WORDS:

1. DON'T COPY THE BEHAVIOR AND CUSTOMS OF THIS LORWD.
   _____

2. BUT LET GOD TRANSFORM YOU INTO A NEW PERSON BY CHANGING THE WAY YOU KINTH. _____

3. THEN YOU WILL LEARN TO KNOW GOD'S WILL FOR YOU, WHICH IS DOGO AND LAGIPENS AND FERCTEP. _____,
   _____, _____

4. GOD SENT JEREMIAH TO WARN ISRAEL THAT THEY WOULD BE TAKEN CAPTIVE IF THEY DIDN'T GENACH THEIR WAYS.
   _____

5. ISRAEL'S FINEST GOUNY PEOPLE WERE TAKEN CAPTIVE BY BABYLON BECAUSE THEY REFUSED TO REPENT. _____

6. DANIEL WAS DETERMINED NOT TO DEFILE HIMSELF BY GAITEN THE FOOD AND WINE GIVEN TO THEM BY THE KING. _____

7. "PLEASE TEST US FOR TEN DAYS ON A TEID OF VEGETABLES AND WATER," DANIEL SAID. _____

8. (DANIEL CONTINUED,) "AT THE END OF THE TEN DAYS, SEE HOW WE LOOK COMPARED TO THE OTHER YOUNG MEN WHO ARE EATING THE GNIK'S FOOD. THEN MAKE YOUR DECISION IN TILGH OF WHAT YOU SEE." _____, _____

9. AT THE END OF THE TEN DAYS, DANIEL AND HIS THREE FRIENDS LOOKED THELIREHA AND TEBRET NOURISHED THAN THE YOUNG MEN WHO HAD BEEN EATING THE FOOD ASSIGNED BY THE KING.
   _____, _____

10. GOD GAVE THESE FOUR YOUNG MEN AN UNUSUAL APTITUDE FOR UNDERSTANDING EVERY ASPECT OF LITERATURE AND SWODIM.
    _____

Notes: _____

_____

_____

_____

_____

_____

_____

_____

_____

_____

_____

_____

_____

_____

_____

_____

_____

_____

_____

_____

_____

_____

_____

_____

_____

_____

_____

_____

_____

_____

_____

_____

_____

WEEK 3: LIVING IN THE BUBBLE— MAKING GOD'S WORD OUR CREED

 Memory Verse: *I have chosen to be faithful; I have determined to live by your regulations.* —Psalm 119:30

WEEK 3: SNAPSHOT

LIVING IN THE BUBBLE— MAKING GOD'S WORD OUR CREED

DAY	TYPE OF LESSON	LESSON TITLE	SUPPLIES
Day 1	Bible Lesson	Taking the Heat	None
Day 2	Storybook Theater	Stickin' to Yer Guns Part 2	Optional Costumes, Props, Art supplies
Day 3	Giving Lesson	Rebuke the Devourer	A bag of candy, 2 Gallon-sized resealable food storage bags, Black wardrobe and mask, A helper or puppet, Money (optional)
Day 4	Object Lesson	Bubble Blower	Wooden dowels, Rope, Metal washer for weight, Bucket, Dishwashing liquid, Strong tape or rubber bands
Day 5	Game Time	Don't Pop the Bubble	Large container of bubbles, Hula hoop, Duct tape, Stopwatch
Bonus	Activity Page	Finding God's Words	1 Copy for each child

Lesson Introduction:

Since Volume 1, we have reiterated the need for our Superkids to CHOOSE. Life doesn't just happen to go God's way, and THE BLESSING doesn't just fall on us because we are Christians. We choose to do things God's way so we are BLESSED (Deuteronomy 30:11-20).

When our Superkids understand this, living this way will become first nature to them.

As we train our Superkids, remember what this will do for their future. They will be easily led by the Spirit and full of His wisdom. Your extra effort, study or preparation that may be required is so worth it. Be encouraged today! You are making an impact on this generation—and beyond!

Love,

Commander Kellie

Commander Kellie

Lesson Outline:

This week, your children will learn about the power of CHOICE. Every parent wants his or her Superkids to be safe. There's no better way to see that happen than to teach your Superkids their creed! The safest place you can ever be is in the will of God…even if you're in the middle of a furnace, like Hananiah, Mishael and Azariah!

I. WE MUST CHOOSE TO DO THINGS GOD'S WAY

a. Jesus knew He must obey His Father, no matter what He Himself wanted to do. John 5:30, AMP

b. As Jesus heard instructions from His Father, He decided that His Father's way is right. So Jesus is always right!

c. When we choose God's way, our understanding gets bigger—we can be right, too! Psalm 119:30-32

II. STORE HIS WORD IN YOUR HEART Proverbs 3:1-4

a. God wants to put His Word into your heart. Jeremiah 31:33

b. All we have to do is receive it and treasure it, and we can live in His bubble! Proverbs 2:1-8

c. How do you store the Word in your heart?

    1. Read and study the Word.

    2. Listen to the Holy Spirit, your parents, and your leaders at church.

    3. Say the Word out loud.

    4. Be a doer of the Word.

III. HANANIAH, MISHAEL AND AZARIAH WERE TOLD TO BOW TO ANOTHER GOD Daniel 3:7-15

a. They chose their God above their own protection, and <u>declared</u> their choice. Daniel 3:16-18

b. When their actions honored God, He protected and promoted them! Daniel 3:25-30

c. Jeremiah had declared that those who trust in the Lord aren't bothered by the heat. Jeremiah 17:7-8

d. They lived in God's bubble—just like you!

Notes: _____

_____

_____

DAY 1: BIBLE LESSON — TAKING THE HEAT

Memory Verse: I have chosen to be faithful; I have determined to live by your regulations.
—Psalm 119:30

When Shadrach, Meshach and Abednego choose to follow God's command and not bow down to the graven image of the king, they are thrown into a fiery furnace! But God sends help to them in the fire, and they come out unharmed. So, the king worships the true God and promotes Shadrach, Meshach and Abednego again.

Read Daniel 3:1-15:
God's Men Won't Bow

(Note: Remind your Superkids that Shadrach, Meshach and Abednego are Hananiah, Mishael and Azariah.)

King Nebuchadnezzar made a gold statue ninety feet tall and nine feet wide and set it up on the plain of Dura in the province of Babylon. Then he sent messages to the high officers, officials, governors, advisers, treasurers, judges, magistrates, and all the provincial officials to come to the dedication of the statue he had set up. So all these officials came and stood before the statue King Nebuchadnezzar had set up.

Then a herald shouted out, "People of all races and nations and languages, listen to the king's command! When you hear the sound of the horn, flute, zither, lyre, harp, pipes, and other musical instruments, bow to the ground to worship King Nebuchadnezzar's gold statue. Anyone who refuses to obey will immediately be thrown into a blazing furnace."

So at the sound of the musical instruments, all the people, whatever their race or nation or language, bowed to the ground and worshiped the gold statue that King Nebuchadnezzar had set up.

But some of the astrologers went to the king and informed on the Jews. They said to King Nebuchadnezzar, "Long live the king! You issued a decree requiring all the people to bow down and worship the gold statue when they hear the sound of the horn, flute, zither, lyre, harp, pipes, and other musical instruments. That decree also states that those who refuse to obey must be thrown into a blazing furnace. But there are some Jews—Shadrach, Meshach, and Abednego—whom you have put in charge of the province of Babylon. They pay no attention to you, Your Majesty. They refuse to serve your gods and do not worship the gold statue you have set up."

Then Nebuchadnezzar flew into a rage and ordered that Shadrach, Meshach, and Abednego be brought before him. When they were brought in, Nebuchadnezzar said to them, "Is it true, Shadrach, Meshach, and Abednego, that you refuse to serve my gods or to worship the gold statue I have set up? I will give you one more chance to bow down and worship the statue I have made when you hear the sound of the musical instruments. But if you refuse, you will be thrown immediately into the blazing furnace. And then what god will be able to rescue you from my power?"

Answer Discussion Questions 1-3

Read Daniel 3:15-30:

[King Nebuchadnezzar said:] I will give you one more chance to bow down and worship the statue I have made when you hear the sound of the musical instruments. But if you refuse, you will be thrown immediately into the blazing furnace. And then what god will be able to rescue you from my power?"

Shadrach, Meshach, and Abednego replied, "O Nebuchadnezzar, we do not need to defend ourselves before you. If we are thrown into the blazing furnace, the God whom we serve is able to save us. He will rescue us from your power, Your Majesty. But even if he doesn't, we want to make it clear to you, Your Majesty, that we will never serve your gods or worship the gold statue you have set up."

Nebuchadnezzar was so furious with Shadrach, Meshach, and Abednego that his face became distorted with rage. He commanded that the furnace be heated seven times hotter than usual. Then he ordered some of the strongest men of his army to bind Shadrach, Meshach, and Abednego and throw them into the blazing furnace. So they tied them up and threw them into the furnace, fully dressed in their pants, turbans, robes, and other garments. And because the king, in his anger, had demanded such a hot fire in the furnace, the flames killed the soldiers as they threw the three men in. So Shadrach, Meshach, and Abednego, securely tied, fell into the roaring flames.

But suddenly, Nebuchadnezzar jumped up in amazement and exclaimed to his advisers, "Didn't we tie up three men and throw them into the furnace?"

"Yes, Your Majesty, we certainly did," they replied.

"Look!" Nebuchadnezzar shouted. "I see four men, unbound, walking around in the fire unharmed! And the fourth looks like a god!"

Then Nebuchadnezzar came as close as he could to the door of the flaming furnace and shouted: "Shadrach, Meshach, and Abednego, servants of the Most High God, come out! Come here!"

So Shadrach, Meshach, and Abednego stepped out of the fire. Then the high officers, officials, governors, and advisers crowded around them and saw that the fire had not touched them. Not a hair on their heads was singed, and their clothing was not scorched. They didn't even smell of smoke!

Then Nebuchadnezzar said, "Praise to the God of Shadrach, Meshach, and Abednego! He sent his angel to rescue his servants who trusted in him. They defied the king's command and were willing to die rather than serve or worship any god except their own God. Therefore, I make this decree: If any people, whatever their race or nation or language, speak a word against the God of Shadrach, Meshach, and Abednego, they will be torn limb from limb, and their houses will be turned into heaps of rubble. There is no other god who can rescue like this!"

Then the king promoted Shadrach, Meshach, and Abednego to even higher positions in the province of Babylon.

Answer Discussion Questions 4-10

Discussion Questions:

1. **What would you do if you were Shadrach, Meshach and Abednego?**

   Answers will vary, but make sure your children understand the passage.

2. **What would be their punishment if they refused the king?**

They would be thrown into the fiery furnace—a furnace hot enough to kill them.

3. **Shadrach, Meshach and Abednego got in trouble with the king's officials when they refused the royal command. And now, the king himself is giving the young men one more chance to CHOOSE to bow and worship him. But if they follow GOD's command and don't bow, they'll be thrown into the furnace. Have you ever chosen to do the right thing, but then more pressure came—and you either gave in to sin or chose the right way?**

Answers may vary. This is a great opportunity for your Superkids to hear an example from your life. It's even better sometimes if you can tell them a true story of when you gave in to pressure, and what those results led to. But also, try to get them to share, as well.

4. **What were some character traits of Shadrach, Meshach and Abednego?**

   • Courage/bravery

   • Trust/faith in God

   • Faithfulness to God

   • Obedience to God's Word ("You must not have any other god but me"/no idols.)

5. **ACT IT OUT: Give the following speech to one of your best readers and have him or her read it with intensity. You can also split it up on sheets of paper between your Superkids and have each one read a portion:**

"O Nebuchadnezzar, we do not need to defend ourselves before you. If we are thrown into the blazing furnace, the God whom we serve is able to save us. He will rescue us from your power, Your Majesty. But even if he doesn't, we want to make it clear to you, Your Majesty, that we will never serve your gods or worship the gold statue you have set up."

How did you feel when you read Shadrach, Meshach and Abednego's statement to the king?

The answers should be similar to Question #4.

6. **How much hotter did the king make the furnace after he heard Shadrach, Meshach and Abednego's response?**

Seven times hotter

7. **How many people did the king end up seeing in the fire?**

Four

8. **Who did the king say the fourth man in the fire looked like?**

A god

9. **Who has said He will be with us in the fire and flood and through whatever trouble we face? Read Deuteronomy 31:6 and Isaiah 43:2:** "So be strong and courageous! Do not be afraid and do not panic before them. For the Lord your God will personally go ahead of you. He will neither fail you nor abandon you." "When you go through deep waters, I will be with you. When you go through rivers of difficulty, you will not drown. When you walk through the fire of oppression, you will not be burned up; the flames will not consume you." God said He would never leave us nor forsake us!

10. **At the end of the day, whom did King Nebuchadnezzar end up bowing down to worship?**

God (Shadrach, Meshach and Abednego's God)

DAY 2: STORYBOOK THEATER | STICKIN' TO YER GUNS PART 2

Concept: The second part of a two-week series about Daniel, Hananiah, Azariah and Mishael, from Daniel 3, but set in the Wild, Wild West! A memorable way to tell a wonderful Bible story.

Teacher Tips:
- DO NOT USE REAL GUNS OR KNIVES! Purchase toy guns/knives at toy stores or costume shops.
- Select some western-style music from a good, old-fashioned Western movie soundtrack. Ennio Morricone (Italian composer and conductor) is brilliant for this. Play the music while the narrator talks, to give it a little more excitement and flow.
- Try to read with the Western accent it's written in.

List of Characters/Optional Costumes and Props
- Narrator: Good reader, country-Western accent
- Buck: Big presence, very tough and intimidating/ranger badge
- Cookie: Craggy, old, chuck-wagon cook/apron
- Daniel: Natural leader/FAKE shotgun, ranger badge
- Hananiah: Brainiac/ maybe wears old-fashioned eyeglasses, smaller FAKE gun—Colt .45, ranger badge
- Mishael: The funny guy/rope, ranger badge
- Azariah: More sensitive type; looks up to Daniel/FAKE knives, ranger badge
- Pickle: A real sleaze-bucket and bootlicker; the brains of the operation
- Joey: Pickle's sidekick
- Jimmy: Not the brightest tool in the shed
- Fourth Cowboy: Angelic, God-like being/white shirt, white jeans, white boots and white hat
- More rangers (optional)

All Costumes: Jeans (cowboy style preferred), Button-down flannel or country-style shirts (always better if they've been rolled in dirt to look more Western era), Cowboy boots, Cowboy hats, Spurs, Chaps; Daniel, Hananiah, Mishael, Azariah: Stuffing for muscles (polyester fiberfill or partially inflated swim floaties)

Supplies: ■ Whiteboard, chalkboard or easel with paper, ■ Dry-erase markers if using whiteboard, colored chalks if using chalkboard, or pencil (art pencils work best) and eraser, black marker and rags (to blend chalks) if using paper, ■ Art smock (to keep your artist's clothes clean)

Props: FAKE shotgun/rifle (for Daniel), Rope (for Mishael), FAKE knives (for Azariah), Smaller FAKE gun—Colt .45 (for Hananiah), 5 Sheriff/Texas Ranger badges (try a dollar store), Cooking pot and spoon, Bowls, Campfire: easy to make with wooden logs resting on top of an upturned fan with red and yellow tissue paper taped to the top of the fan and threaded between the logs. Turn fan to lowest setting. Paper will flutter upward between logs, simulating flames, Music, Smoke machine and red lighting to show the fire growing hotter and hotter (optional).

Optional Backdrop: Brown or gray (color of a mountain) roll of LARGE construction paper. With a dark, GRAY marker, draw the face of the actor who is playing Buck, on the construction paper. You can just draw his mouth and chin, or a particular part of his face, so it makes the mountain look bigger. Think Mount Rushmore.

Variation No. 1:

Read the story as part of your read-aloud time.

Variation No. 2:

Read like a campfire story. Because it's a Western, this is a fun story to read in front of a fire. You can even have the option of making your own dinner as you talk about how Mishael, Azariah and Hananiah wouldn't bow even when the flames were so hot! Imagine, they walked out not even smelling like smoke!

Variation No. 3:

Read the story as an old-time radio skit, complete with different actors for each part. If you are limited on participants, then assign more than one part per person, and change the voice. Make copies of the skit, and have each actor highlight his/her lines. This is great for a community Bible study or co-op.

Variation No. 4:

Act out the story as a fun skit. Perhaps your children can practice during the day (even creating costumes from everyday items), and then perform the skit in the evening before the whole family or community. Before beginning your skit, remember to introduce your cast! If you are limited on participants, have each person play more than one part. This is great for a community Bible study or co-op.

Variation No. 5:

Create a storybook theater where one or more family members sketch the story on a whiteboard, chalkboard or artist's easel as another member reads the story. Initially, there will be a few supplies to purchase but don't let this be a deterrent from using the illustrated story option! Once the supplies have been purchased, they'll be long-lasting and reusable.

To make your presentation easier, lightly sketch the drawing with a pencil prior to presentation. Time may not allow the picture to be completely drawn and colored at the time of the lesson. Erase pencil lines, so light lines are visible to the artist but not visible to your children. Review the story ahead of time to determine the amount of time needed to complete the illustration while telling the story. When the story begins, use black markers to "draw" the picture, following the sketched pencil lines. Next, apply color using the pastel chalk. Then, blend the color with the rags. Finally, cut the illustration from the board, roll it up, secure it with rubber bands, and share it with one of your children!

Story:

[OPTIONAL: PLAY MUSIC]

Well, howdy again, folks! Hope you enjoyed our last story. And by story, I mean *history.* Ya know—where Daniel, Hananiah, Mishael and Azariah had to stick to their guns, and refused to eat the stuff Buck was tryin' to feed 'em? 'Course ya know they came out on top. Yup, a whole 10 times better than everyone else in their outfit. Wish I could tell ya that were the last time them boys was between a rock and a hard place. But, as many o' y'all know, livin' with a creed ain't no pony ride. And not much longer after Buck put them boys in charge, they was once again faced with a choice. But this time, it was a choice of life or death....

Buck had just been promoted to senior captain over the Texas Rangers. But this step up got 'im a bit too big for his boots, perty fast. One stormy day, as the rangers were protectin' the plains, Buck saw a mountain in the distance that drew his attention.

"Hoo! Looky yonder!" Buck hollered. "Come on, rangers! The mountain looks like it could give us some real coverin' from the storm."

As the rangers followed Buck up the mountain, they discovered that the shape of it highly resembled Senior Captain Buck's face.

[FADE MUSIC OUT]

Buck reached the mountain first, with new Sergeants Hananiah, Mishael and Azariah following closely behind. Buck dismounted and looked at the rock that eerily matched his own ugly mug. "Is it just me," Buck began, "or has nature carved this here rock to look like my face?"

Jimmy, a newer ranger, whose brain wasn't always fully loaded, if ya catch my meanin', was happy to be able to catch on fast when he saw Buck's resemblance to the big rock. "Hot dog!" Jimmy exclaimed. "It sure do look like you!"

Buck continued to look on in wonder. "Now, why would there be such a thing like that?"

Pickle, who was as slippery as his name, sidled right up next to Buck. "Well, sir," he said in a flatterin' tone, "you're the sharpest shooter in the West!"

Pickle's sneaky sidekick, Joey, added, "And you ride horses better'n anybody!"

Jimmy didn't know about that, but he did know one thing for sure about his captain, so he added in earnest, "And, Captain Buck, you play the harmonica like a god!"

"Ha-ha," Buck chuckled. "You got a point there, Jimmy."

Tryin' to find a new way into his captain's good graces, Pickle got real serious: "Pardon me, but this ain't no laughin' matter, boss. Nature done singled you out."

Buck tapped his chin with a low, "Hmm...."

Right on cue, Joey added, "Oh yeah, we should be givin' honor where it's due, sir."

Pickle continued to water the idea. "What about a sacrifice. Captain, sir, I'd hate for nature to hit us with a worse storm just 'cause we ain't givin' some sort of sacrifice in your honor!"

Buck, who'd begun to really see himself from his own high horse, considered it. And with a snap he said, "I got it! Ever' time I play my harmonica, you gotta bow down and worship this rock that looks like my face!"

Pickle was proud his idea had sparked such a response. "Splendid idea, sir!"

Jimmy agreed. "Yee-haw! Mother nature will love us!"

"How 'bout a practice round?" Pickle suggested.

Buck pulled his harmonica out of his pocket and began to play. And quickly, all the rangers but Sergeants Hananiah, Mishael and Azariah took off their hats and bowed down to worship the mountain.

Now, Buck was so into his own perty playin', with his eyes closed and all, that he didn't even notice his top sergeants hadn't bowed. But Pickle, of course, saw it all, and he was just jumpin' at any chance to get one o' them shiny sergeant badges.

As Buck's song ended, everyone stood. Jimmy had tears in his eyes and Buck felt mighty good about himself.

"Look!" Joey pointed up at the sky. "I think the sky just cleared up a bit."

Buck looked up as the rain faded away, then looked back down at his harmonica.

Anxious to see his evil plot succeed, Pickle said, "Captain, sir, you *must* be a god...for your music to have such power."

Astounded, Buck looked at his harmonica again and smiled. "Well, I guess so. If my playin' stopped that storm, I really am a god." He yawned. "I'm gonna go take myself a god-nap. I think I earned it."

As Buck haughtily strode off, Hananiah whistled to Mishael and Az. He motioned with his head for them to follow, and they all disappeared behind the rock as Pickle and some of the other rangers started to build a campfire.

"Hey, boys," Pickle said as he started pilin' the wood on, "did you notice that Sergeants Hananiah, Mishael and Azariah weren't bowin'?"

Jimmy shook his head, "Nope."

"Sure did." Joey nodded.

"Oh yeah, uhhh... me, too!" Jimmy pretended.

Pickle rolled his eyes, but got the two rangers' attention. "Looks like an opportunity for promotion if you ask me."

"Huh?" Jimmy asked.

"How you figure?" Joey wanted that shiny sergeant badge, too.

"Well..." Pickle began, "I got myself a perty good idea...." He rubbed his hands together greedily and began layin' out his nasty plot against Hananiah, Mishael and Azariah.

Well, as you can well guess, this meant big trouble for our boys. And, as you well know, them boys weren't about to start worshipin' another god...especially not one that smelled like dirty, old beans on a hot summer day.

As night turned on, the rangers came out to sit by the campfire for some grub. Pickle, Jimmy and Joey stood together as Buck walked out with a big yawn.

"Look. It's the great one!" Pickle announced.

All the rangers tipped their hats in recognition. Jimmy removed his hat and put it over his heart. "May you live forever!" he said.

Buck walked to the three conspirators and put a hand on Jimmy's shoulder. "Well, I just might, Jimmy."

Pickle slid in between Jimmy and the captain. "We was just wonderin', sir...if there was any sort of punishment for not worshipin' yer almightiness, sir."

"Punishment?" Buck hadn't even considered it.

"Ya know…" Jimmy added, "just in case someone decided not to bow down to you, sir."

Buck crossed his arms, "I don't know.…"

Emphatically, Jimmy burst out, "I think anyone who don't worship you oughta be roasted in the campfire!"

Even Buck was taken aback at Jimmy's fervor. "Boys, I hardly think it necessary to…"

But Pickle cut him off. "You ain't goin' soft on us just 'cause yer a god now, are ya?"

"No! Never!" Buck retorted.

Next, Joey sidled up to Buck like they was the best o' friends. "Sir, you oughta make a punishment. I saw with my own eyes a few rangers who didn't bow today."

"What?!" Buck was outraged. "Impossible!"

"No, sir," Joey replied. "And I'd swear it on this holy rock that they ain't never gonna bow. They looked real defiant-like while you was playin' yer harmonica.…"

Buck's hand tapped the edge of his gun holster and his eyes got all squinty and serious. "You point 'em out," Buck said with a low drawl, "and we'll throw 'em in the campfire, now!"

Joey pointed straight at Hananiah, Mishael and Azariah.

Pickle exclaimed as if shocked, "No…yer own sergeants, sir?"

"Sergeants!" Buck's yell echoed from his exquisite rock.

The three boys turned to salute.

Buck approached Hananiah, Mishael and Azariah. "Is this true? My own sergeants won't bow when I play?"

The sergeants nodded in unison. "Yes, sir," they replied.

"Of all the.…" Buck was angry and hurt that his favorites had been the perpetrators. "You boys have one more chance!" He spat at the young sergeants' faces. "I'm gonna get out my harmonica, and if yer not bowin' to my mountain, I'm gonna throw you into this here campfire!"

Azariah looked at his brothers. They nodded. "Sir," Az said, "we won't bow."

"What?" Buck was astonished.

Mishael added, "We won't worship any other god than the One, true livin' God!" He pointed up, but Buck laughed. "What God?! I'm the one rulin' the skies right now. You boys is gonna burn for yer insubordination! An' ain't nobody here gonna be able to pull you out!"

Hananiah remembered his old teachings and pushed his ol' glasses up on his nose. "With all due respect, sir, our Pastor Jeremiah said, if we trust in the Lord, we won't be afraid when the heat comes."

This really made Buck spit! "Well, yer ol' preacher, Jeremiah, ain't here. An' ain't nobody gonna pull ya'll out!"

Mishael took a step closer to the spittin'-mad captain. "Well, God will deliver us. An' even if ya don't throw us in the fire, we're still not gonna serve your god...or anyone else for that matter!"

"Arghhhhhhh!" Buck screamed, "That's it! Rope these boys up! An' build up this campfire!"

Pickle, Joey and Jimmy happily tied up Hananiah, Mishael and Azariah, as Buck paced before the fire. "I want it seven times bigger an' hotter!" Buck exclaimed, and the rangers added more kindling to the fire.

"That's it, rangers! Ha-ha-ha! I'll teach you boys to defy Captain Buck, god of the frontier!" Buck motioned with his hankie for Hananiah, Mishael and Az to be brought forward. "Wooohooo, that's hot!" Buck backed away from the fire as he dabbed the hankie to his neck.

The three conspirators stopped at the fire's edge. Pickle couldn't stand the heat. "We can't take 'em any closer, boss. It's too hot!" he exclaimed.

Buck retorted, "Shove 'em in, you sissies!"

So the three men shoved the brothers right into the middle of the fire. But its heat got to them even from the edge. Pickle cried out, "Ow, my hands!"

"Mommy!" Jimmy wailed in pain as they all ran to Buck.

But as the fire grew hotter, the rope tying Hananiah, Mishael and Az rolled off, and the white-hot flame revealed a Fourth Cowboy! Now, this here Cowboy was all bright in white. And what's more—the sergeants weren't burnin' at all!

Buck looked at the fire, confused. "Who in the sand dunes is that?" he asked.

Jimmy exclaimed, "Hot diggity dog!"

They all watched, amazed, as Hananiah, Mishael, Azariah and the Fourth Cowboy stood in that fire like it was nothin'.

Buck counted, and then counted again. "Didn't we just throw *three* men in there?"

Pickle was flabbergasted. Jimmy tried to count on his fingers, but couldn't get past two.

Buck rubbed his eyes. Was he seein' straight? "How many people do you see in there?"

Jimmy still hadn't gotten past counting to two, but Joey answered, "I see four."

Pickle gulped. "Me too.... an'... an' that fourth one looks like a real God!"

They all stared at the Fourth Cowboy with reverence and very great fear.

Joey's knees was a-bucklin'. "I hope their God ain't plannin' on punishing us!"

Even big ol' Buck was scared. "Hananiah, Mishael, Az, please come out," he yelled.

The brothers looked at their captain. Buck added, "You DO serve the One, true living God. Please come out of the fire!"

"Yeah," Pickle added. "Please, before your God sends fire on us!"

Perfectly healthy, the three brothers strode from the fire. Buck bowed and the other rangers did, too.

Face to the ground, Buck exclaimed, "Blessed be your God, who sent His angels to deliver you because you trusted in Him!"

The three brothers agreed in unison, "Amen!"

As the men stood back up, Jimmy sniffed the sergeants. "Say, you boys don't even smell like smoke!" He was shocked.

Buck sniffed 'em too. True, Hananiah, Mishael and Az may have needed a bath, but Buck didn't catch a whiff of any smoke on 'em. Buck exclaimed, "It's truly a miracle!"

And all the rangers who saw that day said, "Aaaaaaa-men!"

Buck whistled to the rangers: "Listen here, I'm makin' a new law, if anyone ever so much as says a bad word about these boys' true and livin' God, we'll tear 'em up limb from limb!"

Hananiah, Mishael and Az were shocked, but Jimmy yelled out a perty, "Hallelujah!"

Buck moved back and put his arms around his sergeants once more. "And uh…just so there's no hard feelins 'tween me and yer God, I'm promotin' you boys to captains!"

Everyone cheered, except an embittered Pickle. "Not again!" He stomped with his boot, but even Jimmy knew better.

Giving Pickle a hard elbow to the ribs, Jimmy pointed to the sky. "Shhhhhh!"

Pickle clamped his hands on his mouth, and at least pretended to smile for the rest of the evening.

[PLAY WESTERN OUTRO MUSIC]

An' that there's how Hananiah, Mishael and Azariah once again got promoted 'cause they stuck to their guns and they refused to bow down to other gods. Boy, I tell ya, it sure pays to be faithful to yer creed!

[FADE MUSIC]

Notes: _____

_____

_____

_____

_____

DAY 3: GIVING LESSON | REBUKE THE DEVOURER

 Suggested Time: 10-15 minutes

 Offering Scripture: "Bring all the tithes into the storehouse so there will be enough food in my Temple. If you do," says the Lord of Heaven's Armies, "I will open the windows of heaven for you. I will pour out a blessing so great you won't have enough room to take it in! Try it! Put me to the test! Your crops will be abundant, for I will guard them from insects and disease. Your grapes will not fall from the vine before they are ripe," says the Lord of Heaven's Armies. "Then all nations will call you blessed, for your land will be such a delight," says the Lord of Heaven's Armies. —Malachi 3:10-12

 Teacher Tip: Make this offering as much fun as you want to. It does require the help of another older child, parent or adult, but if you really can't find someone you can use a puppet to be the "Devourer."

Supplies: ■ A bag of candy, ■ 2 Gallon-sized resealable food storage bags, ■ Black wardrobe and mask for thief, ■ Money Superkids can tithe from (optional)

Prior to Lesson:

Have your oldest child, helper or another parent dress up as the "Devourer." Be sure to practice the candy snatching and the "fight scene," where the teacher defends the Superkid's candy stash. This should be lots of fun for everyone. So, feel free to work out some fight choreography. Just make sure no one (especially your Superkid volunteer) gets hurt!

Lesson Instructions:

Who likes candy? Talk about *your* favorite candy. *(Put a dreamy look on your face and pretend to be thinking about how good it tastes.)* Since you like candy, too, would one of you like to be my helper?

Pick one of your kids who likes candy, and give him/her the empty resealable food storage bag. OK, I'm going to give you 10 pieces of candy. Help me count, please. *(Count out 10 pieces of candy, and put it into the Superkid's resealable food storage bag.)* As practiced, the "Devourer" comes out of nowhere and snatches the bag from the Superkid without warning and leaves!

Whoa! We're going to try this again. *(Give the Superkid the other resealable food storage bag and count out 10 more pieces of candy for your Superkid helper.)* Here you go! Now, would you mind giving one of these back? Just trust me that if you give me one of these, I'll be your partner and help you keep your candy stash safe.

Your Superkid will give back one candy, but... "Uh, oh! Here comes the Devourer again!" Suddenly, the Devourer comes back to steal the candy! This time, you protect the Superkid and the candy stash.

Fight scene.... The Devourer retreats, clearly beaten.

Thanks for letting me help you out! Here you go! *(Open your bag wide and pour the contents of your candy bag out so fast that some of them even fall on the floor.)*

You can keep all of this candy. *(If your Superkid listened, he/she may try to tithe again!)*

Let's read Malachi 3:10-12 together. Superkids, God wants to partner up with us to make us prosper. That means He doesn't want us to lack *any* GOOD thing. Another translation says that He'll rebuke the devourer for our sakes. But if we ignore Him when He blesses us, we're not allowing Him to help defend us from the "devourer," the devil. The devil is like that thief who stole all of (Superkid's name)'s candy. The tithe is just 10 percent of what God blesses us with. We're supposed to give that 10 percent to God; otherwise we become God robbers.

That means if you have $10 given to you, how many do you give back to God? That's right—$1. What if you have $100? Think about it…. *(Help your Superkids to come up with 10 percent of $100.)*

Was it better to give me 10 percent of what I gave (Superkid's name), or was it better when (he/she) kept it for himself/herself?

(If your Superkid did not tithe again after you emptied out the big candy bag, have the thief come back to steal again.)

Uh-oh. Quick, you tithe, and I'll hold the Devourer back. *(Hold the Devourer at bay until the Superkid gives the tithe. Then push the Devourer back again.)*

Isn't God good? He makes it so easy for us. We give one to Him, and we get to keep the other nine! Just like I was able to pour that candy into (Superkid's name)'s bag, God wants to pour blessings out on our lives. And He can, if we tithe. The verse said to test Him on it, and see if He'll not bless us with more than we can even take in!

Praise God! Let's prepare our offering for next week together. I'm going to go around, and we can all do the math to make sure our tithes are correct. (If some Superkids don't have money, feel free to give them something they can tithe from.)

Notes: _____

_____

_____

_____

_____

_____

_____

_____

_____

_____

_____

_____

_____

DAY 4: OBJECT LESSON   BUBBLE BLOWER

 Suggested Time: 10 minutes

 Memory Verse: I have chosen to be faithful; I have determined to live by your regulations.
—Psalm 119:30

 Teacher Tip: Make sure to do a trial run. When you dip the ropes in the soap, then spread the dowels in and out, you can make a huge bubble.

Supplies: ☐ Wooden dowels, ☐ Rope, ☐ Metal washer for weight, ☐ Bucket, ☐ Dishwashing liquid, ☐ Strong tape or rubber bands

Lesson Instructions:

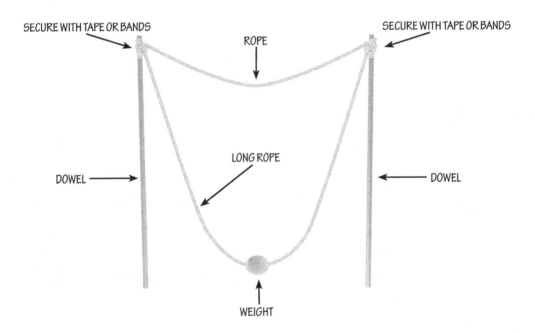

SECURE WITH TAPE OR BANDS   SECURE WITH TAPE OR BANDS
ROPE
LONG ROPE
DOWEL   DOWEL
WEIGHT

Who likes bubbles? I need someone to help me. Someone who REEEEAAAALLLY likes bubbles!

There are all different sizes of bubbles. Small bubbles, medium bubbles and even HUGE bubbles.

Today, we're talking about living in the bubble of Blessing. When we follow the instructions of the Lord, we remain in that bubble. And let me tell you, that bubble is a HUGE bubble!

Psalm 91 even talks about being completely covered, where no harm or disease can touch you. That's what happens when you live in the shelter of the Most High and make God and His ways your refuge.

Notes: _____

_____

_____

_____

_____

_____

_____

_____

_____

_____

_____

_____

_____

_____

_____

_____

_____

_____

_____

_____

_____

_____

_____

_____

_____

_____

_____

_____

_____

_____

_____

_____

_____

_____

_____

_____

DAY 5: GAME TIME — DON'T POP THE BUBBLE

Suggested Time: 10 minutes

Memory Verse: I have chosen to be faithful; I have determined to live by your regulations.
—Psalm 119:30

Supplies: ■ Large container of bubbles, ■ Hula hoop, ■ Duct tape, ■ Stopwatch

Prior to Game:

Place a small strip of tape on the ground to identify a start line. Be ready to hold the hula hoop 15 feet from the start line.

Game Instructions:

This game requires at least two teams. At the start line, have the contestants blow a soap bubble with the wand contained in the bubble bottle. Using only their mouths, the contestants must blow the soap bubble and keep it airborne all the way through the hula hoop that will be placed 15 feet away. If the bubble bursts any time during the game, the contestant must go back to the start line and begin again.

Each player will have 30 seconds to blow the bubble through the hula hoop. This is a 5-minute, timed game. You can play several rounds.

Game Goal:

The team that moves the most bubbles through the hoop, wins.

Final Word:

Ask your children: What came out of the bubble when it burst? That's right! SOAP!

Why did soap come out of the bubble instead of something like soda pop or peanut butter? Was there anything else like that in the bubble? No, there was only soap, so nothing else could come out of it. Did you know we live in a bubble, too? We live in God's bubble. When we obey His Word and listen to His direction, we are safe inside His bubble. Just like soap is on the inside of a bubble, we are on the inside of God's protective bubble, and that bubble can NEVER burst!

Notes: _____

_____

_____

_____

_____

_____

_____

_____

_____

_____

_____

_____

_____

_____

_____

_____

_____

_____

_____

_____

_____

_____

_____

_____

_____

_____

_____

_____

_____

_____

ACTIVITY PAGE   FINDING GOD'S WORDS

 Memory Verse: I have chosen to be faithful; I have determined to live by your regulations.
—Psalm 119:30

ANSWER KEY:

FINDING
GOD'S WORD

```
.  F  .  D  E  T  E  R  M  I  N  A  T  I  O  N  .  .
.  A  .  .  B  L  E  S  S  I  N  G  P  E  A  C  E  .
.  I  .  .  .  .  .  .  .  .  .  .  .  .  .  O  .
C  T  .  .  .  G  I  V  I  N  G  .  S  .  .  .  B  .
O  H  S  U  P  E  R  K  I  D  .  .  T  .  P  .  E  .
U  F  M  E  R  C  Y  .  .  .  .  .  R  .  U  L  D  H
R  U  P  R  O  T  E  C  T  I  O  N  E  .  R  I  I  O
A  L  .  J  O  Y  .  .  L  I  F  E  N  .  P  G  E  N
G  N  .  L  O  V  E  .  .  .  .  G  .  O  H  N  O
E  E  .  .  .  S  E  R  V  A  N  T  T  .  S  T  C  R
.  S  .  .  W  I  S  D  O  M  .  .  H  .  E  .  E  .
.  S  .  .  .  A  B  U  N  D  A  N  C  E  .  .  .  .
```

Name: _____

FINDING
GOD'S WORD

```
I F C D E T E R M I N A T I O N P J
G A M H B L E S S I N G P E A C E M
P I I U Z E N J H U W T U H S W O A
C T I H I G I V I N G M S M C L B P
O H S U P E R K I D M B T Q P P E R
U F M E R C Y B Z J X Q R T U L D H
R U P R O T E C T I O N E M R I I O
A L M J O Y C N L I F E N D P G E N
G N D L O V E R G T C C G F O H N O
E E Z H L S E R V A N T T X S T C R
U S C O W I S D O M X E H Z E F E W
W S E L Y A B U N D A N C E K D K M
```

FIND THE FOLLOWING
WORDS IN THE PUZZLE.
WORDS ARE HIDDEN

➡️ AND ⬇️ .

ABUNDANCE	LOVE
BLESSING	MERCY
COURAGE	OBEDIENCE
DETERMINATION	PEACE
FAITHFULNESS	PROTECTION
GIVING	PURPOSE
HONOR	SERVANT
JOY	STRENGTH
LIFE	SUPERKID
LIGHT	WISDOM

WEEK 4: I AM A SUPERKID!

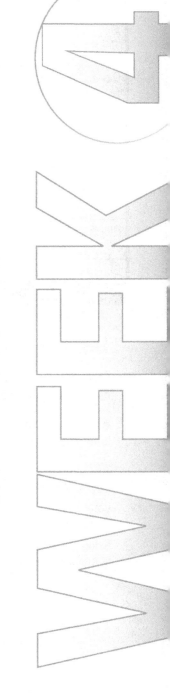
 Memory Verse: *You are of God, little children, and have overcome them, because He who is in you is greater than he who is in the world.* —1 John 4:4 NKJV

WEEK 4: SNAPSHOT — I AM A SUPERKID!

DAY	TYPE OF LESSON	LESSON TITLE	SUPPLIES
Day 1	Bible Lesson	Knowing Who You Are...a Superkid	Art supplies: (whatever art supplies you have handy) paper, pens, crayons, paint, markers, clay or chalk
Day 2	Academy Lab	My Heavenly Power Circuit	At least 1 foot of electrical wire, A 1.5V C-size battery, Flashlight bulb, Tape, Scissors
Day 3	Giving Lesson	I Believe and Obey	Lamb stuffed toy, Small props you have on hand that are referenced in the story, Sign with "Isaac" written on it, Sign with "Abraham" written on it, Baseball cap, Robe, Chair
Day 4	Food Fun	Salt of the Earth	Beef jerky, 3-Day-old hamburger (unrefrigerated), 2 Plates or food boxes with coverings
Day 5	Game Time	My Mission	2 Manila folders with sides stapled, 42 Notecards, 6 Envelopes, Table
Bonus	Activity Page	Decoding the Truth	1 Copy for each child, Bible

Lesson Introduction:

Again (and so soon!), we are calling on our kids to make choices. Point out to them that even Jesus had to choose. When faced with pressure, He chose to believe what the Word and His Father said about Him.

Have your Superkids name some things the Word says about them. Encourage them to say these things out loud and often. The act of speaking the Word over ourselves is one of the most powerful things we can do.

After making sure your Superkids have accepted Jesus into their hearts, encourage them to tell others about Jesus. Since this week is all about being a Superkid, encourage your cadets to be bold and to be a witness. Let your Superkids know how easy it is to tell others about Jesus. Find time this week while you are all out together and show them how to share God's love with others by giving to someone in need as Jesus would, and asking them if they have a relationship with Him. When you know who you are and how awesome He is, what is there to be afraid of?!

Love,

Commander Kellie

Commander Kellie

Lesson Outline:

This week your children will learn more about the power of CHOICE—and HOW to be a Superkid, just as JESUS did!

With Jesus in Us, We Can Be Just Like Him!

I. JESUS FOUND HIMSELF IN THE SCRIPTURES AND SAID SO
Luke 4:16-21

   a. He honored what the Father said about Him. John 5:39

   b. He didn't care what others thought of Him. John 5:40-44

   c. When He said, "I am," He was saying:

      1. I know who I am—the light of the world. John 8:12-14

      2. I don't belong to this world—I belong to My Father. John 8:23-27

      3. He accepted God's plan for Him. John 8:28-30

II. BELIEVE AND DECLARE WHAT GOD SAYS ABOUT YOU

   a. What does the Word say about you?

      1. You are chosen, blessed, you'll do greater works, etc.

      2. Have the Superkids name more things the Word says about them.

   b. Don't be afraid to stand out and be different—we're supposed to! 2 Corinthians 6:14-18

   c. When you say, "I am a Superkid," you are saying:

      1. I know who I am—He's made me the light of the world. Matthew 5:14-16

      2. I don't belong to this world. John 17:16; 1 John 4:4-6

      3. I accept and believe God's plan for me. Ephesians 2:4-10 (Read verse 10 in *The Amplified Bible.*)

III. HOW TO BE A SUPERKID

   a. Accept Jesus as your Lord and Savior. Romans 10:9

   b. Listen to the Holy Spirit, and obey His voice. John 10:27

   c. Honor and obey your parents. Ephesians 6:1-3

   d. Tell others about Jesus. Mark 16:15

DAY 1: BIBLE LESSON

KNOWING WHO YOU ARE... A SUPERKID

Memory Verse: *You are of God, little children, and have overcome them, because He who is in you is greater than he who is in the world.* —1 John 4:4 NKJV

Supplies: Whatever art supplies you have handy : ■ Paper, ■ Pens, ■ Crayons, ■ Paint, ■ Markers, ■ Clay or chalk

Jesus explained to His disciples and the Pharisees who He was—the Light of the World, the Son of God. God created us masterfully so we can be His sons and daughters, too. We have this by believing in Jesus.

Read John 8:12-18, MSG, Verses 23-30, NLT:
Jesus Knows Who He Is

Jesus once again addressed them: "I am the world's Light. No one who follows me stumbles around in the darkness. I provide plenty of light to live in."

The Pharisees objected, "All we have is your word on this. We need more than this to go on."

Jesus replied, "You're right that you only have my word. But you can depend on it being true. I know where I've come from and where I go next. You don't know where I'm from or where I'm headed. You decide according to what you can see and touch. I don't make judgments like that. But even if I did, my judgment would be true because I wouldn't make it out of the narrowness of my experience but in the largeness of the One who sent me, the Father. That fulfills the conditions set down in God's Law: that you can count on the testimony of two witnesses. And that is what you have: You have my word and you have the word of the Father who sent me."

Jesus continued, "You are from below; I am from above. You belong to this world; I do not. That is why I said that you will die in your sins; for unless you believe that I am who I claim to be, you will die in your sins."

"Who are you?" they demanded.

Jesus replied, "The one I have always claimed to be. I have much to say about you and much to condemn, but I won't. For I say only what I have heard from the one who sent me, and he is completely truthful." But they still didn't understand that he was talking about his Father.

So Jesus said, "When you have lifted up the Son of Man on the cross, then you will understand that I am he. I do nothing on my own but say only what the Father taught me. And the one who sent me is with me—he has not deserted me. For I always do what pleases him." Then many who heard him say these things believed in him.

Do Discussion Questions 1-2

Read Psalm 139:1-18, 23-24:
Who Did God Make YOU to Be?

O Lord, you have examined my heart
    and know everything about me.

You know when I sit down or stand up.
    You know my thoughts even when I'm far away.

You see me when I travel
    and when I rest at home.
    You know everything I do.

You know what I am going to say
    even before I say it, Lord.

You go before me and follow me.
    You place your hand of blessing on my head.

Such knowledge is too wonderful for me,
    too great for me to understand!

I can never escape from your Spirit!
    I can never get away from your presence!

If I go up to heaven, you are there;
    if I go down to the grave, you are there.

If I ride the wings of the morning,
    if I dwell by the farthest oceans,
    even there your hand will guide me,
    and your strength will support me.

I could ask the darkness to hide me
    and the light around me to become night—
    but even in darkness I cannot hide from you.

To you the night shines as bright as day.
    Darkness and light are the same to you.

You made all the delicate, inner parts of my body
    and knit me together in my mother's womb.

Thank you for making me so wonderfully complex!
    Your workmanship is marvelous—how well I know it.

You watched me as I was being formed in utter seclusion,
    as I was woven together in the dark of the womb.

You saw me before I was born.
    Every day of my life was recorded in your book.

Every moment was laid out
    before a single day had passed.

How precious are your thoughts about me, O God.
    They cannot be numbered!

I can't even count them;
    they outnumber the grains of sand!

And when I wake up,
    you are still with me!

Search me, O God, and know my heart;
    test me and know my anxious thoughts.

Point out anything in me that offends you,
    and lead me along the path of everlasting life.

Do Discussion Questions 3-6

Discussion Questions:

1. **Who did Jesus say He was in this passage of Scripture? (2 things)**

   Light of the world, and He referred to what He had already said about Himself as the Son of God.

2. **What did Jesus say the Pharisees needed to do to not "die in their sins"?**

   Believe that He was who He claimed to be.

3. **Who is the Creator and Father of our eternal spirits—crafting us in our mothers' wombs?**

   Our heavenly Father—God

4. **How do you choose to become a son or daughter of God?**

   Ask Jesus to come into your heart.

5. **Discuss salvation with your Superkids. Make sure that they have received Jesus into their hearts and understand how this allows them to claim God as their heavenly Father.**

   Feel free to refer back to point III in the Lesson Outline:

   a. Accept Jesus as your Lord and Savior. Romans 10:9

   b. Listen to the Holy Spirit, and obey His voice. John 10:27

   c. Honor and obey your parents. Ephesians 6:1-3

   d. Tell others about Jesus. Mark 16:15

6. **Art Time**

   Pull out some paper, pens, crayons, paint or markers—whatever art supplies you have handy or you know your Superkids enjoy (even clay or sidewalk chalk—feel free to think outside the box). Read Psalm 139 again to them a few times as they draw, paint or create a picture that this psalm makes them think about.

Notes: _____

_____

_____

_____

_____

_____

_____

_____

_____

_____

_____

_____

_____

_____

_____

_____

_____

_____

_____

_____

_____

_____

_____

_____

_____

_____

_____

_____

_____

_____

_____

_____

_____

_____

DAY 2: ACADEMY LAB — MY HEAVENLY POWER CIRCUIT

Suggested Time: 10 minutes

Key Scripture: Jesus spoke to the people once more and said, "I am the light of the world. If you follow me, you won't have to walk in darkness, because you will have the light that leads to life." —John 8:12

Teacher Tip: Do a practice run prior to the lesson.

Supplies: ☐ At least 1 foot of electrical wire (this includes extra, if needed), ☐ A 1.5V C-size battery, ☐ Flashlight bulb, ☐ Tape, ☐ Scissors (You can find all these items at a hardware store.)

Prior to Lesson:

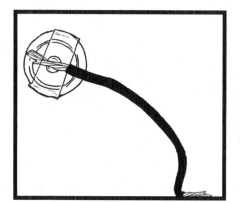 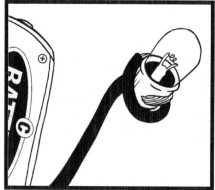 

Be sure to do a practice run before the lesson! Using scissors, cut a 5-inch strip from the electrical wire. Then, gently cut the plastic coating off each end (about an inch from the end, leaving the metal wire exposed). Make sure you do NOT cut the wire part. Pull the plastic away from the ends so that the bare wires stick out.

Lesson Instructions:

Today, we're going to get this flashlight bulb to light up! To do that, we'll need a power source and a good circuit. A *circuit* is what carries the electricity from the battery to the lightbulb.

We'll use this electrical wire to create the circuit. The electrical current we need has to run from the negative charge on the bottom of the battery (flatter side) to the lightbulb, and then to the positive side (the top) of the battery.

I have a C-cell battery here that's large enough to be the power source to light up this bulb.

First, we need to tape our electrical wire to the bottom, which is the negative charge for this battery. We have to make sure that the wire part is actually touching the center of the charge area on the battery.

Next, we must make sure that this electrical wire is connected to our battery to continue the flow (or circuit) of electricity. So, we'll wrap the other end of the electrical wire to the metal part of the lightbulb and tape it.

But wait! We still have to make sure that the lightbulb is connected to the positive end of the charge. So, while our wire is connected to the battery and lightbulb, we're going to touch the tip of the lightbulb base to the top part (the positive end) of the battery and, LET THERE BE LIGHT!

Now, our bulb is lit up!

This is a really cool example of how God can give us the power to light up. Jesus said in John 8:12, "I am the light of the world. If you follow me, you won't have to walk in darkness, because you will have the light that leads to life."

Just like we need an electrical current to get power into this lightbulb, there is a heavenly current that has to be connected for us to receive the power from God.

This battery is like God, our heavenly Father! He's got the power to make us live SUPERNATURAL lives on this earth. John 10:9 (AMP) calls Jesus "the Door"—the only way to salvation. This battery only has one way to power. You have to connect through a charge. If I tried to connect this electrical wire to another part of the battery other than the charge areas, I couldn't get power to run through it.

This wire is a lot like the Holy Spirit who is our connector to God on the earth. Jesus said in Acts 1:8, "You will receive power when the Holy Spirit comes upon you." Jesus is connected to the Holy Spirit (like the flat end of the battery). The Holy Spirit moves the current of power through Jesus who is in us, just like the current runs up through the wire and into the metal part of this bulb.

Now, we are being Spirit-led, but we still need to be connected to Jesus—the only Way, Truth and Life to God—our power Source.

So, at our *base*—in our *hearts*—we must connect to Jesus through the only Door of power, which is like the positive end of the battery.

To really receive God's power, we have to be connected to Jesus *and* the Holy Spirit, and stay connected at all times to keep the power running. (Show what happens if you disconnect either end of the lightbulb and break the electrical circuit.)

If we break the connection to the Holy Spirit (the wire) or with our Door—Jesus (the positive charge)—we break our circuit of power!

Notes: _____

_____

_____

_____

_____

_____

_____

_____

DAY 3: GIVING LESSON | I BELIEVE AND OBEY

 Suggested Time: 10-15 minutes

 Offering Scripture: Some time later, God tested Abraham's faith. "Abraham!" God called. "Yes," he replied. "Here I am."

"Take your son, your only son—yes, Isaac, whom you love so much—and go to the land of Moriah. Go and sacrifice him as a burnt offering on one of the mountains, which I will show you."

The next morning Abraham got up early. He saddled his donkey and took two of his servants with him, along with his son, Isaac. Then he chopped wood for a fire for a burnt offering and set out for the place God had told him about. On the third day of their journey, Abraham looked up and saw the place in the distance. "Stay here with the donkey," Abraham told the servants. "The boy and I will travel a little farther. We will worship there, and then we will come right back."

So Abraham placed the wood for the burnt offering on Isaac's shoulders, while he himself carried the fire and the knife. As the two of them walked on together, Isaac turned to Abraham and said, "Father?"

"Yes, my son?" Abraham replied.

"We have the fire and the wood," the boy said, "but where is the sheep for the burnt offering?"

"God will provide a sheep for the burnt offering, my son," Abraham answered. And they both walked on together.

When they arrived at the place where God had told him to go, Abraham built an altar and arranged the wood on it. Then he tied his son, Isaac, and laid him on the altar on top of the wood. And Abraham picked up the knife to kill his son as a sacrifice. At that moment the angel of the Lord called to him from heaven, "Abraham! Abraham!"

"Yes," Abraham replied. "Here I am!"

"Don't lay a hand on the boy!" the angel said. "Do not hurt him in any way, for now I know that you truly fear God. You have not withheld from me even your son, your only son."

Then Abraham looked up and saw a ram caught by its horns in a thicket. So he took the ram and sacrificed it as a burnt offering in place of his son. Abraham named the place Yahweh-Yireh (which means "the Lord will provide"). To this day, people still use that name as a proverb: "On the mountain of the Lord it will be provided."

—Genesis 22:1-14

Supplies: ■ Lamb stuffed toy, ■ Small props you have on hand that are referenced in the story, ■ Sign with "Isaac" written on it, ■ Sign with "Abraham" written on it, ■ Baseball cap for Isaac, ■ Robe for Abraham, ■ Chair (this will be your altar)

Lesson Instructions:

Can someone help me with this lesson? *(Choose two of the children to be your helpers. If there is only one child, you can be Abraham.)*

In our Bible passage today, God asked Abraham to do something that most people would think was very hard. But, do you think Abraham BELIEVED God would provide a ram to be sacrificed instead of his son, Isaac?

You're right! Yes, Abraham believed God with all his heart. But why do you think he believed? Abraham believed God because God had promised Abraham that He would provide for him.

Abraham BELIEVED God and declared what he believed with his mouth. (Read Genesis 22:8 again.) Abraham BELIEVED God had promised him his son, Isaac, so he knew God would not take him away.

Abraham BELIEVED what God said and obeyed it without questioning. And because of Abraham's faith, God provided the ram as a substitute for Abraham's offering of Isaac.

Listen to your heavenly Father's voice, BELIEVE and OBEY what He says, and watch how He will always provide for *you.*

Let's look up to our heavenly Father and say this out loud:

- "I BELIEVE and OBEY God."
- "He always provides for me."

Decide on a giving challenge today! Pray together with your children and have them ask God if there is something He wants them to give away.

God may challenge them to give something just as difficult as it may have been for Abraham to think about giving up Isaac. Make sure it's THEIR choice, and they are able to sense what the Lord wants them to give. Don't be shocked if it's a big gift or a challenge to you as well! Make sure that whatever they give, they can do it cheerfully and wholeheartedly.

As you make plans to give, tell your heavenly Father how thankful you are that He always takes care of you and provides for your every need!

Notes: _____

_____
_____
_____
_____
_____
_____
_____
_____
_____
_____
_____
_____
_____
_____
_____
_____

DAY 4: FOOD FUN

SALT OF THE EARTH

Suggested Time: 10 minutes

Key Scripture: You are the salt of the earth. But what good is salt if it has lost its flavor? Can you make it salty again? It will be thrown out and trampled underfoot as worthless. —Matthew 5:13

Supplies: ☐ Beef jerky, ☐ 3-Day-old hamburger (unrefrigerated), ☐ 2 Plates or food boxes with coverings

Prior to Lesson:

Place the 3-day-old, unrefrigerated hamburger (it should look somewhat gross) and the beef jerky onto two separate, covered plates or covered boxes. Make sure the Superkids won't be able to guess what's inside.

Lesson Instructions:

Bring out the two plates, covered. Set them down like a meal.

I'm sure some of you must be very hungry! Well, I have some food here. Can someone help me with these? *(Have your Superkid helper put one of the plates on the table for you.)*

We have two choices of food for you today. I'm sure you're excited! Well, the food on plate No. 1 is months old, and the food on plate No. 2 is just a few days old. But, I just thought I'd tell you that neither one has been in the refrigerator—at all! Sounds yucky, doesn't it?!

So, who can guess what's under each lid? Lift the lids one at a time, and show Superkids the two choices. *(Let the children guess what each item is. You can give them the beef jerky and then let them smell the gross hamburger meat. DON'T LET THEM, OR ANYONE ELSE, EAT IT! (Feel free to let everyone enjoy the beef jerky if you have enough.)*

You know, the jerky is months older than the hamburger, but it is *preserved,* so it's still healthy to eat—it won't make you sick like the spoiled meat will.

Jesus had something to say about things being preserved like this jerky. He said in Matthew 5:13, "You are the salt of the earth. But what good is salt if it has lost its flavor? Can you make it salty again? It will be thrown out and trampled underfoot as worthless."

So, Superkids, what do you think Jesus meant when He called us the "salt of the earth"?

Did you know that in Jesus' time, salt was very valuable because it was used as a *preservative?* Even back then, meats were dried and salted to make them last much, much longer without needing to be refrigerated. Salt was also valuable because it gave flavor to food.

Jesus was telling us that we, as believers, are the preservers of the earth. We are supposed to be giving good "flavor" to the places where we live and keeping them from going bad like this burger did.

But, what if this beef jerky/salted beef were to lose its saltiness? It would spoil, wouldn't it, just like this burger, which would taste disgusting and make people sick.

Our world needs us to be *good* salt and not weak salt. We must stand out for God and not be weak Superkids. If we become weak, we are as helpful to the world as this old hamburger. Even though there's some salt in the meat naturally, there's not enough to make a difference. It's still disgusting.

Let's help God, and be super-salty! So when He needs someone to be a Superkid to our world, He knows He can choose us to add some flavor and help our world not to rot!

Notes: _____

_____

_____

_____

_____

_____

_____

_____

_____

_____

_____

_____

_____

_____

_____

_____

_____

_____

_____

_____

_____

_____

_____

_____

_____

_____

_____

DAY 5: GAME TIME

MY MISSION

Suggested Time: 10-15 minutes

Memory Verse: You are of God, little children, and have overcome them, because He who is in you is greater than he who is in the world. —1 John 4:4 NKJV

Teacher Tip: Depending on the age and size in your group, you can: Write the confessions down on puzzle pieces and have the kids unscramble and put the puzzle pieces together, OR play as a timed game for 1 child.

Supplies: ■ 2 Manila folders with sides stapled, ■ 42 Notecards, ■ 6 Envelopes: each labeled 1, 2 or 3, ■ Table

Prior to Game:

Divide the 6 envelopes into 2 groups. For Group 1, write each word of the following Superkid confessions on a separate notecard. Scramble the notecards before placing them in the envelopes.

Contents of envelope 1: I am a light to the world (7 notecards).

Contents of envelope 2: I don't belong to the world (6 notecards).

Contents of envelope 3: I accept and believe God's plan for me (8 notecards).

For Group 2, repeat the procedure with the 3 remaining envelopes. Then, on the front of each of the stapled manila folders, write "TOP SECRET," and place the 3 envelopes with the scrambled verses inside each.

Game Instructions:

Who's ready to go on a mission today?

Divide children into 2 groups, or if you only have 2 children, they can each participate alone. Have each team open 1 envelope from their manila folder at a time, unscrambling the words to accurately form the correct phrase. Make sure there is enough space between your players so they can't see what the other player(s) are doing.

When each team completes a phrase and believes they have cracked the code, ask them to hold up the TOP SECRET folder. Check to make sure the phrase is correct, and if not, ask them to continue. When each phrase is correct, ask the team to open the next envelope and unscramble the phrase, until phrases in all 3 envelopes are complete. Whichever team cracks the codes first, wins.

Ask the winning team to read the phrases out loud. Depending on your time, you can repeat the game several times using new phrases (prepared ahead of time!).

Game Goal:

The first team to accurately put the phrases together and crack the code, wins.

Final Word:

God's plan is never hidden from us. His plan for your life is a mission only you can complete. All you have to do is accept it, believe in the mission and ask Him to reveal it to you!

Ask your Superkids to repeat the 3 confessions aloud with you:

1. I am a light to the world.

2. I don't belong to the world.

3. I accept and believe God's plan for me.

Notes: _____

_____

_____

_____

_____

_____

_____

_____

_____

_____

_____

_____

_____

_____

_____

_____

_____

_____

_____

ACTIVITY PAGE   **DECODING THE TRUTH**

 Memory Verse: You are of God, little children, and have overcome them, because He who is in you is greater than he who is in the world. —1 John 4:4 NKJV

Supplies: ☐ 1 Copy of puzzle for each child, ☐ Bible

ANSWER KEY:

DECODING
THE TRUTH

UNSCRAMBLE MESSAGE #1:
ANSWER: YOU ARE THE LIGHT OF THE WORLD

UNSCRAMBLE MESSAGE #2:
ANSWER: JOHN ONE VERSE FIVE (JOHN 1:5)

USING YOUR BIBLE AS THE KEY, DECODE MESSAGE №3

ANSWER: THE LIGHT SHINES IN THE DARKNESS, AND THE DARKNESS CAN NEVER EXTINGUISH IT.

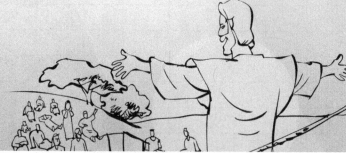

Name: _____

God's Word is the key to how we should live our lives in a dark world. Can you decode the message below using the key given?

DECODING
THE TRUTH

A	B	C	D	E	F	G	H	I	J	K	L	M
1	2	3	4	5	6	7	8	9	10	11	12	13

N	O	P	Q	R	S	T	U	V	W	X	Y	Z
14	15	16	17	18	19	20	21	22	23	24	25	26

UNSCRAMBLE MESSAGE #1:

25 15 21   1 18 5   20 8 5   12 9 7 8 20   15 6   20 8 5

23 15 18 12 4

UNSCRAMBLE MESSAGE #2:

10 15 8 14   15 14   5   22 5 18 19 5

6 9 22 5

USING YOUR BIBLE AS THE KEY,
DECODE MESSAGE №3

_____   _____   _____

_____   _____

Notes: _____

_____

_____

_____

_____

_____

_____

_____

_____

_____

_____

_____

_____

_____

_____

_____

_____

_____

_____

_____

_____

_____

_____

_____

_____

_____

_____

_____

_____

_____

_____

_____

_____

_____

WEEK 5: SERVANT AND CHILD OF THE MOST HIGH GOD

 Memory Verse: And He said to them, How is it that you had to look for Me? Did you not see and know that it is necessary [as a duty] for Me to be in My Father's house and [occupied] about My Father's business?
—Luke 2:49 AMPC

WEEK 5: SNAPSHOT

SERVANT AND CHILD OF THE MOST HIGH GOD

DAY	TYPE OF LESSON	LESSON TITLE	SUPPLIES
Day 1	Bible Lesson	Son or Servant	None
Day 2	Read-Aloud	The Prodigal Circus	Popcorn, candy or peanuts (optional)
Day 3	Giving Lesson	Hand in Hand	$5 Bill, Dishcloth and towel, 2 Containers—1 with dishwater and 1 with rinse water, Dish soap, 3-4 Dirty dishes, Table
Day 4	Food Fun	Cadet Brooke's Thumbprint Cookies	Oven/toaster oven with fitted cooking tray (not rack), 1 Electric hand mixer, Cooking whisk, 1 Medium bowl, 1 Large mixing bowl, Wooden spoon, Measuring cups and spoons, Aprons (optional), 1¾ Cups all-purpose flour, ½ Teaspoon baking powder, ½ Teaspoon finely ground salt, ¾ Cup (1½ sticks) unsalted butter, 2/3 Cup sugar, 1 Large egg, 1 Teaspoon vanilla extract, Jam
Day 5	Game Time	Go on Green	2 Waiter trays, Several items to place on each tray: empty beverage bottle, fork, plastic plate, etc., 2 Chairs, Mismatched/clumsy shoes: swimming flippers, big boots, large tall-heeled shoes, clown feet, etc., Small prize(s) for the winner(s)
Bonus	Activity Page	A-Mazing Love	1 Copy for each child

Lesson Introduction:

This is one of those weeks where I have (lovingly) included a lot of scripture. Remember it's for you! Fill up on God's Word. Allow the reality to get inside your heart: You are God's child. He loves you with all His heart. Selah! And because we love Him, we serve Him.

Minister to your kids this week out of that place as His child and servant. After you meditate on these scriptures, the message will flow out of you the way your kids need to hear it. Do you focus on servanthood? Being His child? Do you talk about the kids being servants at home and loving Mom and Dad?Choose your discussion questions based on your focused direction

The Holy Spirit knows exactly what your Superkids need to hear and which scriptures you should focus on. John 12:26 and Matthew 18:5 are great verses for YOU, today. As you follow Jesus, the Father honors you. And, so do I!

You are a great child and servant of the Lord to teach His little ones. It is no small thing to Him. Selah!

Love,

Commander Kellie

Commander Kellie

Lesson Outline:

This week your children will learn about being the servant and child of the Most High God. Like the prodigal son and his older brother, we must learn the balance of serving God with the heart of a child...specifically HIS child!

I. THE FATHER WANTED HIS SONS TO ACT LIKE SONS
Luke 15:11-31

    a. When the lost son came home, he thought he should be a servant. Verses 17-21

    b. The other son had been acting like a servant, but he was a son all along. Verses 28-31

    c. A servant does what his master wants, without question.

    d. A child loves, honors and obeys his/her parents.

II. JESUS SHOWS US HOW TO BE BOTH SERVANT AND CHILD
Luke 2:41-52

    a. Even when He was about your age, what the Father wanted was most important to Him. Verse 49

    b. He was about His Father's business. (Read verse 49 in *The Amplified Bible.*)

    c. Like a servant, Jesus does exactly what the Father tells Him. John 5:30

III. WE LET HIM LEAD US LIKE A SERVANT, BUT HE'S MADE US HIS CHILDREN Romans 8:14-16

    a. We choose wholeheartedly to obey Him as servants. Romans 6:16-18

    b. But we've been made so much more by the Most High God. Hebrews 12:23

    c. Everything the Father has is ours—we are His kids, and He's our Daddy! Galatians 4:6-7

Notes: _____

_____

_____

_____

_____

_____

_____

_____

DAY 1: BIBLE LESSON   **SON OR SERVANT**

 Memory Verse: And He said to them, How is it that you had to look for Me? Did you not see and know that it is necessary [as a duty] for Me to be in My Father's house and [occupied] about My Father's business? —Luke 2:49 AMPC

Even after the Lord freed them from slavery in Egypt, the children of Israel doubted Him and created a false idol in His place. This passage is a great reminder of how far we can move away from God when left to our own devices. God desires that we follow Him faithfully and remember the Sweet Life He has given us through His Son Jesus.

Read Luke 15:11-32, MSG:
The Prodigal Son

Then he said, "There was once a man who had two sons. The younger said to his father, 'Father, I want right now what's coming to me.'

"So the father divided the property between them. It wasn't long before the younger son packed his bags and left for a distant country. There, undisciplined and dissipated, he wasted everything he had. After he had gone through all his money, there was a bad famine all through that country and he began to hurt. He signed on with a citizen there who assigned him to his fields to slop the pigs. He was so hungry he would have eaten the corncobs in the pig slop, but no one would give him any.

"That brought him to his senses. He said, 'All those farmhands working for my father sit down to three meals a day, and here I am starving to death. I'm going back to my father. I'll say to him, Father, I've sinned against God, I've sinned before you; I don't deserve to be called your son. Take me on as a hired hand.' He got right up and went home to his father.

"When he was still a long way off, his father saw him. His heart pounding, he ran out, embraced him, and kissed him. The son started his speech: 'Father, I've sinned against God, I've sinned before you; I don't deserve to be called your son ever again.'

"But the father wasn't listening. He was calling to the servants, 'Quick. Bring a clean set of clothes and dress him. Put the family ring on his finger and sandals on his feet. Then get a grain-fed heifer and roast it. We're going to feast! We're going to have a wonderful time! My son is here—given up for dead and now alive! Given up for lost and now found!' And they began to have a wonderful time.

"All this time his older son was out in the field. When the day's work was done he came in. As he approached the house, he heard the music and dancing. Calling over one of the houseboys, he asked what was going on. He told him, 'Your brother came home. Your father has ordered a feast—barbecued beef!—because he has him home safe and sound.'

"The older brother stalked off in an angry sulk and refused to join in. His father came out and tried to talk to him, but he wouldn't listen. The son said, 'Look how many years I've stayed here serving you, never giving you one moment of grief, but have you ever thrown a party for me and my friends? Then this son of yours who has thrown away your money on [sin*] shows up and you go all out with a feast!'

"His father said, 'Son, you don't understand. You're with me all the time, and everything that is mine is yours—but this is a wonderful time, and we had to celebrate. This brother of yours was dead, and he's alive! He was lost, and he's found!'"

Discussion Questions:

1. **What did the son who left home want from his father before he left?**

   Money—his inheritance

2. **What made him come to his senses?**

   He was so hungry, he wanted to eat the trash people fed to the pigs. Yuck!

3. **What did the prodigal want when he came back?**

   Just to be a farmhand or servant for his father

4. **Before the prodigal son made it home, his father recognized him from far away and began running to him. How is this the way God feels about us? Can you think of any other scriptures that talk about God going out of His way to show His love for us—even when we've made mistakes?**

   Answers may vary:

   - "Come close to God, and God will come close to you." James 4:8a

   - "But God is so rich in mercy, and he loved us so much, that even though we were dead because of our sins, he gave us life when he raised Christ from the dead. (It is only by God's grace that you have been saved!)" Ephesians 2:4-5

   - "For this is how God loved the world: He gave his one and only Son, so that everyone who believes in him will not perish but have eternal life." John 3:16

5. **When the father heard his son repent, what did he give his son instead of punishment?**

   His father dressed him in nice clothes and gave him a ring to show he was part of the family again.

6. **How did the father celebrate when the prodigal son returned home?**

   They killed a calf for a feast and a party with joyous music and dancing.

7. **Luke 15:10 says: "In the same way, there is joy in the presence of God's angels when even one sinner repents." How does this story reflect how God feels when one of His children repents and asks to be a son again?**

   He is excited—and there is joyous celebrating in heaven.

*Changed at the discretion of the Commander.

8. **The older son was angry and jealous of the younger son receiving a party, new clothes, and a huge feast when he returned home. All the time the younger son was gone, his older brother had been faithfully serving his father.**

   The older son didn't realize that everything he had worked for belonged to him as a son. He had nothing to be jealous about. He could have thrown a party anytime! "His father said, 'Son, you don't understand. You're with me all the time, and everything that is mine is yours.'"

9. **Fill in the blank: The younger brother didn't know how to be a _____, but the older brother didn't know how to be a _____.**

   Servant, Son

10. **How could the older son have lived his previous years had he realized his place as a son?**

    • He would have realized all he was working for would benefit him one day.

    • He would have known his father loved him just as much as his father loved the younger son.

    • He would have known that everything his father had belonged to him.

    • He would have known he could have thrown a party anytime because the calf was actually his as the one who ran the farm.

11. **Discuss the two sons and how their choices affected their lives.**

    • **Who lived a better life? Older or younger?** older

    • **Who ended up with more inheritance?** older

    • **Who was able to spend more years with his father?** older

    • **Who was able to learn more about taking care of his property and land?** older

    • **Who spent time sleeping with pigs and going hungry?** younger

    • **Who lost his inheritance though he was still loved by the father?** younger

12. **How do you want to spend your life? Do you want to live close to the Father or would you like to lose everything, spend time with pigs and eat their food? Discuss real examples of how choices can lead you to be a SERVANT and a SON. Are you ready for your inheritance?**

    Answers may vary. It is a good place to discuss Ephesians 2:10 here: This is God's good plan for our lives. We're not just expecting a worldly inheritance or just treasures in this world, but we're also laying up for ourselves treasure in heaven (Matthew 6:20). Living a godly life will always be rewarded!

Notes: _____

_____

_____

_____

_____

_____

DAY 2: READ-ALOUD | THE PRODIGAL CIRCUS

 Suggested Time: 15 minutes

 Memory Verse: And He said to them, How is it that you had to look for Me? Did you not see and know that it is necessary [as a duty] for Me to be in My Father's house and [occupied] about My Father's business? —Luke 2:49 AMPC

 Concept: A modern-day story of the prodigal son, but with a twist!

Supplies: ☐ Popcorn, candy or peanuts (optional)

Story:

There once lived two brothers of the same age who were nothing alike. The elder was named Peter, and the younger was named Hiro. They were born two days apart, but Hiro was adopted from Japan. And though the two boys were nothing alike in appearance or action, their mom and dad loved them equally.

Since the boys were so close in age, they shared everything: their room, toothpaste, a bathroom, bunk beds and once a year, they shared a birthday party. But because they shared so much, their parents failed to notice a trend that had developed since the boys had first shared their birthday party together at age 7.

On their seventh birthdays, Hiro had just been adopted. The orphanage he came from was very strict, and he had never been given anything before. He had to work very hard just to be able to earn the right to sleep on a real bed. So when his parents gave him his first toy at age 7, Hiro felt he did not deserve it.

Peter, on the other hand, did not share that same feeling. He loved getting gifts, especially on his birthday. So when Hiro received the front half of the train set, Peter received the back half. At first, Peter was upset because he got the caboose end instead of the conductor end. But shortly after the party was over, Hiro handed the front part of the train to him and said, "This is yours. I did nothing to earn it."

Peter was speechless, but he didn't argue because he had really wanted that conductor piece in the first place. So began their tradition of gifts. Every time the boys would get gifts, Hiro, feeling so undeserving, gave them over to Peter. Over the years, Peter began telling Hiro what to ask for, so that he could get it.

Sadly, this did not end with gifts. Hiro did not feel like he deserved anything he received. So, with every hug and kiss from his parents, he felt as if he were stealing them away from Peter. He could never quite hug his parents back or kiss them good night without feeling a bit out of place. Although he loved his new mommy and daddy, he felt that it wouldn't be fair for them to love him as much as they loved Peter. So Hiro always felt a little out of place in his own home, and always, always tried to make up for the burden he thought he was by working for it.

Peter, however, knew that his parents would love him no matter what. Even if he didn't clean his room, do his chores or if he complained. And although he loved Hiro deep down, he had not adjusted to having a brother very well....until, of course, he realized what a hard worker Hiro was.

When the boys were told to clean their room, Hiro would always offer to clean it by himself. And the day Peter realized that Hiro would gladly do all his chores, he never picked up a broom again…unless, of course, Mom was watching.

By the time their eleventh birthdays rolled around, Hiro was completely exhausted. He worked so hard to be perfect, do his chores and homework, and tried so very hard to not get in Peter's way in their room.

Just that afternoon, the boys had gotten into a fight because Peter wanted to switch from the bottom to the top bunk. Hiro began to cry because he always felt like that top bunk was the only space in their whole room that was truly his. It was his territory. As little tears slipped down Hiro's cheeks, Peter pushed him to the floor and laughed at him.

"Get up, you big baby!" Peter taunted Hiro. "I'm surprised you're not scared to sleep up there, you…."

Just then their dad shouted, "Come to the kitchen, boys. Mom and I have a surprise for you!"

Peter knocked Hiro back down and raced to the kitchen. Hiro got back up and followed Peter in as quickly as he could. They arrived one right after the other, and Peter practically tore into his package on the table, while Hiro opened his more reservedly.

"Tickets to the circus!" Peter shouted. "Wow! Thanks." He immediately hugged his mom and dad. When Hiro realized he'd received the same thing, he didn't know how to respond. How could he give his ticket to Peter? He would have to take it for himself, though that didn't seem like the right thing to do.

Mom noticed the worried look that began to cover Hiro's face. "What's the matter, Hiro?" she asked. "Do you not want to go?"

Hiro was in shock. What kid didn't want to go to the circus? "I want to go!" he said without thinking. His mom smiled and hugged Hiro, and then Dad joined the bunch. But even as Hiro's arms wrapped tightly around his parents, he was filled with worry. Would Peter be upset if he had to take this gift? He knew he didn't deserve to go, but it sounded like such fun.

Maybe if I promise to stay more out of Peter's way and give him my top bunk, he won't be so mad, he thought to himself.

At the circus, both Peter and Hiro had the time of their lives! They watched in awe as the elephants did tricks, people swung from rope to rope, and a clown went across a tiny wire on a bicycle as he juggled. Hiro had never seen anything more fascinating.

Throughout the night, he ate all the popcorn his parents bought for him. And even though Peter gave him an angry look when he did not hand over his cotton candy, Hiro decided to keep every gift his parents were buying him. He ate the popcorn, and proudly wore the cap and shirt his parents bought for him.

Peter was having fun too, but it irked him that Hiro was getting equal treatment, since he was so used to Hiro relinquishing everything his parents bought him. As Hiro finished his last bite of cotton candy, Peter decided he was going to say something about it.

By the time they got home, Peter was really irritated. He didn't like the feeling that his parents liked Hiro more than him. It was bad enough that Mom was always talking about what a hard worker and a great straight-A student Hiro was. So at the end of the night, as Mom and Dad were tucking them in, Peter got up the nerve to ask his mom a question.

"Mom…" Peter whispered so his brother wouldn't hear from the top bunk, "do you love Hiro more than me?"

Mom was shocked that Peter would ask such a question. "Of course not, Sweetie," she answered. Peter took a sigh of relief until she added, "You know Daddy and I love you both the same."

Peter was stunned. He had always hoped that his parents felt a little more affection for him since he was their natural-born son. His dad came to hug him next, but Peter was so upset, he could barely think straight. He didn't even realize how mad he was until his parents quietly shut their door. And then…

"How could you, Hiro?" Peter whisper-yelled to him from the bottom bunk.

"Huh?" Hiro wasn't sure what Peter was talking about, but he was beginning to feel really guilty for taking so much attention away from Peter all night.

"Never mind." Peter didn't know what he meant to say either. He just knew he was mad because his birthday turned out most unusual. "The least you could do is let me have your top bunk."

Hiro began to cry once more. That day was the most fun he'd ever had in his entire life. He sniffed back the tears.

"Are you crying again, crybaby?" Peter spat out.

Hiro didn't want to answer. He knew anything he said would just give him away.

"Ugh," Peter snorted in disgust. "You're such a freak, Hiro, you should join the circus." Then he rolled over and went to sleep.

But Hiro was wide awake. Wide awake and miserable. He lay in his top bunk for hours pondering what Peter had said. Should he really join the circus? Hiro knew Peter wasn't serious, but he seemed pretty serious about not wanting him around.

Maybe he should run away. It would be sad because tonight he began to feel for the first time that maybe he had done something right. His parents really did seem like they loved him. He would miss Mom and Dad tucking him in at night and helping him with homework. A happy thought struck him. *If I joined a circus, there wouldn't be any homework. The circus looked like one, big family tonight. I bet if I joined them, I could make them love me too, and I wouldn't be stealing Peter's family away from him anymore.*

So, with that thought, he was finally able to get some sleep. It would be hard, but he would wake up in the morning, pack his few items that he kept for himself, and run off to join the cargo of circus people.

The next morning when Peter awoke, he found Hiro's bed made and a note on top. "Dear Peter, you can have the top bunk. Love, Hiro." At first Peter was thrilled…. Then, he noticed Hiro's backpack and clothes were missing along with the cap and shirt his parents had bought him the night before. Peter screamed at the top of his lungs, "Mom! Dad! Hiro's gone!" He crumpled the note up and threw it in the trash.

As the year passed on, Hiro worked three times as hard with his new circus family as he had with his old family. Every other day, he would remember his mom's sweet notes in his lunch or how his dad would play ball with him. He would get miserably homesick, until he reminded himself that it was Peter who deserved their time and affection. So, he stuck it out at the circus. His job mostly included cleaning the animals…and their waste. It was not a pretty job, but he had resigned himself to it. After all, he had to earn his keep, somehow.

Hiro worked so hard that he had hardly noticed it was a mere week until his twelfth birthday. Peter, however, was dreading the upcoming week. Birthdays had always been a time of joy for Peter in the past, but this week had been worse than ever. Since Hiro's disappearance, their parents had searched high and low, but were unable to find Hiro anywhere. Every night, as they tucked Peter into bed, they cried longingly as they looked at the empty top bunk where Hiro had once slept.

Today was the worst birthday he'd ever had. He had always felt a little guilty about Hiro leaving. After Hiro had left, nothing was the same. Not only were his parents constantly sad and weepy, but he also found that he missed Hiro much more than he thought possible.

One night, as Peter watched TV with his parents, a commercial came on about the upcoming circus that next week. Mom immediately started crying and a thought struck Peter as he watched the commercial. What if Hiro had joined the circus as Peter had so meanly suggested the year before? It was then that Peter decided to write Hiro a letter. It may never reach him, but it was certainly worth a try.

> *Dear Hiro,*
>
> *We all miss you so much. Mom and Dad cry every day that you are gone. It's not the same without you. We love you. I apologize. Come back home soon.*
>
> *Your brother,*
>
> *Peter*

Hiro read this letter a few days later. They had just gotten into town, and it was waiting for him when they arrived. And now, with tears streaming down his face, Hiro realized for the first time that it must have been true when his parents told him they loved him. He immediately packed his bags and used what little money he had to take a cab home.

An hour later, Hiro stood on the porch of his home. He held a shaky hand over the doorbell, took a deep breath, and then pressed the bell with all his might. Within seconds Hiro found himself surrounded by the arms of his family. Everyone was crying tears of joy. And of all people, Peter spoke up first. "We missed you, Hiro!"

Dad barely got out a, "Welcome home!" And Mom couldn't speak, she was weeping so loudly with joy. And, for the first time ever, Hiro allowed himself to feel truly loved by these people. He knew he was home. And from that day forth, Hiro never felt out of place again. His family loved him and nothing would ever change that.

Peter made sure that Hiro always felt welcome, too. He helped with chores and even made space in their room for just Hiro's stuff. He also gave back every present that he ever took from Hiro. And, the two boys began sharing the one thing they had never shared before…the friendship of a lifetime.

The End

Variation: Circus Theme

Feel free to go with the circus theme and give your kids popcorn, cotton candy or peanuts, just as if they were really at the circus!

DAY 3: GIVING LESSON

HAND IN HAND

Suggested Time: 10 minutes

Offering Scripture: And it is impossible to please God without faith. Anyone who wants to come to him must believe that God exists and that he rewards those who sincerely seek him. —Hebrews 11:6

Supplies: ■ $5 Bill, ■ Dishcloth and towel, ■ 2 Containers—1 with dishwater, 1 with rinsing water, ■ Dish soap, ■ 3-4 Dirty dishes, ■ Table

Lesson Instructions:

So, who loves to get their hands dirty? I can see that not many of you like to do that!

Well then, how many of you love to wash dirty dishes? Some of you do! Who'd like to help me to clean these dishes while we're talking about how God rewards those who are diligent and serve Him? *(Choose one of the children and ask him/her to clean the dishes while you teach the lesson. Let him/her know that you will bless his/ her diligence in cleaning the dishes and staying focused.)*

While _____ (name of child) is doing that, does anyone know what a *reward* is? A reward is something given or received in return for a service.

(Ask your helper if he/she believes you will bless him/her when he/she is finished cleaning the dishes. Read Hebrews 11:6 out loud to the children.)

I believe you're going to do a great job! Thank you for lending your hands to me! *(When your helper is finished, have him/her dry their hands and then bless him/her with a $5 bill.)*

So, Superkids, how should you act when Mom or Dad asks you to help out around the house? When you're asked to wash dishes, clean up your room or take out the trash, it might not sound like the most fun thing to do. But, doing what's right should be what you choose every time!

You know, we have a wonderful Father God who is a great Daddy to us. He always does what He says. He is a giver, and His hands are always ready to bless His children! He always rewards those who sincerely seek Him.

Let's all say this out loud:

I live to please God.

I have faith in God.

I work hand in hand with my heavenly Daddy.

I believe as I give today, my Daddy wants to and will reward me!

(Have the children bring their offerings for the week and hand them over to God, their heavenly Daddy.)

Notes: _____

DAY 4: FOOD FUN

CADET BROOKE'S THUMBPRINT COOKIES

Suggested Time: 10-15 minutes

Memory Verse: And He said to them, How is it that you had to look for Me? Did you not see and know that it is necessary [as a duty] for Me to be in My Father's house and [occupied] about My Father's business? —Luke 2:49 AMPC

Ingredients: ☐ 1¾ Cups all-purpose flour, ☐ ½ Teaspoon baking powder, ☐ ½ Teaspoon finely ground salt, ☐ ¾ Cup (1½ sticks) unsalted butter—softened, ☐ 2/3 Cup sugar, ☐ 1 Large egg, ☐ 1 Teaspoon vanilla extract, ☐ Jam

Prior to Lesson:
☐ If you don't have 10-12 minutes to wait for your cookies to bake, bake at least 1 batch of cookies to let your Superkids taste.
☐ Pre-measure ingredients to cut down on prep time.
☐ If using a toaster oven, be sure to plug the toaster oven in to a power outlet before the segment begins. Use an extension cord if necessary.

Supplies: ☐ Oven/toaster oven with fitted cooking tray (not rack), ☐ Electric hand mixer (For safety reasons, only allow adults to operate the electric mixer.), ☐ Cooking whisk, ☐ Medium bowl, ☐ Large mixing bowl, ☐ Wooden spoon, ☐ Measuring cups and spoons, ☐ Aprons (optional)

Lesson Instructions:

If you know Cadet Brooke from Commander Kellie's Superkid Academy, then you know she loves to cook! Today, we're going to make her family's secret recipe for her thumbprint cookies!

We're going to divide up the jobs we need to get done so we can enjoy our yummy cookies. We'll each have a job to do while we're having fun making our treat!

Let's do first things, first! When you bake something, you need to have your oven already hot so your recipe turns out just right. So, let's preheat our toaster oven to 350°.

The next thing we need to do while our toaster oven is heating up is to combine our dry ingredients. We'll put together 1¾ cup of all-purpose flour and ½ teaspoon of baking powder. Then, so that our yummy recipe doesn't taste flat, we need to add ½ teaspoon fine salt. Now, we'll whisk them all together and set this aside to add to the wet ingredients later.

Here's our large mixing bowl. With our electric mixer, we're going to whip ¾ cup of butter and 2/3 cup of sugar together until it's nice and fluffy. Then, we'll need to beat in 1 egg and 1 teaspoon of vanilla extract.

With this wooden spoon, I'm going to stir in the combined dry ingredients from the medium-sized bowl that we set aside, into the wet ingredients. Now that our ingredients are combined, we have a nice bowl of dough.

We're going to spoon it into 1-inch balls and put them on a cookie sheet. Before we put them into our pre-heated oven, we'll need to make a thumbprint on the top of each 1-inch ball to make a nice dent so we can put 1 teaspoon of our tasty jam into each one.

Now that the jam is nicely settled into our thumbprints, we'll put the cookies into the oven and let them bake for 10-12 minutes. I know you all want to taste Cadet Brooke's Thumbprint Cookies! *(If you don't have time to wait for your cookies to bake, bring out the pre-cooked thumbprint cookies for your Superkids to enjoy.)*

Brooke got this recipe from her mom, and she bakes it all the time. Brooke loves to spend time with her mom in the kitchen!

In fact, I hope you had fun with me today, even though I was giving you things to do. You didn't mind obeying because we were spending time together. And when you listened to what I said to do, we came out with these yummy cookies!

Being God's servant is the same way. He's not looking for people to boss around. He wants you to know Him as your heavenly Father. But He also wants to know that you will be faithful to obey Him, so that He can trust you to do some pretty amazing works with Him as the head Chef of your life!

Let's enjoy your cookies together. I'm going to eat one, too! *Mmmmm!*

Notes: _____

_____

_____

_____

_____

_____

_____

_____

_____

_____

_____

_____

_____

_____

_____

_____

_____

_____

_____

DAY 5: GAME TIME

GO ON GREEN

 Suggested Time: 10 minutes

 Memory Verse: And He said to them, How is it that you had to look for Me? Did you not see and know that it is necessary [as a duty] for Me to be in My Father's house and [occupied] about My Father's business? —Luke 2:49 AMPC

 Teacher Tip: Depending on the age and size of your group, obstacles can be placed for players to step over or maneuver around.

Supplies: ☐ 2 Waiter trays, ☐ Several items to place on each tray: empty beverage bottle, fork, plastic plate, etc., ☐ 2 Chairs, ☐ Mismatched/clumsy shoes: swimming flippers, big boots, large tall-heeled shoes, clown feet, etc., ☐ Small prize(s) for the winner(s)

Game Instructions:

This will be a relay race! We'll choose several of you for teams. Each of our players may only use 1 hand to play, holding it out flat to balance the waiter tray. Our players stand behind the starting line. Before we begin, players will have to put on as many mismatched, clumsy shoes as they can.

We're going to put these two chairs at a distance far enough from the starting line for each of our players to walk toward and circle around.

Have any of you ever played "red light/green light"? Well, this game is a lot like that. I'll call out, "Green light!" which means you can move forward toward the chair. If I say, "Red light!" that means you have to stop moving toward the chair or circling around it.

The idea is that each player has to move toward the chair, circle it and then head back to the starting line to hand the tray off to the next player on his/her team.

To make it more fun and exciting, if an item falls off a tray, the player must pick it up, head back to the starting line and wait for the next "green light." And, if a player doesn't complete the correct command for the color I call out (red light or green light), he/she must return to the starting line and wait for the next "green light"!

So, Superkids, do you think you can do all that?! Of course you can! Let's get started!

Game Goal:

The first team to have all members complete the relay 1 time through, with all the items on their tray, wins!

Final Word:

It's really hard to win a race wearing the wrong shoes, isn't it? God made it His business for you to be a winner—

every time. No matter what obstacle you face in life, make it your business to be a servant and child of the Most High God who listens for His "green light," and you'll always be a winner!

Notes: _____

_____

_____

_____

_____

_____

_____

_____

_____

_____

_____

_____

_____

_____

_____

_____

_____

_____

_____

_____

_____

_____

_____

_____

_____

_____

_____

_____

_____

ACTIVITY PAGE | A-MAZING LOVE

Memory Verse: And He said to them, How is it that you had to look for Me? Did you not see and know that it is necessary [as a duty] for Me to be in My Father's house and [occupied] about My Father's business? —Luke 2:49 AMPC

ANSWER KEY:

Name: _____

MAZE: Help the Prodigal Son Find His Way Home

Memory Verse: *So why do you keep calling me "Lord, Lord!" when you don't do what I say? —Luke 6:46*

WEEK 6: SNAPSHOT

JESUS IS MY SAVIOR AND MY LORD

DAY	TYPE OF LESSON	LESSON TITLE	SUPPLIES
Day 1	Bible Lesson	Building on the Rock	8 Connecting blocks (Legos® or connectable pieces that will make a house), Marker, 8 Labels (optional)
Day 2	Food Fun	Recipe for Success	Muffin tin, Mixer, Mixing bowl, Mixing spoon, ½ Cup butter, 1 Cup granulated sugar, 2 Large eggs, 1 Teaspoon vanilla, ¼ Teaspoon salt, 2 Teaspoons baking powder, 2½ Cups blueberries, 2 Cups all-purpose flour, ½ Cup milk, Spray or butter to grease pan
Day 3	Giving Lesson	Secret Superhero	Superhero mask and cape, Superhero props, Bowl, Slips of paper
Day 4	Real Deal	Corrie ten Boom	Photos of the secret room in the ten Booms' house, Photos of Corrie and her family, Optional Costume: Grandmother wig and shawl
Day 5	Game Time	Do What I Say	2 Blindfolds, Small objects (1 per child), Timer (optional)
Bonus	Activity Page	Connect the Romans Road	1 Copy for each child

Lesson Introduction:

Remember, one of the requirements to being a Superkid is to OBEY the Holy Spirit. Jesus says in John 16 that the Holy Spirit will tell us what Jesus tells Him. How can we be a Superkid on a mission from God, if He can't get us to listen and obey? Making Him Lord means He gets to tell us what to do.

Jesus spoke to His disciples about this in Luke 6. It's a great word for us today! Many Christians know Him as their Savior, but haven't made Him Lord over their lives. Jesus wants to be both.

As our Superkids determine to obey and let Him be Lord (in charge) over their lives, they will develop an acute sense of His leading. We know obedience is key—The Sweet Life is waiting!

Love,

Commander Kellie

Commander Kellie

Lesson Outline:

This week, your children will learn about making Jesus their SAVIOR *and* their LORD. When your children understand the importance of going beyond just asking Jesus into their hearts for their eternal salvation, they make their own commitment to obey and follow Him as SUPERKIDS!

I. JESUS CAME TO BE YOUR SAVIOR Romans 5:6-11

a.   Adam's sin brought sin to all—Jesus came to free us from sin. Romans 5:12, 17-21

b.   Jesus became like us, and He defeated Satan so we can, too. Hebrews 2:14-15

c.   Because Jesus is faithful and He loves us, we can trust Him to lead us. Hebrews 2:16-18

II. JESUS WANTS TO BE LORD OVER YOUR LIFE Luke 6:46-49

a.   Asking Him into your heart and making Him Lord of your life are two different things.

b.   He loves you, even when you don't obey Him.

c.   He can be your Savior and live in your heart, but if you don't listen to and obey Him, He isn't your Lord.

III. IS JESUS YOUR SAVIOR AND YOUR LORD?

a.   If you haven't already, make Jesus your Savior. Romans 10:8-11
(Lead in prayer of salvation.)

b.   If you haven't been obeying Him and His Word, ask Him to forgive you. 1 John 1:9
(Lead in prayer of repentance.)

c.   Make Jesus the Lord of your life. John 10:27
(Lead in a confession of commitment to hear and obey Jesus.)

Notes: _____

_____

_____

_____

_____

_____

_____

_____

_____

DAY 1: BIBLE LESSON

BUILDING ON THE ROCK

Memory Verse: *So why do you keep calling me "Lord, Lord!" when you don't do what I say?*
—Luke 6:46

Supplies: ■ *8 Connecting blocks (Legos® or connectable pieces that will make a house),* ■ *Marker,*
■ *8 Labels (optional)*

Without Jesus, we are powerless to overcome obstacles in our lives.

This Bible lesson comes with a small object lesson to bring the Scriptures to life in your Superkids' minds. Some scriptures are often more easily grasped when we have a clear image to build on. You're going to create a house—one that can stand a lot of turmoil.

Prior to Lesson:

Prepare your 8 blocks (Legos or connectable pieces that will make a house): You'll need: 1 foundation block, 4 walls (better if they're 2 blocks high), 1 roof block, and 2 (at least) filler blocks. Before writing on the blocks, read over the directions and the Interactive Discussion Questions (on the next 3 pages) to design your house. You can use more blocks if needed. Next, use the marker to write on the blocks, or use labels if you don't want to write on them.

1. *Foundation* block—print **"Lord Jesus"** on this block. This is the largest block. Or, you can use many blocks connected into 1 piece (they must be connected to make a firm foundation).
2. *Roof* block—print **"Father God"** on this block.
3. *Faith* wall block—print **"Faith"** on this one. This should be built like a wall, preferably 2 blocks high.
4. *Endurance* wall block—print **"Endurance"** on this block. It should be built like a wall, preferably 2 blocks high.
5. *Strength of character* wall block—print **"Strong Character"** on this block. It should be built like a wall, also, preferably 2 blocks high.
6. *Hope* wall block—print **"Hope"** on this block. It should be built like a wall, also 2 blocks high.
7. *Love* filler block—print **"Love"** on this one and connect to the "Father God" roof block to fill the house.
8. *Holy Spirit* block—print **"Holy Spirit"** on this block and connect it to the *Lord Jesus* foundation block and the *Love* filler to fill the house.

Read Romans 5:1-5:
Building Blocks

Therefore, since we have been made right in God's sight by **faith,** we have peace with God because of what **Jesus Christ our Lord** has done for us. **Because of our faith,** Christ has brought us into this place of undeserved privilege **where we now stand** *[our foundation],* and we confidently and joyfully look forward to sharing God's glory.

We can rejoice, too, when we run into problems and trials, for we know that they help us develop **endurance.** And endurance develops **strength of character,** and character strengthens our confident **hope** of salvation. And this hope will not lead to disappointment. **For we know how dearly God loves us,** because he has given us the Holy Spirit to fill our hearts with his **love.**

Do Discussion Questions 1–9

Read Luke 6:46-49:
Withstanding the Storms

So why do you keep calling me "Lord, Lord!" when you don't do what I say? I will show you what it's like when someone comes to me, listens to my teaching, and then follows it. It is like a person building a house who digs deep and lays the foundation on solid rock. When the floodwaters rise and break against that house, it stands firm because it is well built. But anyone who hears and doesn't obey is like a person who builds a house without a foundation. When the floods sweep down against that house, it will collapse into a heap of ruins.

Do Discussion Questions 10-11

Read Romans 5:1-5 MSG:
Standing Tall in God's Grace and Glory!

By entering through faith into what God has always wanted to do for us—set us right with him, make us fit for him—we have it all together with God because of our Master Jesus. And that's not all: We throw open our doors to God and discover at the same moment that he has already thrown open his door to us. We find ourselves standing where we always hoped we might stand—out in the wide open spaces of God's grace and glory, standing tall and shouting our praise.

Do Discussion Question 12

Interactive Discussion Questions:

1. **Who should be the foundation on which we stand?**

   Jesus Christ our Lord

   Pull out your foundation block that says *Lord Jesus* and lay your foundation.

2. **What connects us with God and His Son, Jesus, and makes us right in God's eyes?**

   Faith in Jesus Christ as our Lord

Take out the *Faith* wall, and connect it to the *Lord Jesus* foundation and *Father God* as the roof. Here is a great place to remind them of Psalm 91—our Father God is our protector, and He keeps us safe from danger. He covers us like a roof on a house.

3. What do problems and trials help us to develop?

Endurance

Take out the *Endurance* wall. Show something coming against your house, and how building another wall connected to the roof and foundation helps keep bad things out and the house standing tall. Endurance keeps our house and faith in God intact, even when hard times come our way. When someone makes fun of us because of Jesus or because we decide to do the right thing—every time we say no, or even get back up and repent when we make a mistake—we are developing endurance!

4. What does endurance develop?

Strength of character (Strong Character)

Take out the *Strong Character* wall, and place it next to the endurance wall. Now your house is even more fortified. Your house is growing more glorious. A strong character is one that's steady. Someone with strong character doesn't lie about things—big or small. That person doesn't choose to disobey the Lord and do something he/she knows is a sin. In fact—the person of strong character is in the habit of CHOOSING THE RIGHT WAY.

5. What does a strong character develop?

Hope

When you've seen Jesus come through for you and save your "house" again and again—when you've seen His blessings firsthand because He blesses you when you CHOOSE LIFE, your hope grows stronger and stronger. Your heart becomes full of hope in God. You can't be talked or pushed out of being a Superkid because you have that strong HOPE that you serve a SUPER God!

6. How much more powerful is your house now that it is built strong?

Much steadier

7. Could your house get even stronger? How?

Yes. Fill it up.

8. How do we know God's hope will not disappoint us?

Because we know God loves us (verse 5): "And this hope will not lead to disappointment. For we know how dearly God loves us, because he has given us the Holy Spirit to fill our hearts with his love."

First John 4:8 says God is love. Connect the *Love* block.

Being filled with the Spirit is not just speaking in other tongues. It's listening to and obeying God every day. When we ask, "What would Jesus and God, or more practically, LOVE do?" God is always connected to love because it's who He is. And, just like this love block becomes part of the roof to make it stronger—God's love makes Him who He is. It's His love that's protecting our lives. Love makes this roof even stronger. NEVER make the mistake of thinking that love makes you weak or wimpy! Love strengthens and fortifies you.

9. **Who has God given us to connect His love to the foundation of our lives?**

The Holy Spirit (verse 5): "He has given us the Holy Spirit to fill our hearts with his love."

Connect the *Holy Spirit* block. See, the Holy Spirit helps us to connect to God's love! The Holy Spirit fills our house with God's love! And just look at how powerful this house is now!

Make sure all the pieces are pressed together, then pass the house around to show everyone how strong it is.

10. **Read Luke 6:46-49. According to this scripture, how do we build a good foundation?**

Hearing what Jesus says and doing it

Remove the foundation layer, and show how your blocks can be easily torn apart and broken. How much steadier is it when we keep Jesus as our Lord by OBEYING Him? Without Jesus as our Lord, our faith is weak and our endurance isn't strong. Our character can't be as strong, either. And then our hope can fail (show it being crushed when you toss it or push on it).

11. **Why do we need all this? Why do we need a strong house with a strong foundation?**

God wants us to be equipped to take on anything that comes our way and live the sweet life He has for us. When we build the foundation of our lives with Jesus as our Lord and Savior (begin building again with your foundation—*Lord Jesus* block—we can have strong lives that can withstand any attack of the enemy. We have faith (connect *Faith* block to *Lord Jesus* block) that Jesus is our Lord. Our faith connects us to our Father God and His love, which is our protection (connect the *Faith* wall to the *Father God* block), and the Holy Spirit fills our hearts with love (connect *Holy Spirit* block). When problems come, we develop endurance (put up *Endurance* wall). Then endurance develops strong character (put up *Strong Character* wall). Then, our strong character produces hope (put up *Hope* wall). And now, our hope won't be disappointed (Make sure everything is well connected, then push on the *Hope* wall) because we are filled with God's love! Now, we have strong houses that, like Jesus said, won't break down because of a wind or be pushed around by a bully (push on your structure to show how strong it is) or break down, because of the pressure of the world (stack books on top and see how it holds).

12. **Read Romans 5:1-2 again—but in *The Message*. How should our house/life look?**

Glorious and standing tall—"out in the wide open spaces of God's grace and glory, standing tall and shouting our praise."

(Show the house.) Just like we can keep building this house, God can keep building our lives, if we'll let Him. How do we do that? By obeying Him. When times get tough, or even when life is easy, making the RIGHT CHOICES by obeying Jesus and believing in Him allows God to form us into HIS Superkids. We stay connected to the Father through faith, following the Holy Spirit's leading, walking in love, letting our good Father God protect us, renewing our hope daily, and getting back up with endurance when we fail, until we have super-strong character. Then we'll live the glorious life with Him that we were created for!

Notes: _____

_____

_____

_____

DAY 2: FOOD FUN

RECIPE FOR SUCCESS

Suggested Time: 10-15 minutes

Memory Verse: *So why do you keep calling me "Lord, Lord!" when you don't do what I say?* —Luke 6:46

Teacher Tip: Memorize the recipe! Also, your lesson will go faster if you prepare and divide everything ahead of time. Make sure to bake some of the muffins before the lesson so everyone can taste them, if you won't have the time to wait for the muffins to finish baking.

Ingredients: ☐ ½ Cup butter at room temp, ☐ 1 Cup granulated sugar, ☐ 2 Large eggs, ☐ 1 Teaspoon vanilla, ☐ ¼ Teaspoon salt, ☐ 2 Teaspoons baking powder, ☐ 2½ Cups blueberries, ☐ 2 Cups all-purpose flour, ☐ ½ Cup milk, ☐ Spray or butter to grease pan

Recipe:
1. Heat oven to 375°F.
2. Grease 18 regular-sized muffin cups (or 12 large-sized muffin cups).
3. In bowl, mix butter until creamy. Add sugar, and beat until pale and fluffy.
4. Add eggs, 1 at a time, beating each with the mixer.
5. Beat in vanilla, baking powder and salt.
6. With spoon, fold half the flour, then half the milk, into batter; repeat.
7. Fold in blueberries.
8. Spoon into muffin cups.
9. Bake 20-30 minutes until golden brown and springy to touch.

Supplies: ■ Muffin tin, ■ Mixer, ■ Mixing bowl, ■ Mixing spoon

Lesson Instructions:

Today, we'll be making some yummy blueberry muffins in the kitchen.

Who likes blueberry muffins?

Mmmmm, I can see most of you do! Since they're so tasty and can be a great snack, I've memorized the recipe. *(Make sure to not do anything during this speech.)*

Well, let's see *(stare off into space, as if thinking intently)*. First, you mix your ½ cup of butter, then 1 cup of sugar, and 2 eggs together with a mixer, beating the eggs separately. Then, you beat in the vanilla, baking powder and salt. Then you spoon in, not with the mixer, 1 cup of flour and ¼ cup of milk. Then you repeat and spoon in another 1 cup of flour and ¼ cup of milk. Add the 2½ cups of blueberries with a spoon, and after putting the whole thing in the oven—that you already preheated to 375° and placed the batter in a greased muffin pan, and baked for 20-30 minutes—whew!—you have blueberry muffins!

*Mmmm…*can't you just smell them? Ask your kids… Can't you? *(They should say no.)* Well, can't you just see them—they're nice and brown and delicious-looking! No? I'm not talking about seeing them just in your mind—but like you are eating them! What? You can't? And, you can't pick them up and put them in your mouth to taste them? Well, why not? Well, of course! We haven't put together the recipe yet, have we?

So, Superkids, even if I have an amazing blueberry muffin recipe memorized, and I want to eat blueberry muffins, what do I have to do? Oh, my goodness, you're right! I have to make them. I have to do something with this recipe I have stored in my heart.

Will knowing that I need to heat the oven to 375° magically turn an oven on to start making the muffins? No.

You know what's interesting? It's how things work for us where faith in God is concerned. It's not hard to ask Jesus into our hearts and want Him to be our Savior. In fact, it was probably more difficult to memorize this recipe, than it was for me to say, "Jesus, come into my life, and be my Savior!" But if I want to taste what God has for me, and see Jesus perform miracles through my life, and get to hear and know His voice, I have to ACT. I have to let what has gone into my heart become an action in my life.

I could go my whole life knowing this awesome blueberry muffin recipe, but if I never, ever do anything with it, what a waste! I could have fed the hungry and even enjoyed some yummy muffins myself.

So, what am I saying, Superkids?

Knowing that the oven needs to be heated to 375°, I can turn the oven on to 375°, (do step 1) and I am a whole step closer to having blueberry muffins ready to eat and share with others.

And then, I can prepare my pan by greasing it (do step 2); I am even closer.

Do steps 3-8, and have fun doing it! Put your muffins in the oven to bake.

Now (step 9) we wait. God wants to show up in our lives and Jesus is always there for us. But, it's just like the blueberry muffin recipe. If I woke up in the middle of the night with a craving for these blueberry muffins, I know the recipe, and I know I can go and get the ingredients and make them anytime.

But unless I actually get out of bed, and get the right ingredients—even turn on the oven—I won't be able to eat the "fruits of my labor" unless I put together all the ingredients and bake the muffins in the oven.

It's great to have Jesus be your Savior, but if you want to see Him work in your life, it requires commitment. You have to DO something. Listen when He speaks. Obey when He commands. Always be growing in your relationship with Him, and you'll truly get to "taste and see" how good He is!

Notes: _____

_____

_____

_____

_____

_____

DAY 3: GIVING LESSON — SECRET SUPERHERO

 Suggested Time: 10 minutes

 Offering Scripture: But when you give to someone in need, don't let your left hand know what your right hand is doing. Give your gifts in private, and your Father, who sees everything, will reward you. —Matthew 6:3-4

 Teacher Tip: Get creative if you don't want to buy a cape and mask. You can use a blanket tied around you and cut the sleeve off an old T-shirt to create a mask.

Supplies: ■ Superhero mask and cape, ■ Superhero props, ■ Bowl, ■ Slips of paper with one child's name on each

Lesson Instructions:

(Come out dressed as a superhero, and speak in your superhero voice.)

Hey, Superkids! Have any of you ever served someone? Raise your hand. Can you tell me what you did to serve? *(Call on children with their hands raised, and let them tell you about their experiences.)* Wow, you were really being a blessing to the people you served!

So, why would a superhero like me be asking you about serving? Because all superheroes have something in common. Does anyone know what it is? *(Allow children to guess.)* Well, all superheroes have a SECRET IDENTITY!

Because I'm a superhero, I have many special talents and abilities I use to fight evil and to help people. *(Explain the special talents and abilities your specific character possesses that set you apart for your fighting-evil job, and showcase the props you're using.)*

Let's read Matthew 6:3-4. *(Read this scripture out loud to your Superkids.)* Did you know that REAL superheroes offer their secret talents and abilities to save and to serve others, without anyone knowing their real identity? That's just like Jesus. He is a true Superhero who came to save and to serve us.

You can be just like Him. You can serve your family in secret this week, and see how your heavenly Father will reward you! He loves us so much. He is always watching us and watching over us with love.

Let's each pick a name from our bowl. Sometime this week, everyone can do something special, in secret, for the person whose name you picked!

Notes: _____

_____

_____

_____

DAY 4: REAL DEAL

CORRIE TEN BOOM

 Memory Verse: *So why do you keep calling me "Lord, Lord!" when you don't do what I say? —Luke 6:46*

 Concept: Highlighting an interesting historical place, figure or event that illustrates the theme of the day. The theme of the day is knowing Jesus as your Savior and Lord.

 Teacher Tip: This segment has many possible variations. Choose the best that fits your family and have fun! We suggest becoming as familiar as possible with the script prior to teaching this lesson.

Supplies: ■ Photos of the secret room in the ten Booms' house, ■ Photos of Corrie and her family

Optional Costume: ■ Grandmother wig and shawl

Intro:

This week, we're learning about Jesus as our Savior and Lord. Can anyone tell me what a *savior* is? A savior is a person who saves or rescues. Jesus did that for us, didn't He? Jesus is the ultimate example of unfailing love. He chose to love, even when He wasn't loved in return. And, He chose to love even His persecutors.

Today, we'll learn about a woman who demonstrated this God kind of love, just like her Lord and Savior, Jesus, and gave her life to save people's lives and to love them.

This person we're learning about today is the REAL DEAL because she rescued and saved many people. She was a Dutch woman. She was never married and never had any children, but she gave her life to help others. She and her family had a secret room in their house—a "hiding place" that was built into her room. And, this woman was a Nazi concentration camp survivor.

Can anyone guess who she was? *(Allow children to guess for a few minutes, if they have some ideas who it might be.)*

About Corrie ten Boom:

Corrie ten Boom was born April 15, 1892, in Haarlem, Holland. She had two sisters, Betsie and Nollie, and a brother named Willem. She worked as a watchmaker in the shop her grandfather started in 1837.

May 14, 1940, Holland surrendered to the Nazis. The Nazis did not want Jewish people to have privileges that other people had, so they put many in jail. If people were helping or letting Jewish people stay in their homes, their lives were in danger.

Corrie said her father inspired her to help the Jewish people. He always said, "In this household, God's people are always welcome."

The ten Booms helped many of their Jewish neighbors find safety, and even housed seven Jewish people in their home. It wasn't easy hiding all those people. Helping Jews and hiding them was illegal. So, housing and hiding seven Jewish people was already dangerous, but feeding them was another story. Due to the war, everyone—except the Jewish people—was issued ration cards. A ration card is kind of like going to the store, but only being allowed to buy certain products, and only a certain amount of those products.

Corrie needed to feed the people living in her house. She went to an old friend who was in charge of the local ration office, and received 100 ration cards, enough to feed not only her guests, but also the ones she had helped to find other housing.

Corrie and her family were very cautious about the police discovering all those people living in their house. Since what they were doing was made illegal by the Nazis, the ten Booms built a secret room in the highest point of the house, which was Corrie's room.

The ten Booms smuggled in bricks and building supplies in briefcases and folded newspapers. Finally, when the secret room was finished, the Jewish people were able to hide in it safely if the police ever raided the ten Booms' house. *(This would be a good time to show pictures of the secret room.)* The secret room was built behind a false wall in Corrie's room. It was only about 30 inches wide and had a built-in ventilation system in it so the people hiding there could breathe.

Arrest and Suffering:

On February 28, 1944, a man came into the ten Booms' watch shop and asked Corrie if she could help him. The man told her the police had arrested his wife and he needed 600 guilders (about $340 U.S. dollars) to bribe the police for her freedom. Corrie agreed to help.

The same day, the ten Booms' home was raided and the family was arrested and sent to concentrations camps. But the people staying in their house made it to the hiding place, and later to safety.

Corrie's father and sister both died in the concentration camps, but Corrie survived and later traveled all over the world, telling of God's goodness, love and protection. She wrote books telling the story of the hiding place and told many people about how God had rescued her and set her free.

On a Mission:

After the war, Corrie continued to help the Jewish people who had been hurt, put in prison camps and terrorized by the Nazis.

Corrie even learned to forgive one of the guards who had been at the camp where she and her sister had been prisoners.

Corrie lived to be 91 years old. She lived her life to the fullest.[6]

Outro:

Corrie and her family saved the lives of many Jewish people who would have died horribly in concentration camps during World War II. She put her own life and safety aside for others.

---

6 Historical information is from *The Hiding Place,* Corrie ten Boom and Elizabeth and John Sherrill (Grand Rapids: Chosen Books, 2006); corrietenboom.com/history.htm (7/11/11).

There may be some times in your life that are hard, and you wonder what might happen. Remember Corrie's story and how God rescued her. And because God sent Jesus to be your Savior, He will rescue you, too!

Variation No. 1: Dress Up

Entering in costume is an attention grabber for the Superkids. Feel free to present the information as if you were Corrie ten Boom herself!

Variation No. 2: Interview

If you are in a co-op and have other teens or adults involved, consider having another person play Corrie ten Boom and you can be the interviewer.

Notes: _____

_____

_____

_____

_____

_____

_____

_____

_____

_____

_____

_____

_____

_____

_____

_____

_____

_____

_____

_____

_____

_____

_____

DAY 5: GAME TIME

DO WHAT I SAY

Suggested Time: 10 minutes

Key Scripture: *After he has gathered his own flock, he walks ahead of them, and they follow him because they know his voice.* —John: 10:4

Supplies: ■ 2 Blindfolds, ■ Small objects (1 per child), ■ Timer (optional)

Game Instructions:

Divide players into 2 teams. (See Variation No. 1.) Then, line up the teams in two straight lines, except for the designated leader. The first person in each line will give commands first. Put a blindfold on the 2nd team member in each line. Spread out the objects in the game area. When you yell, "Go!" start the timer. At that time, the first person in line must shout out instructions to guide the blindfolded teammate to an object and back to the line. The leader can yell instructions such as "Go straight," "Go to the right," "You've reached the object!" The blindfolded teammate must listen to the instructions of the person ahead of him/her until he/she reaches and picks up the object and returns to the line, tagging the next contestant and passing on the blindfold. Then, it's his/her turn to give instructions. This can be a challenge over the screams of the other kids. Repeat this process until all of the team's objects have been picked up and the last contestant makes it back to the line.

Game Goal:

To be the first team to retrieve all the objects by each team member listening to and obeying their leader, as the leader gives specific directions to reach each object. Whichever team has picked up all their objects first and brings them successfully back "home," wins!

Final Word:

Just as these Superkids had to listen to their leader to get their directions, we must not only listen, but do what our Leader, Jesus, says to do. Despite the fact that there were loud voices all around them, these Superkids tuned their ears to hear the leader's voice. They recognized their leader's voice. The Bible says in John 10:4 that the sheep know the shepherd's voice. We know and recognize Jesus' voice when we hear Him speaking!

Tune your ear to hear what He is saying as He directs you and guides you. Once you hear what He says, then do it! You'll win every time!

Variation No. 1:

Use the timer: If the game area is not large enough to safely play with both teams at the same time, you can time each team. The team to finish in the least amount of time, wins.

Variation No. 2:

If the group is small, make the game work for you.

1 Child: Just you and 1 child, feel free to lay out a few different objects for your child, blindfold them and time them as you give them instructions. Then switch off and let them give you commands.

2-3 Children: Time them as they switch off between giving the commands and being blindfolded and picking up the objects.

Notes: _____

_____

_____

_____

_____

_____

_____

_____

_____

_____

_____

_____

_____

_____

_____

_____

_____

_____

_____

_____

_____

_____

ACTIVITY PAGE  **CONNECT THE ROMANS ROAD**

Memory Verse: *So why do you keep calling me "Lord, Lord!" when you don't do what I say?*
—Luke 6:46

The Romans Road helps us to connect the points in our lives to see our need for a Savior. Follow the steps that leads like a road through these scriptures in the book of Romans. Cut out illustration on the next page, then have children fold it into squares, like a booklet. Your kids can and take it with them whenever they need a reminder of how to share God's good news, the gospel, with their friends!

(Versions are paraphrased or from the *King James Version*.)

1. **Romans 3:23:** "All have sinned and fallen short of the Glory of God."

2. **Romans 6:23:** "For the wages of sin is death, but the gift of God is eternal life."

3. **Romans 10:9:** "That if you confess with your mouth, "Jesus is Lord," and you believe in your heart God raised Him from the dead, you will be saved."

4. **Romans 10:10:** "It is with your heart you believe and are justified, and with your mouth you are saved."

CONNECT THE
ROMANS ROAD

4. ROMANS 10:10 IT IS WITH YOUR HEART YOU BELIEVE AND ARE JUSTIFIED, AND WITH YOUR MOUTH YOU ARE SAVED.

1. ROMANS 3:23 ALL HAVE SINNED AND FALLEN SHORT OF THE GLORY OF GOD.

3. ROMANS 10:9 THAT IF YOU CONFESS WITH YOUR MOUTH, "JESUS IS LORD," AND YOU BELIEVE IN YOUR HEART GOD RAISED HIM FROM THE DEAD, YOU WILL BE SAVED.

2. ROMANS 6:23 FOR THE WAGES OF SIN IS DEATH, BUT THE GIFT OF GOD IS ETERNAL LIFE.

Notes: _____

_____

_____

_____

_____

_____

_____

_____

_____

_____

_____

_____

_____

_____

_____

_____

_____

_____

_____

_____

_____

_____

_____

_____

_____

_____

_____

_____

_____

_____

_____

_____

_____

_____

_____

WEEK 7: I AM FILLED WITH HIS HOLY SPIRIT

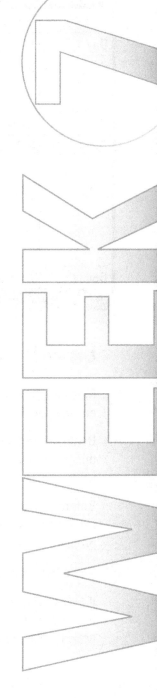

Memory Verse: All of them were filled with the Holy Spirit and began to speak in other tongues as the Spirit enabled them. —Acts 2:4 NIV

WEEK 7: SNAPSHOT — I AM FILLED WITH HIS HOLY SPIRIT

DAY	TYPE OF LESSON	LESSON TITLE	SUPPLIES
Day 1	Bible Lesson	Peter: From Rocky to Rock	None
Day 2	Academy Lab	Filled	Balloon, About 3 tablespoons of water, Large (2 liter) soft-drink bottle, Stir stick or straw, Lemon juice or vinegar, 1 Teaspoon of baking soda
Day 3	Giving Lesson	God's Partner	Bible
Day 4	Object Lesson	Most Holy Faith	Pictures of weight lifters/athletes, Real weights or pictures of weights, Bible
Day 5	Game Time	Tic-Tac-Treat	9 Lunchboxes (fun colors and designs), 9 Lunch-style treats (fruit pies, cupcakes, etc.), Clipboard, Sticky-backed hook and loop fastener (or tape), 5 Large laminated X's and 5 large laminated O's, Game-show music, glitzy costume (optional)
Bonus	Activity Page	The Right Place for Peter	1 Copy for each child

Lesson Introduction:

Many teachers and ministers are nervous about teaching on the Holy Spirit. They shouldn't be! Kids are the easiest people to lead in their new prayer language. Don't allow fear to enter in.

Begin at the point of telling the kids what the ministry of the Holy Spirit is. I've listed in your outline several things the Holy Spirit does for us, but there is so much more! Anything Jesus did for His disciples in the Gospels, the Holy Spirit does for US—comfort, help, instruction, etc.

Before you lay hands on your kids to receive the Holy Spirit and speak with tongues, make sure the Word regarding it is in you. Faith comes by hearing the Word. Believe in the gift of the Holy Spirit. You won't have any problem ministering to your Superkids.

One other tip: Encourage your Superkids to pray loudly and boldly in the spirit—not just today, but often.

It may take some time to develop them in this, but it's awesome when you say, "Let's pray in tongues," and they blast you out of the room! Open your services like this as the Lord leads. Just remind the Superkids, "No wimpy praying! We are giving the Lord our mouths! What an honor that He would speak through us!"

Love,

Commander Kellie

Commander Kellie

Lesson Outline:

This week, your children will learn about the power of the Holy Spirit. He is the ONE who will lead and guide us into the SWEET LIFE that God has planned, but we need to learn to hear from Him, and let Him lead our lives.

I. WHEN JESUS WAS PREPARING TO LEAVE, HE COMFORTED THE DISCIPLES BY PROMISING TO SEND THE HOLY SPIRIT
John 14:15-21, 26-27

    a.   The disciples didn't want Jesus to leave them.

    b.   The Father will send another Helper—the Holy Spirit.
         Another means "one of the very same kind."[6]

    c.   Jesus told the disciples to wait in Jerusalem until the Holy Spirit came. Acts 1:4-5, 8

    d.   They did—and He did! Acts 2:1-4

II. THE HOLY SPIRIT GIVES US THE POWER TO DO ALL OUR LORD WANTS US TO DO!

    a.   The Holy Spirit guides us into all the Father has prepared for us. John 16:12-15

    b.   He imparts God's nature into us and helps us do what is right. Galatians 5:16, 22-23

    c.   He prays the right prayer through us to receive God's best. Romans 8:26-27

III. THE BEST OFFER IN THE WORLD: BE FILLED WITH THE HOLY SPIRIT AND SPEAK IN OTHER TONGUES!

    a.   It's easy to receive your new language when you believe. Mark 16:17

    b.   The Father will give the Holy Spirit to those who ask Him. Luke 11:10-13

    c.   So...

       1.   Ask!

       2.   Believe—no fear!

       3.   Receive—that means you have to open your mouth in faith.
          Give the Holy Spirit your mouth—He will give you His words.

Notes: _____

_____

_____

---

6 *Another*—From *Sparkling Gems From the Greek,* Rick Renner (Tulsa: Teach All Nations, 2003) p. 195.

DAY 1: BIBLE LESSON

PETER: FROM ROCKY TO ROCK

 Memory Verse: All of them were filled with the Holy Spirit and began to speak in other tongues as the Spirit enabled them. —Acts 2:4 NIV

This week's Bible lesson focuses on one man's life that was radically changed the day he was filled with the Holy Spirit and began speaking in other tongues…Peter! The same man who denied even knowing Jesus Christ, proclaimed knowing Him to thousands on the day of Pentecost.

Read Matthew 16:15-23:
A Rocky Start for Peter

Then he asked them, "But who do you say I am?"

Simon Peter answered, "You are the Messiah, the Son of the living God."

Jesus replied, "You are blessed, Simon son of John, because my Father in heaven has revealed this to you. You did not learn this from any human being. Now I say to you that you are Peter (which means 'rock'), and upon this rock I will build my church, and all the powers of hell will not conquer it. And I will give you the keys of the Kingdom of Heaven. Whatever you forbid on earth will be forbidden in heaven, and whatever you permit on earth will be permitted in heaven."

Then he sternly warned the disciples not to tell anyone that he was the Messiah.

From then on Jesus began to tell his disciples plainly that it was necessary for him to go to Jerusalem, and that he would suffer many terrible things at the hands of the elders, the leading priests, and the teachers of religious law. He would be killed, but on the third day he would be raised from the dead.

But Peter took him aside and began to reprimand him for saying such things. "Heaven forbid, Lord," he said. "This will never happen to you!"

Jesus turned to Peter and said, "Get away from me, Satan! You are a dangerous trap to me. You are seeing things merely from a human point of view, not from God's."

Do Discussion Questions 1-4

Read Mark 14:27-31, 66-72:
Peter Fails His Promise to Jesus

On the way, Jesus told them, "All of you will desert me. For the Scriptures say, 'God will strike the Shepherd, and the sheep will be scattered.' But after I am raised from the dead, I will go ahead of you to Galilee and meet you there."

Peter said to him, "Even if everyone else deserts you, I never will."

Jesus replied, "I tell you the truth, Peter—this very night, before the rooster crows twice, you will deny three times that you even know me."

"No!" Peter declared emphatically. "Even if I have to die with you, I will never deny you!" And all the others vowed the same....

[After Jesus had been betrayed, arrested, and put on trial]
Meanwhile, Peter was in the courtyard below. One of the servant girls who worked for the high priest came by and noticed Peter warming himself at the fire. She looked at him closely and said, "You were one of those with Jesus of Nazareth."

But Peter denied it. "I don't know what you're talking about," he said, and he went out into the entryway. Just then, a rooster crowed.

When the servant girl saw him standing there, she began telling the others, "This man is definitely one of them!" But Peter denied it again.

A little later some of the other bystanders confronted Peter and said, "You must be one of them, because you are a Galilean."

Peter swore, "A curse on me if I'm lying—I don't know this man you're talking about!" And immediately the rooster crowed the second time.

Suddenly, Jesus' words flashed through Peter's mind: "Before the rooster crows twice, you will deny three times that you even know me." And he broke down and wept.

Do Discussion Questions 5-6

Read Acts 2:1-41:
Filled With the Holy Spirit, Peter Becomes the Rock

On the day of Pentecost all the believers were meeting together in one place. Suddenly, there was a sound from heaven like the roaring of a mighty windstorm, and it filled the house where they were sitting. Then, what looked like flames or tongues of fire appeared and settled on each of them. And everyone present was filled with the Holy Spirit and began speaking in other languages, as the Holy Spirit gave them this ability.

At that time there were devout Jews from every nation living in Jerusalem. When they heard the loud noise, everyone came running, and they were bewildered to hear their own languages being spoken by the believers.

They were completely amazed. "How can this be?" they exclaimed. "These people are all from Galilee, and yet we hear them speaking in our own native languages! Here we are—Parthians, Medes, Elamites, people from Mesopotamia, Judea, Cappadocia, Pontus, the province of Asia, Phrygia, Pamphylia, Egypt, and the areas of Libya around Cyrene, visitors from Rome (both Jews and converts to Judaism), Cretans, and Arabs. And we all hear these people speaking in our own languages about the wonderful things God has done!" They stood there amazed and perplexed. "What can this mean?" they asked each other.

But others in the crowd ridiculed them, saying, "They're just drunk, that's all!"

Then Peter stepped forward with the eleven other apostles and shouted to the crowd, "Listen carefully, all of you, fellow Jews and residents of Jerusalem! Make no mistake about this. These people are not drunk, as some of you are assuming. Nine o'clock in the morning is much too early for that. No, what you see was predicted long ago by the prophet Joel:

'In the last days,' God says, 'I will pour out my Spirit upon all people. Your sons and daughters will prophesy. Your young men will see visions, and your old men will dream dreams. In those days I will pour out my Spirit even on my servants—men and women alike—and they will prophesy. And I will cause wonders in the heavens above and signs on the earth below—blood and fire and clouds of smoke. The sun will become dark, and the moon will turn blood red before that great and glorious day of the Lord arrives. But everyone who calls on the name of the Lord will be saved.'

"People of Israel, listen! God publicly endorsed Jesus the Nazarene by doing powerful miracles, wonders, and signs through him, as you well know. But God knew what would happen, and his prearranged plan was carried out when Jesus was betrayed. With the help of lawless Gentiles, you nailed him to a cross and killed him. But God released him from the horrors of death and raised him back to life, for death could not keep him in its grip. King David said this about him: 'I see that the Lord is always with me. I will not be shaken, for he is right beside me. No wonder my heart is glad, and my tongue shouts his praises! My body rests in hope. For you will not leave my soul among the dead or allow your Holy One to rot in the grave. You have shown me the way of life, and you will fill me with the joy of your presence.'

"Dear brothers, think about this! You can be sure that the patriarch David wasn't referring to himself, for he died and was buried, and his tomb is still here among us. But he was a prophet, and he knew God had promised with an oath that one of David's own descendants would sit on his throne. David was looking into the future and speaking of the Messiah's resurrection. He was saying that God would not leave him among the dead or allow his body to rot in the grave.

"God raised Jesus from the dead, and we are all witnesses of this. Now he is exalted to the place of highest honor in heaven, at God's right hand. And the Father, as he had promised, gave him the Holy Spirit to pour out upon us, just as you see and hear today. For David himself never ascended into heaven, yet he said, 'The Lord said to my Lord, "Sit in the place of honor at my right hand until I humble your enemies, making them a footstool under your feet."'

"So let everyone in Israel know for certain that God has made this Jesus, whom you crucified, to be both Lord and Messiah!" Peter's words pierced their hearts, and they said to him and to the other apostles, "Brothers, what should we do?"

Peter replied, "Each of you must repent of your sins and turn to God, and be baptized in the name of Jesus Christ for the forgiveness of your sins. Then you will receive the gift of the Holy Spirit. This promise is to you, to your children, and to those far away—all who have been called by the Lord our God." Then Peter continued preaching for a long time, strongly urging all his listeners, "Save yourselves from this crooked generation!"

Those who believed what Peter said were baptized and added to the church that day—about 3,000 in all.

Do Discussion Questions 7-10

Discussion Questions:

1. What name did Jesus give to Simon?

Peter

2. **What does *Peter* mean, and how did that correspond with Peter's calling?**

Peter means "rock." Jesus said Peter was a little rock, but on the mighty rock of the revelation that Peter had received from God that Jesus is the Christ, the Son of the living God, He was going to build His Church.

3. **Jesus said He would give Peter the "keys of the Kingdom of Heaven." What does that mean?**

Jesus was talking about power to unlock (like keys do) God's heavenly plan into the earth realm. So with those "keys," Peter and all believers would have God's authority in the earth.

4. **Not long after Jesus prophesied over Peter, Jesus told Peter he was being used by Satan, tempting Jesus to not obey God's plan! Does this Peter seem like the powerful *rock* Jesus called him to be? Discuss.**

No. It seems that Peter is being used by Satan to say the wrong thing. Also note that only a little earlier, Jesus had said to Peter that he was blessed because God had revealed the truth to him. Make sure your Superkids understand the imbalance that Peter shows without the Holy Spirit.

5. **Peter promised to never desert Jesus, but Jesus knew that Peter would break under peer pressure. Do you think Peter knew how much pressure he'd face when he promised Jesus that he'd never deny Him? Discuss.**

No. Peter ended up denying Jesus just as Jesus had said.

6. **How many times did Peter deny Jesus?**

Three

7. **Who gave the disciples the ability to speak in other tongues?**

The Holy Spirit

8. **How many people did Peter lead to Jesus and baptize that day?**

About 3,000!

9. **Discuss the automatic change that Peter experienced on the day when he was filled with the Holy Spirit. How can the Baptism in the Holy Spirit change your Superkid's life, as well?**

Peter experienced a very obvious transformation, especially where fear and preaching the gospel was concerned. Just days before, he was scared to admit that he even knew Jesus. After he received the Baptism in the Holy Spirit on the day of Pentecost, Peter proclaimed to thousands that Jesus is the Son of God, the Messiah, sent to save us from sins. He overcame his fear through the power of the Holy Spirit, and began a ministry of proclaiming Jesus that day. *(If you have any stories of how the power of the Holy Spirit changed your life or helped you overcome fear, take time to share that experience.)*

10. **Take the time to make sure your Superkids are filled with the Holy Spirit, with the evidence of speaking in other tongues, and know how to use their heavenly language by praying in tongues together for a while.**

Notes: _____

_____

_____

_____

DAY 2: ACADEMY LAB — FILLED

 Suggested Time: 15 minutes

 Memory Verse: All of them were filled with the Holy Spirit and began to speak in other tongues as the Spirit enabled them. —Acts 2:4 NIV

 Teacher Tip: It is helpful to stretch out the balloon before the lesson to make it easy to inflate.

Supplies: ☐ Balloons, ☐ About 3 tablespoons water, ☐ Large (2 liter) soft-drink bottle, ☐ Stir stick or straw, ☐ Lemon juice or vinegar, ☐ 1 Teaspoon baking soda

Prior to Lesson:

Practice this experiment a couple of times before you teach the lesson.

Lesson Instructions:

Does anyone know how to inflate a balloon? *(Pass out balloons, and let the kids try inflating them.)* Some of you were able to do it, but does anyone know how to inflate a balloon without using your mouth? Is that even possible?

Actually, yes it is! But, to show you how to do this, I'm going to need some help. Would anyone like to help me with this? *(Choose one of the Superkids to be your assistant.)*

First, I'm going to pour some water into this bottle and stir in 1 teaspoon baking soda until it's dissolved.

Now, I'm going to pour some lemon juice into the bottle with the baking soda and water mixture and quickly place the balloon over the mouth of the bottle. I'm going to hold the balloon tightly so it doesn't pop off. *(The balloon should inflate.)*

Cool, huh? Because we added the lemon juice to the baking soda, it created a reaction that filled the balloon with carbon dioxide—which caused the balloon to inflate!

In our memory verse today, we see that the disciples were filled with the Holy Spirit and began to speak with other tongues. We're just like this balloon. When the Holy Spirit is added to our lives, we become FILLED with Him. When the Holy Spirit mixes with our faith in Jesus, we can speak out, and it becomes as easy as filling up this balloon. The only difference is, a balloon can't speak, but when *we're* filled up, we get to use *our* mouths to speak what the Spirit is saying through us!

Notes: _____

_____

_____

DAY 3: GIVING LESSON | GOD'S PARTNER

Suggested Time: 10 minutes

Offering Scripture: When the Spirit of truth comes, he will guide you into all truth. He will not speak on his own but will tell you what he has heard. He will tell you about the future. —John 16:13

Lesson Instructions:

Superkids, have you ever wanted to give something away, but you weren't sure you were supposed to? Or worse, have you ever known you were supposed to give something away, and you didn't? You thought about it and maybe prayed about it, but you still weren't sure, or you just didn't want to?

Hearing from the Holy Spirit is always very important, especially when we bring our gifts before God. Whether we're giving money in the offering or helping Mom around the house with extra work, all our giving should be Spirit led. When we become Spirit-led givers, we do away with all the guesswork because He shows us things that are to come.

Let's read John 16:13. *(Read this verse out loud to your Superkids.)*

Superkids, how do we become Spirit-led givers? *(Allow time for answers.)* Well first, we must receive Jesus as Savior and Lord, and be filled with the Holy Spirit. When He is living in our hearts, we can be led by His Spirit, who lives in us. *(This is another great place to make sure all in your group/home have asked the Lord Jesus to live in them and have also been filled with the Holy Spirit.)*

Since the Holy Spirit is living in you now, you can be led by Him in everything you do. So, before you go to church, ask Him what you should give to Him in the offering. It makes a big difference to bring an offering you prepared ahead of time because you prayed and asked God how much He wanted you to give, rather than just plunking the money into the offering basket or bucket.

So, let's put out an offering challenge today. How about every morning when you wake up, pray in tongues for a few minutes and ask God, "What would You like me to give today?" You might be thinking, *You mean, I'm supposed to give something every day?* We're supposed to live a lifestyle of giving because it's part of living the love walk. God is love. He's a giver. In fact, John 3:16 says, "For God so loved…that He gave…" (NKJV). We're to be just like Him. You don't always have to give money. It could be a pencil to a friend at school or a nice note to Dad. But if you get really quiet on the inside, the Holy Spirit will tell you what you should be giving, and it WILL CHANGE YOUR LIFE, EVERY DAY!

In fact, why don't we do that right now for the offering? Let's pray in tongues for a few minutes. *(Have your kids pray in tongues for 1-2 minutes.)* Very good! Now, let's all say: "Holy Spirit, I know You are going to lead me and guide me into all truth in my giving. I know You show me the future. I am asking You, Holy Spirit, what You want me to give."

Let's get really quiet and listen inside our spirits. This is the fun part: Now, do what He says! You can never out-give God! You'll *always* be blessed when you obey the Lord!

Notes:

DAY 4: OBJECT LESSON — MOST HOLY FAITH

Suggested Time: 10 minutes

Key Scripture: But you, beloved, building yourselves up on your most holy faith, praying in the Holy Spirit. —Jude 20 NKJV

Supplies: ■ Pictures of weight lifters/athletes, ■ Real weights or pictures of weights, ■ Bible

Prior to Lesson:

Choose pictures of three to five bodybuilders who obviously spend a lot of time lifting heavy weights in the gym. If there are favorite football players or athletes your children enjoy watching, include their pictures, as well. Convey the concept that these people have been lifting some heavy weights!

Include pictures of various weights, like barbells or dumbbells, ranging from 1 to 100 pounds. *(If you happen to have real weights, you can use them for illustration.)*

You can also check online to find a clean video clip of a bodybuilder lifting some really heavy weights. The key is for your Superkids to get a mental image of what happens to their inner man when they pray in tongues.

Lesson Instructions:

Today, we're going to look at some pictures of some really strong people. You can tell they've been working out very hard, haven't they? *(Show your Superkids the pictures, and let them pass them around.)* Just look at those big muscles! What do you think all these people have in common?

Yes, you're right! These people have all been very diligent to work out. They work out with some heavy weights. It takes consistent effort, lifting lots of weight to grow muscles that big!

(Show the pictures of the weights or your collection. If you found a video, play it so the kids can see the person performing some heavy lifting.)

Which of these weights do you think these bodybuilders and athletes used to grow those big muscles? Do you think they used these really light weights *(show the smaller weights),* or do you think they used these really heavy weights? *(Show the larger, heavier weights.)*

That's right! It doesn't look like these men/women bother working out with the really small weights very often. It looks like they really make a point of building the biggest muscles they can, as fast as they can with the bigger, heavier weights. They are going for maximum results in the shortest amount of time. So when they lift the heaviest weight, they expend the maximum, or greatest, effort, and their muscles grow at a maximum rate!

(Show the picture of the heaviest weight.) Superkids, do you know what is *just like* lifting the very heaviest weight—not for your body—but to make <u>your spirit man</u> strong? *(Allow for answers.)* It's when you pray in your heavenly language!

Let's read Jude 20. It says, "But you, beloved, building yourselves up on your most holy faith, praying in the Holy Spirit." So when you pray in tongues, it's as if your spirit man is going to the gym and lifting and bench pressing weights like these. *(Show the picture of the heaviest weights again.)*

Can anyone tell me why praying in your heavenly language is like lifting heavy weights and growing big muscles for your spirit man? It's because when you pray in tongues, you're praying out God's will for your life. Romans 8:26-27 says, "And the Holy Spirit helps us in our weakness. For example, we don't know what God wants us to pray for. But the Holy Spirit prays for us with groanings that cannot be expressed in words. And the Father who knows all hearts knows what the Spirit is saying, for the Spirit pleads for us believers in harmony with God's own will."

I think we need to do some heavy lifting for our spirit man today! Let's spend some time right now, praying in our heavenly language, and see how the Lord strengthens us!

Notes: _____

_____

_____

_____

_____

_____

_____

_____

_____

_____

_____

_____

_____

_____

_____

_____

_____

_____

_____

_____

_____

_____

_____

DAY 5: GAME TIME

TIC-TAC-TREAT

Suggested Time: 10 minutes

Memory Verse: *All of them were filled with the Holy Spirit and began to speak in other tongues as the Spirit enabled them.* —Acts 2:4 NIV

Supplies: ■ 9 Lunchboxes (fun colors and designs), ■ 9 Lunch-style treats to place in each box (fruit pies, cupcakes, etc.), ■ Clipboard (for questions), ■ Questions from previous 6 weeks' teaching, ■ Sticky-backed hook and loop fastener (or tape) to place X's and O's on the lunchboxes, ■ 5 Large laminated X's and 5 large laminated O's (see pages 131-132 for templates, ■ Game-show music, ■ Glitzy costume (optional)

Prior to Game:

This is a "game series" that corresponds with the teaching series. The initial preparation may take more effort, but it's a favorite! Let your Superkids know that they will be playing this game for the next few weeks of your series. Watch how excitedly your group pays attention!

On the back of each lunchbox, place 2 pieces of sticky-backed loop fastener. You'll want to place them in good positions to hold the laminated X or O. Copy 5 X's and 5 O's onto brightly colored paper (yellow is good). We recommend using the same color for all X's and O's, in case some Superkids catch a glimpse of the color behind the lunchbox. Super-smart cadets will figure out different colors! Laminate the X's and O's so they will not tear when being switched from box to box during following weeks. Place the corresponding pieces of sticky-backed fastener on your laminated X's and O's.

With sticky fastener, fasten an X or O to each lunchbox. You'll have 1 X or 1 O left over. If you used more X's than O's, for instance, next time you will want to do the opposite.

Now, place a treat in each lunchbox, and place the lunchboxes at the front of the room—with the X's and O's facing away from the Superkids.

Place review questions on the clipboard. *(Write your own, or use the ones provided.)*

Game Instructions:

Begin playing the game-show music immediately. This game is all about presentation. To kick it up a notch, use a game-show assistant to turn the lunchboxes around (like a glamorous game-show assistant would, with dramatic hand gestures). We also recommend glitzy host costumes. Thrift stores are great places to find these.

Hey, Superkids! Welcome to Tic-Tac Treeeeeaaaat—the game where lunchboxes go from dull to delicious!

I'm going to choose 2 Superkids to answer our first question. *(Read question No. 1.)* If you know the answer, you must raise your hand. Whoever gets the right answer first, will get to pick whether he/she will be X's or O's and choose a lunchbox. But, I'll be the one to turn the lunchbox around. *(Call on the first player to raise his/*

her hand. Use this time to hype things up, like a game-show host.)

Will it be an X or an O? Let's find out!

(After Player 1 has correctly answered a question and picked a box, ask a question of Player 2. If he/she is correct, a box may be chosen. If not, the play returns to Player 1, and so on, until someone has 3 X's and 3 O's, at which time, loudly declare: "We have a Tic-Tac-Treat!" Allow the winning Superkid to open the 3 winning lunchboxes, and take the treats as their game prize.

(Note: This game is rather involved, so only 1 round is usually needed.)

Game Goal:

Whichever Superkid answers all the questions correctly and has 3 X's or 3 O's, wins!

Final Word:

When we pay close attention to God's Word, there are lots of awesome "treats" waiting for us—even better than "Tic-Tac-Treats"!

Variation No. 1: Original Questions

Questions and answers have been provided, but if you would like to write your own questions, there is a question template provided.

Variation No. 2: Dress Up

Make it a game-show night, complete with a host/assistant's costumes—glitzy jackets, sunglasses, dress, etc.

Variation No. 3: Applause

Have someone hold up an "applause" sign at appropriate moments, as on a TV game show.

Variation No. 4: Brown Paper Bags

Lunch-sized, brown paper bags could be used instead of lunchboxes for your game. Your children can even decorate them with stickers before your game to build anticipation.

Variation No. 5: Family vs. Family

If you know of another family or have a co-op studying *Superkid Academy's Home Bible Study for Kids,* consider joining together—and facing off—for a fun evening or dinner and a round of Tic-Tac-Treat. It's an exciting way to celebrate Bible study and godly friendships!

TIC-TAC-TREAT QUESTIONS:

(Review Taken From Weeks 1-6)

BIBLE LESSON:

#1 Q: What is the Superkid Creed?

A: A list of decisions we make that come from God's Word, a belief system/way of living.

#2 Q: When Israel was taken captive, who were the four boys we learned about who chose to honor God in Babylon?

A: Daniel, Hananiah, Mishael and Azariah, OR Daniel, Shadrach, Meshach and Abednego

#3 Q: We learned about living in God's bubble, and found that God wants us to put WHAT in our hearts?

A: His Word

#4 Q: There are four things you must do in order to be a Superkid. What are two of them?

A: 1. Accept Jesus as your Lord and Savior.

2. Listen to the Holy Spirit, and obey His voice.

3. Honor and obey your parents.

4. Tell others about Jesus.

#5 Q: We are no longer just servants, but we were made God's _____ through Christ.

A: Children

GIVING LESSON:

#6 Q: Why is God a great Daddy? (Must give one of three answers.)

A: 1. He always does what He says.

2. God is a giver and His hands are always ready to bless His children.

3. He rewards those who sincerely seek Him.

#7 Q: TRUE OR FALSE: Matthew 6:3-4 says we should give loudly and arrogantly so everyone can see us giving.

A: False

MEMORY VERSE:

#8 Q: When the Creed was introduced, what was the memory verse we learned? *(They can quote it or say the reference.)*

A: "As pressure and stress bear down on me, I find joy in your commands." Psalm 119:143

OBJECT LESSON:

#9 Q: What type of seasoning/spice does Matthew 5:13 say we need to be to the world?

A: Salt

STORYBOOK THEATER:

#10 Q: When Buck played his harmonica, what were Hananiah, Mishael and Azariah supposed to do?

A: Bow down and worship the mountain that looked like Buck's face.

TIC-TAC-TREAT (10 QUESTIONS TOTAL)

BIBLE LESSON: 5 QUESTIONS

#1 Q: _____
_____

A: _____
_____

#2 Q: _____
_____

A: _____
_____

#3 Q: _____
_____

A: _____
_____

#4 Q: _____
_____

A: _____
_____

#5 Q: _____
_____

A: _____
_____

Notes: _____
_____
_____
_____

TIC-TAC-TREAT (10 QUESTIONS TOTAL)

GIVING LESSON: 2 QUESTIONS

#6 Q: _____

_____

A: _____

_____

#7 Q: _____

_____

A: _____

_____

MEMORY VERSE: 1 QUESTION

#8 Q: _____

_____

A: _____

_____

WILD CARD: 2 QUESTIONS

#9 Q: _____

_____

A: _____

_____

#10 Q: _____

_____

A: _____

_____

ACTIVITY PAGE

THE RIGHT PLACE FOR PETER

Memory Verse: All of them were filled with the Holy Spirit and began to speak in other tongues as the Spirit enabled them. —Acts 2:4 NIV

ANSWER KEY:

Name: _____

Fear and unfaithfulness have no place in a Superkid's life, but with the Holy Spirit's help, we can learn to drive out fear and unfaithfulness the way Peter did. Can you spot the things that are out of place in this picture?

THE RIGHT PLACE FOR PETER

Notes: _____

_____

_____

_____

_____

_____

_____

_____

_____

_____

_____

_____

_____

_____

_____

_____

_____

_____

_____

_____

_____

_____

_____

_____

_____

_____

_____

_____

_____

_____

_____

_____

_____

WEEK 8: I OBEY HIS WRITTEN WORD

Memory Verse: Study this Book of Instruction continually. Meditate on it day and night so you will be sure to obey everything written in it. Only then will you prosper and succeed in all you do. —Joshua 1:8

WEEK 8: SNAPSHOT

I OBEY HIS WRITTEN WORD

DAY	TYPE OF LESSON	LESSON TITLE	SUPPLIES
Day 1	Bible Lesson	Living by God's Word	Paper, Pens, Pencils, Crayons, Paint, Markers, Clay or chalk
Day 2	Read-Aloud	What Would Word Do?	None
Day 3	Giving Lesson	Blessed to Be a Blessing	Pictures of The Salvation Army (optional)
Day 4	Object Lesson	Study Tools	Printouts of quiz, Pens or pencils
Day 5	Game Time	Picture Perfect	6 Sheets of paper per player, 2 Tables, 1 Pencil or crayon per player, 6 Photos, Tarp, 2 Boxes of markers and colors, Stopwatch, Dry-erase board and marker (optional)
Bonus	Activity Page	God's Word Unscrambler	1 Copy for each child

Lesson Introduction:

Making a decision early in life to honor and obey God's Word will set our Superkids on the right path! That's all God ever needed from His people to be able to bless them. Teach your kids to develop a relationship with their Bibles.

I know I've said it before, and I may say it again! But, it's true. In today's society, it's easy to get used to a device with a Bible on it, and that's fine to use, but let the kids see you using your hard-copy Bible.

I challenge you to read Psalm 119 before teaching this week. Let the Holy Spirit minister to you the importance of His Word. That's who we are. They don't call us Word people for nothing!

Love,

Commander Kellie

Commander Kellie

Lesson Outline:

This week your children will learn about the steadiness and surety of following God's Word. God's Word keeps you and your Superkids protected and in God's GOOD PLAN (Ephesians 2:10). That's why we call the Word of God—our Bibles—THE SUPERKID MANUAL. It's the guide to living, if your kids want to live a SUPER life!

I. GOD'S WORD IS TRUE AND RELIABLE

a.   It is the sure Word of God. 2 Peter 1:16-21

b.   Live your life like Jesus. 1 John 2:3-6

c.   Jesus lived by the written Word. Hebrews 10:7

II. KEEP THE WORD IN YOUR HEART 2 Timothy 3:10-17

a.   Keeps you safe, delivered, corrected, etc.

b.   Ask what you will, and it will be done. John 15:7, 9-11

c.   Brings THE BLESSING. Deuteronomy 28:1; Proverbs 3:1-2
     Remember "The Sweet Life"!

III. PUT THE WORD FIRST

a.   Meditate on the Word, and you'll obey it. Joshua 1:8

b.   Read and listen with the ears of a doer. James 1:21-25

c.   The Word will help you know the difference between the voice of God coming from your spirit and the voice of your flesh and emotions (or what *you* want). Hebrews 4:12

Notes: _____

_____

_____

_____

_____

_____

_____

_____

_____

_____

DAY 1: BIBLE LESSON

LIVING BY GOD'S WORD

Memory Verse: Study this Book of Instruction continually. Meditate on it day and night so you will be sure to obey everything written in it. Only then will you prosper and succeed in all you do.
—Joshua 1:8

Optional Supplies: ☐ Paper, ☐ Pencils, ☐ Pens, ☐ Crayons, ☐ Paint, ☐ Markers, ☐ Clay or chalk, or ☐ Paper and pen to write a song

God's written Word is not to be taken lightly. It is to be taken to heart. He gives us His Word, so we can live blessed with Him. It's His plan for success!

Read 2 Timothy 3:14-17:
Trusting God's Written Word

But you must remain faithful to the things you have been taught. You know they are true, for you know you can trust those who taught you. You have been taught the holy Scriptures from childhood, and they have given you the wisdom to receive the salvation that comes by trusting in Christ Jesus. All Scripture is inspired by God and is useful to teach us what is true and to make us realize what is wrong in our lives. It corrects us when we are wrong and teaches us to do what is right. God uses it to prepare and equip his people to do every good work.

Do Questions 1-3

Read Psalm 19:7-14, MSG
God's Map to the Sweet Life

The revelation of God is whole
and pulls our lives together.

The signposts of God are clear
and point out the right road.

The life-maps of God are right,
showing the way to joy.

The directions of God are plain
and easy on the eyes.

God's reputation is twenty-four-carat gold,
with a lifetime guarantee.

The decisions of God are accurate

down to the nth degree.

God's Word is better than a diamond,
better than a diamond set between emeralds.

You'll like it better than strawberries in spring,
better than red, ripe strawberries.

There's more: God's Word warns us of danger
and directs us to hidden treasure.

Otherwise how will we find our way?
Or know when we play the fool?

Clean the slate, God, so we can start the day fresh!
Keep me from stupid sins,
from thinking I can take over your work;

Then I can start this day sun-washed,
scrubbed clean of the grime of sin.

These are the words in my mouth;
these are what I chew on and pray.

Accept them when I place them
on the morning altar,

O God, my Altar-Rock,
God, Priest-of-My-Altar.

Do Discussion Questions 4-5 (and/or variations)

Discussion Questions:

1. **What did the Scriptures give to Timothy in his childhood?**

   The wisdom to receive salvation in Christ Jesus

2. **Fill in the blanks: Scripture _____ us when we are wrong and teaches us to do what is _____.**

   corrects / right

3. **Fill in the blanks: God uses Scripture to _____ and _____ His people to do every good work.**

   prepare / equip

4. **How does the psalmist describe God's sense of direction and His reputation?**

   His directions are always right and His reputation is as good as gold!

5. **Discuss Psalm 19:7-14. What images does this bring to mind? Talk about some key imagery:**

   - GPS/Maps—God has clear directions for us that are right.

   - God's reputation is pure gold!

- His Word is better than diamonds.

- His Word is sweeter than strawberries.

- His Word warns us of danger.

- His Word directs us to hidden treasure—like a treasure map!

- He cleanses us from sin and gives us fresh, new days.

- God is our Rock.

Art Variation:

Have your Superkids choose their favorite stanza from Psalm 19, and/or select parts for your children to paint, draw, mold, etc., into what they see from their selection. Pull out some paper, pens, crayons, paint or markers—whatever art supplies you have handy or you know your Superkids enjoy. (Even clay or sidewalk chalk will work. Feel free to think outside the box.)

Song Variation:

Have your Superkids choose their favorite stanza and/or select parts for them to create their own song. Encourage them to sing their song or read it aloud, if they would like to.

Notes: _____

_____

_____

_____

_____

_____

_____

_____

_____

_____

_____

_____

_____

_____

_____

_____

_____

_____

_____

DAY 2: READ-ALOUD

WHAT WOULD WORD DO?

 Suggested Time: 10 minutes

 Memory Verse: Study this Book of Instruction continually. Meditate on it day and night so you will be sure to obey everything written in it. Only then will you prosper and succeed in all you do. —Joshua 1:8

 Concept: Jordan discovers that life is as easy as an open-book test. When you know what God's Word says, you'll always know what to do.

Story:

Once upon a Tuesday, in a schoolyard not so far away, Jordan's friends Jamie, Marty and Harry were making fun of him because he told them that his parents wouldn't allow him to see the horror movie at their party.

"You're gonna miss the party of the year because you're not allowed to see horror movies?!" Jamie asked after school one day.

"No...I..." Jordan stuttered a reply, but Marty cut him off.

"What kind of a wimp are you?"

"Yeah, scared of a few zombies, huh?" Harry added.

To be clear, Jordan wasn't afraid. "No," he said. "I just can't disobey my..."

"Hey guys." Now Jamie cut him off this time. "Jordan's a scaredy-cat!" Jamie taunted.

Everybody in the schoolyard laughed.

"Am not," said Jordan.

"Are too!" Jamie threw back at him with a slight push to his shoulder.

"Not."

"Too."

"Take it back!" Jordan yelled as a larger crowd began to form.

"Chicken-liver!" Jamie loved the attention, and began to cluck like a chicken. His friends followed suit.

Jordan closed his eyes as his soul screamed, "What do I do?" He was a Superkid learning to listen to his spirit.

Suddenly, from the inside he heard a Voice that almost sounded like an announcer from a baseball game. "Are you stuck in a bind and don't know what to do?" the Voice asked.

Jordan looked around. Everyone was still laughing and clucking. But for this moment, he ignored everything but what he heard from the inside.

The Voice sounded again. "Do you wish your life were an open-book test with all the answers laid before you?"

Jordan considered it. He tapped his chin.

"Are you tapping your chin wondering whether you should LIE to your parents about seeing a BAD horror film which they specifically told you that you were not allowed to see…?"

"Yes!" Jordan admitted.

"Well, tap your chin no more! Kids everywhere are discovering that by reading their Bibles, they can ensure that they will live the bright and blessed future that the Lord has planned for them! When you carry God's Word in your heart, you will have the right answers with you for every problem you face!"

"OK, great." Jordan looked around him. "But what do I do about right now?"

"Do you know what Proverbs 12:22 says?"

"Uh…no," Jordan replied.

Suddenly Jordan remembered the Bible in his backpack. He unzipped his bag, paying more attention to his spirit than all the other commotion.

Jordan opened it to Proverbs with a "What chapter and verse again?"

"12:22," the Voice replied.

Jordan searched until he found it. "'The Lord detests lying lips, but he delights in those who tell the truth.' So…" Jordan looked up and around. "I shouldn't lie, right?" he asked.

The Voice answered, "That's right."

"But it's supposed to be the awesomest party of the year!" Jordan said.

The inner Voice cleared His throat. "I didn't want to have to do this, but…what about Ephesians 6:1?" He asked.

Jordan frowned—this one he knew by heart. "Ephesians 6:1: 'Children, obey your parents because you belong to the Lord, for this is right,'" Jordan recited with very little enthusiasm.

"Look at *you!*" The big Voice seemed to be quite proud of Jordan. "OK, keep going," He encouraged.

"That's all I know," said Jordan.

Suddenly, Jamie tried to swipe the Bible from Jordan, and he remembered himself. "Hey, that's mine!" Jordan took the Bible back and walked away, completely forgetting what the fuss was about to begin with. He walked to a secluded, nearby bench, and opened his Bible to Ephesians 6:2-3. "'Honor your father and mother.' This is the first commandment with a promise: If you honor your father and mother, 'things will go well for you, and you will have a long life on the earth.'"

"Woohooo! Yeah!" The Voice inside began rejoicing.

But Jordan didn't get it. He slammed the book shut. "What are You so happy about?" he asked. He looked back up, and saw Jamie and Harry practicing a dramatic skit, which involved a lot of pointing in his direction and crying like a baby.

The Voice replied. "You got something against living well and enjoying life?"

"No, of course not," Jordan replied. He could tell that Jamie's comedy act had moved on to involve his parents. Marty was now pretending to be his mom and shaking her finger at Jamie.

But his spirit Voice seemed unfazed. "Then, obey your parents, and don't watch the movie. The heavenly crowd's about to go wild because you now have a great opportunity to OBEY your parents.... Woo-hooo!"

"Is it really that black and white?" Jordan asked. It didn't seem that way. Right now, it seemed like obeying your parents just got you made fun of at school.

"It is on the page, isn't it?" the Voice asked.

Jordan looked back down at the Word of God and nodded.

"Is God a liar?" the Voice asked.

"NO WAY!" Jordan knew that was not the case.

"Then obey, and you'll live a long and happy life! Think about it. The forces of darkness are setting you up for a strikeout! They'd love it if you'd taken the easy way out. But when you say yes to God's Word, you're hitting a home run for your heavenly team. Who cares if you strike out with mean 'friends,' who don't seem to be on your team anyway?"

Finally, it clicked. Jordan was pretty big into playing baseball, and he knew the power of a home run. Jordan smiled and placed the Bible in his backpack. Although their loud bullying and chicken squawking filled the air, in a snap, his so-called "friends" seem to fade into the background.

Jordan ignored the group as he walked to the bus. As he climbed up the steps, he was struck with another thought: *If God wants to bless my life, surely He could bless me with some godly friends!* As Jordan took a seat, he began praying for some friends who were godly. He wanted friends who wouldn't lie to their parents, but obeyed them the way he did.

That was one really lonely week at school. By the end of the week, even the bus ride home was like a ghost town—everyone else was leaving from school to see the movie.

With a sigh, Jordan stepped up into the bus again. But as he made his way to the back, he caught sight of a girl with her Bible open in her lap, speaking quietly to the boy next to her. It looked as if she were praying for him!

Quietly and excitedly, Jordan slipped into the seat behind them and waited for the girl to finish praying.

Well, I'll cut to the chase and let you know that the boy and girl who sat there became some of Jordan's new best friends. He was truly blessed that he didn't go with the flow, but obeyed his parents. Because that Friday, he met Rachel and Sam. The three of them started their own Bible study that continued until they graduated from high school. And between them, they were able to lead more than 50 people at their school to Jesus. Eventually, even Jamie and Marty asked Jesus to come into their hearts! And it all went back to that Tuesday—the day Jordan decided to obey God's written Word, and hit a home run!

Notes: _____

_____

_____

_____

DAY 3: GIVING LESSON

BLESSED TO BE A BLESSING

Suggested Time: 10 minutes

Offering Scripture: And *God* is able to bless you abundantly, so that in all things at all times, having all that you need, you will abound in every good work. —2 Corinthians 9:8 NIV

Supplies: ■ Optional: pictures of The Salvation Army

Lesson Instructions:

Hello, Superkids! Today, we're going to talk about a wonderful organization that helps a lot of people.

But first, can someone help me answer a question? Does anyone know why we believe in prosperity? *(Allow for answers.)* Yes, you're right! Prosperity is having more than enough to meet every need and enough left over to bless others.

Did you know that some people think and act like it's a righteous thing—pleasing to God—to be poor? We need to think about that for a moment. Is it easier to bless people and share with others when you're rich or when you're poor? That's right. It's very difficult to bless others when you are poor or struggling to just get enough for you and your family.

Well, the wonderful organization I was telling you about is one of the most generous groups that helps those in need. Their manifesto is "Doing the Most Good." Does anyone know what a *manifesto* is? It's "a public declaration of intentions, opinions or motives, as issued by a government, sovereign or organization." So, this organization's manifesto is to do good to others. That's just like Jesus, isn't it?

This group or organization is called The Salvation Army. But it's impossible to do what they do without money.

In 1918, The Salvation Army spent about $3 million. *(In today's market, that would equal about $300 million.)* With that money, they were able to help about 3.5 million people.

Ninety-one years later, in 2009, The Salvation Army spent $3.12 billion serving nearly 30 million people. Can you see how The Salvation Army has increased in their giving and ability to "Do the Most Good"? When they had a budget 10 times bigger in today's market, than when they started in 1918, they were able to help 10 times the number of people!

This is a great example of how when God increases our money, He increases our ability to give more and do more good works! We can't do the good works God has called us to do without having enough ourselves, so thank the Lord, He has taken the pressure off us. We don't have to do good works on our own. Let's read 2 Corinthians 9:8 and see what God has to say about our prosperity!

Did you hear that? Jesus doesn't want us to live in poverty and give away everything we own and have nothing left. He has called us to do many good works to help people, for Him. He wants us to have so much that we'll have plenty of everything, so we can *abound*—that means to have more than enough—to do a TON of good things to help others!

DAY 4: OBJECT LESSON

STUDY TOOLS

 Suggested Time: 10 minutes

 Memory Verse: Study this Book of Instruction continually. Meditate on it day and night so you will be sure to obey everything written in it. Only then will you prosper and succeed in all you do. —Joshua 1:8

Teacher Tip: Be ready to help younger kids who need help with their reading skills. Also, feel free to print some information to take home with them about their individual learning style.

Supplies: ■ Printouts of quiz, ■ Pens or pencils

Prior to Lesson:

Be sure to make enough copies of the quiz for each Superkid to have one. Also, have enough pens or pencils on hand for your Superkids to fill out the quizzes.

Lesson Instructions:

Today, we're going to find out what types of learners we are! This will be such a big help to all of us in school, at home and ALSO with our Bible memorization! When we know how we, as individuals, learn and process information, it can make all the difference. Not everyone is alike. God made us each to be unique and special, with abilities and talents that make not one of us quite like anyone else! It's a wonderful thing to understand our unique styles and adjust how we read and study God's Word, how we study for tests at school, and how we remember best to do the things we're asked to do. So, Superkids, are you ready to find out the amazing ways God made you special so you can fulfill His amazing plan for your life?

We're going to hand out the questions, and a pen or pencil for you to be able to answer them. The questions won't take very long, and there are no wrong answers! If you need help, just raise your hand.

(Hand out the quiz and pens or pencils. Give at least five minutes for your children to complete the quiz, and be ready to help if there are questions. If there are children with reading challenges, consider going over the quiz together as you read it aloud.)

Is everyone finished? Let's count the number of a's, b's and c's you got.

If you got mostly:

A's = You are a **visual** learner. You learn best by pictures, diagrams and written instructions. You rely mostly on your sense of SIGHT to learn.

B's = You are an **auditory** learner. You can take in a lot of information when people tell it to you and can often repeat back anything that's said to you. You rely mostly on your sense of HEARING to learn.

C's = You are a **kinesthetic** or "hands-on" learner. You learn best by doing. You mostly rely on your sense of TOUCH to learn.

If you're a Visual Learner, here are some tips that will help you:

- Try to study and read in peace and quiet.
- Ask your parents to write your chores down for you instead of speaking them.
- Draw pictures and diagrams for yourself to better remember things.
- Ask the teacher if he/she can move you closer to the front, or when you can choose, get a seat closer to the front so you can pay attention better.
- Take notes while you listen to the teacher, and use fun colors to highlight important information.
- Study Tip: Use flashcards to help you remember better as you study!

If you're an Auditory Learner, here are some tips that will help you:

- Don't worry about taking tons and tons of notes in class. Just do your best to listen to what the teacher is saying.
- It may be easy for you to listen to the teacher, but a little harder to not voice what you are thinking while he/she speaks. Instead of asking questions out of turn, write them down and ask them later on when you have the opportunity.
- Turn on music while you work or clean, and you'll move faster.
- When learning about a subject, watch movies or plays about it.
- Study Tip: Find another auditory learner and start a study group!

If you're a Kinesthetic Learner, here are some tips that will help you:

- Make sure to take frequent breaks in between study periods.
- When your teachers give you a class break, try to stretch and move around to expend energy.
- Feel free to move around, and try standing while you read.
- When someone is lecturing, try to doodle pictures and notes that go along with what they are saying.
- Study Tip: Turn your lessons into hands-on learning. Make history and even science and other subjects come alive by acting them out in skits!

Make Sure to Note:

You all did such a great job! Did our quiz help you to understand more about how you learn and to realize that God has truly made you special to do great things for Him? I think we can all see that no one is better than anyone else. God loves us all the same, so no learning style is better than another. It just proves, all the more, that God made us all different on purpose!

It's always good to remember that just because you learn mostly one way, don't trash the other types of learning, because we will always have to be learning in different ways. We all need to be adaptable and learn in all the ways that are available to us. Knowing your individual learning style is a big help when you're studying on your own or learning one-on-one.

Learning-Styles Quiz:

1. **I understand what I read the best when I…**

   a. See pictures and diagrams with what I read

   b. Read out loud

   c. Chew gum and tap my foot while I read

2. **I most enjoy…**

   a. Drawing

   b. Telling stories

   c. Playing outside

3. **When I am concentrating I usually…**

   a. Like complete peace and quiet

   b. Hum or whistle while I work

   c. Like to move around and work with my hands

4. **Class is easiest for me when the teacher…**

   a. Draws or shows maps and pictures on the chalkboard or screen

   b. Tells us stories and talks about our lesson

   c. Gives us projects to work on together in groups

5. **Teachers most often get onto me for…**

   a. Reading or solving puzzles instead of listening in class

   b. Talking when I'm not supposed to

   c. Chewing on pencils and doodling in class

6. **I am a…**

   a. Very imaginative person

   b. Great listener

   c. Hard worker

7. **I would rather…**

   a. Read a book

   b. Go to the theater and watch a play

   c. Play sports

8. **I am a very speedy…**

a. Reader

   b. Talker

   c. Worker

9. **It's hardest for me to…**

   a. NOT daydream while the teacher is talking

   b. Understand charts and maps

   a. Sit still

10. **I usually talk…**

   a. Very little

   b. Way too much

   c. With my hands

11. **It is easiest for me to go to sleep whenever…**

   a. My room is clean

   b. I'm listening to soothing music or my parents read to me

   c. I am exhausted from playing too hard

DAY 5: GAME TIME

PICTURE PERFECT

Suggested Time: 10 minutes

Memory Verse: Study this Book of Instruction continually. Meditate on it day and night so you will be sure to obey everything written in it. Only then will you prosper and succeed in all you do. —Joshua 1:8

Supplies: ■ 6 Sheets of paper per player, ■ 2 Tables, ■ 1 Pencil or crayon per player, ■ 6 Photos, ■ Tarp, ■ 2 Boxes of markers and colors, ■ Stopwatch, ■ Dry-erase board and marker to track game points (optional)

Prior to Game:

Choose 6 highly detailed photos from the Internet:

Examples:

- Butterfly with multicolored wings
- Dog with a lot of detail
- Sailboat with multiple sails
- House with many windows or landscaping
- Guitar with a lot of detail
- Fish with multiple colors

Game Instructions:

Plan for 6 rounds of this game. Divide your Superkids into 2 teams. If there are enough children, allow each team to choose a team captain. Or, if there are only a few children, you can be the team captain for both teams. You will need to distribute 6 sheets of paper to each Superkid—one for each round.

Choose 1 of the photos to reveal for each round. Superkids will have 30 seconds to look at the picture before attempting to draw it themselves on the paper provided. Teams will have 1 minute to attempt to draw the picture. At the end of each round, each team will have 30 seconds to discuss which drawing is the best copy of the picture they saw. When time is called, team captains will make the final decision on which picture will represent the team for that round. Hold the Internet pictures up along with the team drawings for everyone to admire, and give 100 points to the winning team. Repeat the game until all the photos have been used.

Game Goal:

The team with the most points, wins!

Final Word:

Everyone did a really great job! It isn't always easy to try to draw a copy of a picture you've only seen once, and for a very short time!

Our memory verse today tells us that we must study and meditate on God's Word so that we can obey it. The Creed is like one of the pictures we saw today. But it's not a sailboat or a butterfly *(or whatever pictures you used)*. It's a picture taken from the Bible of what a Superkid should look like. A Superkid's No. 1 priority is to be obedient to God. The Sweet Life will always follow obedience to Him!

Variation No. 1:

If you only have 1-3 players, have each person be his/her own team. You might see if you can get a teen/parent helper to be the judge.

Notes: _____

_____

_____

_____

_____

_____

_____

_____

_____

_____

_____

_____

_____

_____

_____

_____

_____

_____

_____

_____

_____

_____

ACTIVITY PAGE — GOD'S WORD UNSCRAMBLER

Memory Verse: Study this Book of Instruction continually. Meditate on it day and night so you will be sure to obey everything written in it. Only then will you prosper and succeed in all you do.
—Joshua 1:8

ANSWER KEY:

GOD'S WORD UNSCRAMBLER

1. BLESSING
2. SPIRIT
3. LIGHT
4. STRONG
5. POWER
6. OBEDIENCE
7. TRUTH
8. LOVE
9. COVENANT
10. COMMANDS

Name: _____

God's Word should be the final authority in our lives! Can you unscramble these God words?

GOD'S WORD
UNSCRAMBLER

1. SINGSLEB

2. PITIRS

3. GLITH

4. NORGTS

5. WOREP

6. DOBICEENE

7. THURT

8. EVOL

9. TANNOVEC

10. MONCAMSD

WEEK 9: I HEAR EVERY WORD, AND I OBEY QUICKLY WITHOUT ARGUING!

Memory Verse: *We must quickly carry out the tasks assigned us by the one who sent us.* —John 9:4a

WEEK 9: SNAPSHOT

I HEAR EVERY WORD, AND I OBEY QUICKLY WITHOUT ARGUING!

DAY	TYPE OF LESSON	LESSON TITLE	SUPPLIES
Day 1	Bible Lesson	Jonah and the Attitude	None
Day 2	Food Fun	Quick Caramel Apples	4 Apples (unwaxed preferred), Popsicle sticks, Bag of unwrapped caramel candies or bits, Medium-sized bowl, 2 Tablespoons water, Wax paper, Butter or cooking spray, Tray, Spoon, Other toppings like sprinkles, marshmallows, Oreos, cookies, nuts, cereals or candies (optional)
Day 3	Giving Lesson	Forgiveness: A Powerful Seed	Pitcher of lemonade, 1 Clean, clear cup per child, 1 Clear cup half filled with dirt
Day 4	Real Deal	Paul Revere's Midnight Ride	Map of Paul Revere's ride, Costume (optional)
Day 5	Game Time	Don't Blow It!	2 Hula hoops, 2 Jump-ropes, 2 Baseball bats (can be plastic), 1 Whistle
Bonus	Activity Page	Jonah and the Big Fish	1 Copy for each child

Lesson Introduction:

This week's Creed statement came from instruction that the Lord gave me years ago. I began to say it every day. It has changed my life! Habakkuk 2:1 NIV, says, "I will stand at my watch…I will look to see what he will say to me." This is what you are doing by saying this every day: You are tuning your ear to hear. As He leads you, it's important to obey quickly. Our kids should practice this at home. I tell the kids if you won't obey Mom and Dad, whom you *can* see, how will you obey God whom you *can't* see? Encourage them to practice quick obedience and to stop themselves if they begin to argue. Remind them of our previous lesson. Is Jesus your Lord or not? This is where they walk this out. I believe you will receive some great reports from Mom and Dad!

Love,

Commander Kellie

Commander Kellie

Lesson Outline:

This week, your children will learn about being QUICK to listen and obey! Sometimes that extra moment when we argue with God can cost us and others. Superkids who are quick to listen and obey, without arguing, are WORLD CHANGERS!

I. WE CHOOSE WHOM WE LISTEN TO John 10

a.   His sheep know His voice and follow <u>Him,</u> not a stranger. verses 1-5

b.   Trust Jesus—He will lead you to the good plan of God. verses 9-10

c.   Decide to hear Him—tune your ears. Proverbs 2:2-6

II. GOD NEEDED JONAH TO CHANGE NINEVEH Jonah 1:1-2

a.   Jonah argued with God and went in the opposite direction—right into the belly of a BIG fish! Jonah 1:3-17

b.   Jonah repented, and the fish spit him out. Jonah 2:1, 9-10

c.   Jonah went to Nineveh; the people repented and turned to God. Jonah 3:1-10

d.   When we obey God without arguing, things turn out right!

III. BE QUICK TO LISTEN <u>AND</u> QUICK TO OBEY James 1:22-25

a.   If you listen and obey, you are wise. Matthew 7:24-27

b.   Is He your Lord? Then, you are strong and blessed! Luke 6:46-48

c.   Quickly carry out what your Lord asks—you can change the world! John 9:4-5

Notes: _____

_____

_____

_____

_____

_____

_____

_____

_____

DAY 1: BIBLE LESSON JONAH AND THE ATTITUDE

 Memory Verse: We must quickly carry out the tasks assigned us by the one who sent us.
—John 9:4a

When God calls us to do something, He always has a plan. Jonah's slow obedience to obey God almost cost him and his crew their lives! See how God's plan worked out when Jonah obeyed. Here is a great example to encourage your Superkids that it's not just about finally obeying, but the attitude with which you go about it.

Read Jonah 1-3 MSG:
Jonah's Disobedience (Chapter 1)

One day long ago, God's Word came to Jonah, Amittai's son: "Up on your feet and on your way to the big city of Nineveh! Preach to them. They're in a bad way and I can't ignore it any longer."

But Jonah got up and went the other direction to Tarshish, running away from God. He went down to the port of Joppa and found a ship headed for Tarshish. He paid the fare and went on board, joining those going to Tarshish—as far away from God as he could get.

But God sent a huge storm at sea, the waves towering.

The ship was about to break into pieces. The sailors were terrified. They called out in desperation to their gods. They threw everything they were carrying overboard to lighten the ship. Meanwhile, Jonah had gone down into the hold of the ship to take a nap. He was sound asleep. The captain came to him and said, "What's this? Sleeping! Get up! Pray to your god! Maybe your god will see we're in trouble and rescue us."

Then the sailors said to one another, "Let's get to the bottom of this. Let's draw straws to identify the culprit on this ship who's responsible for this disaster."

So they drew straws. Jonah got the short straw.

Then they grilled him: "Confess. Why this disaster? What is your work? Where do you come from? What country? What family?"

He told them, "I'm a Hebrew. I worship God, the God of heaven who made sea and land."

At that, the men were frightened, really frightened, and said, "What on earth have you done!" As Jonah talked, the sailors realized that he was running away from God.

They said to him, "What are we going to do with you—to get rid of this storm?" By this time the sea was wild, totally out of control.

Jonah said, "Throw me overboard, into the sea. Then the storm will stop. It's all my fault. I'm the cause of the storm. Get rid of me and you'll get rid of the storm."

But no. The men tried rowing back to shore. They made no headway. The storm only got worse and worse, wild and raging.

Then they prayed to God, "O God! Don't let us drown because of this man's life, and don't blame us for his death. You are God. Do what you think is best."

They took Jonah and threw him overboard. Immediately the sea was quieted down.

The sailors were impressed, no longer terrified by the sea, but in awe of God. They worshiped God, offered a sacrifice, and made vows.

Then God assigned a huge fish to swallow Jonah. Jonah was in the fish's belly three days and nights.

Do Discussion Questions 1-4

Jonah Repents (Chapter 2)

Then Jonah prayed to his God from the belly of the fish. He prayed:

"In trouble, deep trouble, I prayed to God.
He answered me.

From the belly of the grave I cried, 'Help!'
You heard my cry.

You threw me into ocean's depths,
into a watery grave,

With ocean waves, ocean breakers
crashing over me.

I said, 'I've been thrown away,
thrown out, out of your sight.

I'll never again lay eyes
on your Holy Temple.'

Ocean gripped me by the throat.
The ancient Abyss grabbed me and held tight.

My head was all tangled in seaweed
at the bottom of the sea where the mountains take root.

I was as far down as a body can go,
and the gates were slamming shut behind me forever—
Yet you pulled me up from that grave alive,
O God, my God!

When my life was slipping away,
I remembered God,

And my prayer got through to you,
made it all the way to your Holy Temple.

Those who worship hollow gods, god-frauds,
walk away from their only true love.

But I'm worshiping you, God,
calling out in thanksgiving!

And I'll do what I promised I'd do!
Salvation belongs to God!"

Then God spoke to the fish, and it vomited up Jonah on the seashore.

Do Discussion Question 5

Nineveh Repents (Chapter 3)

Next, God spoke to Jonah a second time: "Up on your feet and on your way to the big city of Nineveh! Preach to them. They're in a bad way and I can't ignore it any longer."

This time Jonah started off straight for Nineveh, obeying God's orders to the letter. Nineveh was a big city, very big—it took three days to walk across it. Jonah entered the city, went one day's walk and preached, "In forty days Nineveh will be smashed."

The people of Nineveh listened, and trusted God. They proclaimed a citywide fast and dressed in burlap to show their repentance. Everyone did it—rich and poor, famous and obscure, leaders and followers.

When the message reached the king of Nineveh, he got up off his throne, threw down his royal robes, dressed in burlap, and sat down in the dirt. Then he issued a public proclamation throughout Nineveh, authorized by him and his leaders: "Not one drop of water, not one bite of food for man, woman, or animal, including your herds and flocks! Dress them all, both people and animals, in burlap, and send up a cry for help to God. Everyone must turn around, turn back from an evil life and the violent ways that stain their hands. Who knows? Maybe God will turn around and change his mind about us, quit being angry with us and let us live!"

God saw what they had done, that they had turned away from their evil lives. He *did* change his mind about them. What he said he would do to them he didn't do.

Do Remaining Discussion Questions

Discussion Questions:

1. **What did Jonah do that put the sailors' lives in danger?**

   He disobeyed and was running from what God told him to do: Preach to Nineveh, and tell them to repent.

2. **When the sailors heard Jonah's story, they realized that Jonah's disobedience was causing the storm. Has your disobedience ever affected others or caused others to get in trouble? Has your bad attitude ever led others astray, as well?**

   Answers may vary. Parents/teachers, this is a great place to share a story of your own experience.

3. **How could Jonah have avoided almost dying at sea and putting others in harm's way, as well?**

   If Jonah had obeyed right away, he wouldn't have been on the ship.

4. **Once Jonah took responsibility for his actions and confessed to the sailors, was God able to bring about good from the situation?**

Yes. The storm stopped, the sailors believed in God and praised Him for stopping the storm. Plus, God brought a fish to save Jonah from death.

5. **In this chapter, Jonah cries out to God for help, repents and promises to fulfill God's command for him to go to Nineveh. What happened when Jonah did that?**

God spoke to the fish, and the fish spit Jonah up on the beach.

6. **When Jonah obeyed and preached God's warning to the Ninevites, how did they respond? What did the king do?**

The Ninevites repented, and mourned over their sins. They fasted and made sacrifices to God. The king even got down from his throne to repent to God and called for his whole province to fast, repent, make sacrifices to God and pray for His mercy.

7. **Was God faithful to spare Nineveh when they repented?**

Yes.

8. **Jonah, the sailors and the Ninevites saw, firsthand, that when we obey, we allow God to work strongly in our lives. Think of all God could have done, had Jonah only obeyed sooner! Is there something in your life that God is asking you to change, now? Read Hebrews 3:7-8: "That is why the Holy Spirit says, 'Today when you hear his voice, don't harden your hearts....'" Discuss.**

Answers may vary. Encourage your Superkids that if there is something they need to repent of, they can repent to God. But unlike Jonah, they need not be ashamed to repent to the people whom they may have affected in their disobedience.

Help the children to find good, everyday examples of how they can obey quickly, without arguing. For example: when asked to clean their rooms, do their homework or take out the trash.

Notes: _____

_____

_____

_____

_____

_____

_____

_____

_____

_____

_____

_____

DAY 2: FOOD FUN — QUICK CARAMEL APPLES

 Suggested Time: 10-15 minutes

 Memory Verse: We must quickly carry out the tasks assigned us by the one who sent us. —John 9:4a

 Ingredients: ☐ 4 Apples (unwaxed preferred), ☐ Bag of unwrapped caramel candies or bits, ☐ 2 Tablespoons water, ☐ Butter or cooking spray to grease the wax paper, ☐ 2 Tablespoons water, ☐ Other toppings like sprinkles, marshmallows, Oreos or other cookies, nuts, cereals or candies (optional)

Prior to Lesson:
- Wash and thoroughly dry the apples.
- Stab the apples with popsicle sticks and place in the refrigerator for 5-6 hours. If you have challenges inserting the popsicle sticks, stab the apple slightly with a small knife first, then insert the sticks, which should extend from the stem end.

Note: If you plan to add nuts, Oreos or other toppings, make sure they are crunched and placed in separate small bowls, ready to go.

Supplies: ■ Popsicle sticks, ■ Medium-sized bowl for dipping, ■ Wax paper, ■ Tray, ■ Spoon, ■ Small bowls to put the toppings in

Lesson Instructions:

Hello, Superkids! Today we're going to have something really yummy! But, before we get started, has anyone ever heard the expression, "Strike while the iron is hot"? Does anyone know what that means?

Well, that saying usually means, "Do it while you can!" Back in the day when people had to re-shoe their horses, the blacksmith would reshape a horseshoe by heating the iron in his fire until it was superhot. The really hot fire would make the iron glow red and made it temporarily soft enough to shape. But, once the iron cooled, that shoe became hard as a rock again and wouldn't budge. So, you had to strike the metal with a hammer to reshape it while the iron was still hot.

Well, we aren't making shoes for a horse today, but we *will* be making some caramel apples. And, you have to dip while the caramel is hot!

So, first, let's check on our apples. I went ahead and put popsicle sticks in them and placed them on wax paper in the refrigerator. When you start with a cool apple, the caramel sticks to the apple much better and stays thicker. *(Place wax paper on the tray or large plate and grease it with spray or butter so the caramel apples won't stick to the plate.)*

Now let's melt the caramel! Unwrap the candies *(or use the bits),* and place in a microwave oven for 2½-3 minutes, mixed with 2 tablespoons of water. Make sure you remove the caramel mixture from the microwave oven every minute to stir it, and watch it carefully, since microwaves may differ in intensity.

Now that we have our caramel nice and hot, we need to dip our apples. It's a good thing we prepped these apples beforehand. Hold the apples by their popsicle sticks and dip them into the caramel until they're well covered. You can spin the apple around in the bowl using the popsicle stick. Then, pull the apple out, and let the excess drip away. You can also spoon on the caramel, and use a knife or spoon to cut off the excess drips. *(As soon as the apples are coated, pull them out of the bowl and immediately have the children roll them in nuts, crushed cookies or candies, if you had planned to.)* Place the apples back on the greased wax paper to cool.

(Enjoy dipping and decorating the rest of your apples.) You know, Superkids, sometimes, timing really is everything. Just like we have to dip this apple while the caramel is hot, it's important to obey quickly. We saw earlier how Jonah was a very poor example of obeying quickly. But think about what not obeying quickly does to our hearts: It hardens them like this caramel sauce or the iron on the horse's shoe. The more we disobey, the more our hearts get hardened and it becomes more difficult for God to shape us into the people we need to be.

As you enjoy your masterpiece today in the kitchen, remember you are God's masterpiece! Obeying keeps your heart moldable for God. You want to be a masterpiece with purpose, molded by God—not an unwrapped, hard candy that can't be molded to what He has planned for you!

Notes: _____

_____

_____

_____

_____

_____

_____

_____

_____

_____

_____

_____

_____

_____

_____

_____

_____

_____

_____

_____

DAY 3: GIVING LESSON

FORGIVENESS: A POWERFUL SEED

Suggested Time: 10 minutes

Offering Scripture: I tell you, you can pray for anything, and if you believe that you've received it, it will be yours. But when you are praying, first forgive anyone you are holding a grudge against, so that your Father in heaven will forgive your sins, too. —Mark 11:24-25

Supplies: ☐ Pitcher of lemonade, ☐ 1 Clean, clear cup per child, ☐ 1 Clear cup half filled with dirt

Lesson Instructions:

Isn't lemonade on a hot summer day just so refreshing? Mmmm, it tastes so good! I need a helper who's thirsty enough to drink some of this. *(Hold up the pitcher of cold lemonade.)* Doesn't it look delicious? Oh, all of you would like some? Great! Did you notice that all you had to do was ask for some lemonade? I'll give you each a cup. *(Hand a cup to each person, including the cup with dirt in it.)*

What? One of the cups has dirt in it? *(It's probably best to give the cup filled with dirt to someone who wouldn't dare drink it…so maybe not the boy who eats glue! Pour the lemonade into all the cups, including the one with dirt in it.)* So, how does that nice, cold lemonade taste? Isn't it delicious? *(Ask the Superkid with the dirt in his/her cup:)* Why aren't you drinking your lemonade? Because there's dirt in it? *(Show everyone the cup with the dirt in it.)* Oh, so you don't like to drink dirty lemonade?

You know, this reminds me of something Jesus said about receiving. Let's take a few minutes, and read Mark 11:24-25. *(Read verses aloud.)* Wow! Jesus said He would do whatever we asked. That's amazing! But you can't stop there. We must hear every word and obey quickly without arguing, which means we have to do what Jesus says in verse 25, don't we? WE MUST FORGIVE.

Some of you may have asked God for something or you're praying for something right now—like a bike, a game system, friends, money or a new house. *(Hold up the cup with the dirty lemonade.)* Do you realize that this is what happens when we let unforgiveness into our lives? *(Hold up the pitcher.)* Even though Jesus has what you asked for, like this cold, delicious lemonade, and it's totally great and perfect, if there's unforgiveness in your heart, you can't receive what you've asked for.

It's not that God's not willing to give us what we want. But our hearts are too crowded with junk to receive.

Let's take a moment today, just close our eyes and see someone we need to forgive or something that was done to us that we need to forgive. Remember, we don't have to forgive on our own. Jesus said He would help us do that, too! And, if Jesus forgave the people who beat Him and hung Him on the cross, He will also help us to forgive the people who hurt us.

So, with our eyes closed, repeat this prayer after me: "Dear Jesus, help me to let go of the hurtful things others have done to me. Holy Spirit, please reveal to me anything I need to forgive today. *(Pause while God talks to the children.)* I forgive on purpose as an act of my will. Thank You for Your strength and courage. I ask this in Jesus' Name. Amen."

Now, encourage your kids to pray over what they are believing for. Find a seed to sow today and stand in agreement with them for their harvest!

DAY 4: REAL DEAL | PAUL REVERE'S MIDNIGHT RIDE

 Memory Verse: We must quickly carry out the tasks assigned us by the one who sent us. —John 9:4a

 Concept: Highlighting an interesting historical place, figure or event that illustrates the theme of the day. The theme of the day is: I hear every word, and I obey quickly without arguing.

 Teacher Tip: We suggest becoming as familiar as possible with the script prior to teaching this lesson. The following script is a sample outline that may be helpful to follow during class (it can be modified to fit your teaching style).

Supplies: ■ Map of Paul Revere's ride[7], ■ Costume (optional)
It's best if you can print off a large map on which, as you speak, you can note the various stops made by Paul Revere.

Intro:

Today, you will highlight an American hero whose fast action and obedience saved lives! Paul Revere was a silversmith and patriot during the time of the American Revolution who disregarded his own safety to quickly act to warn others of danger and possible death. His fast action and obedience to the call of duty saved the leaders of the American Revolution from being arrested by the British and possibly killed. His warning awakened the American militia to prepare their weapons for battle. While others were sleeping, Paul Revere was making history!

Lesson:

Today, we're going to learn about an American hero named Paul Revere. He was a colonial silversmith who disregarded his own safety to warn the leaders of the American Revolution that they were in danger of arrest and possible execution.

Paul Revere Had a Plan:

Paul was part of a network called the Sons of Liberty who watched British movements and reported them to the leaders of the American Revolution. The Sons of Liberty knew that an attack from the British was close at hand. Paul Revere was prepared. A week before his famous ride, he set up a signal to warn the patriots whether the British troops were coming by land or by sea, across the Charles River.

If the British were traveling across the river by sea, TWO lanterns would hang in the North Church steeple. If the British were marching by land, they would hang ONE lantern.

---

7 Paul Revere Heritage Project, "Map of the Midnight Ride," http://www.paul-revere-heritage.com/midnight-ride-map.html (4/4/16); "Virtual Midnight Ride, an Interactive Map of Paul Revere's Ride," Paul Revere House, https://www.paulreverehouse.org/ride/virtual.html.

When the Call Came, Paul Was Ready:

April 18, 1775, around 10 p.m., Dr. Joseph Warren requested Paul Revere to leave IMMEDIATELY and make haste to Lexington, Massachusetts, to warn their leaders, John Hancock and Samuel Adams, that the British were coming to arrest them and sending troops to stop the American resistance.

Paul found out that another man, William Dawes, had been sent out just ahead of him, taking a western route. Paul Revere left immediately and asked a friend to make the signals in the North Church steeple.

The Perilous Journey:

Paul stopped quickly at home for his boots and overcoat. Then, two of his friends rowed him across the Charles River to Charlestown.

He went to the home of Deacon Larkin to borrow a horse. As the horse was being prepared, Richard Devens told him that he'd seen 10 well-armed British army officers on the road on his way back from Lexington that evening.

At about 11 p.m. Paul mounted the horse and headed north. Just after he'd passed the Charlestown Neck (a narrow place on the peninsula), he saw two British officers under a tree. One officer moved to head him off, but Paul quickly turned his horse the other way and headed in a different direction toward Medford Road. The other British soldier followed but got stuck in clay near a tavern before Medford.

Paul rode through Medford, over the Mystic River Bridge and up to Menotomy.

In Medford, he awakened the captain of the Minute Men and the people in every house he came to, all the way to Lexington, which is why he is so famous for yelling what…? "The British are coming! The British are coming!" HOWEVER, most historians believe he just made a lot of noise to wake up every home, and actually said, "The regulars (British soldiers) are coming out!"[8]

Making History:

Around midnight, Paul Revere arrived in Lexington, where Samuel Adams and John Hancock were staying. As he rode up to the house, a sentry reprimanded him for making too much noise. He replied, "Noise! You'll have noise enough before long. The regulars are coming out!"

He was able to deliver his message to John Hancock and Sam Adams. Mission accomplished!

Paul Revere's ride awakened the American Continental Army to fight their first battle in the Revolutionary War.

Outro:

Paul Revere was made famous by Henry Wadsworth Longfellow's poem "Paul Revere's Ride."[9]

---

8 Historical information is from a letter written in 1798 by Paul Revere to Jeremy Belknap, founder and president of the Massachusetts Historical Society, www.revolutionary-war-and-beyond.com/paul-reveres-ride-2html (4/4/16); "Letter From Paul Revere to Jeremy Belknap, circa 1798," Massachusetts Historical Society, http://www.masshist.org/database/viewer.php?item_id=99 (4/4/16).

There were two other men also assigned the task of warning the patriot leaders: William Dawes and Dr. Samuel Prescott. The two arrived after Revere.

All three men accomplished their goal in Lexington. They were all arrested, but Paul Revere got away when a British soldier, hearing the beginning gunshots of the Battle of Lexington, took Paul's more rested horse to the battle scene and left Paul on foot.

Paul Revere fought bravely in the American Revolution. September 1, 1778, he was promoted to commander of Fort Independence, formerly the British fort that guarded the entrance to Boston Harbor.

Paul Revere was a good example of the parable that Jesus told of the talents in Matthew 25:23, where the master said, "Well done, my good and faithful servant. You have been faithful in handling this small amount, so now I will give you many more responsibilities."

Paul Revere is highly noted in history because of his QUICKNESS to drop everything and obey. His preparation of the lantern signals paid off. Paul was ready to go at any moment!

Variation No. 1: Dress Up

Entering in costume is an attention grabber for the Superkids. Feel free to present the information as if you were Paul Revere himself!

Variation No. 2: Interview

If you are in a co-op and have other teens or adults involved, consider having another person play Paul Revere, and you can be the interviewer.

Variation No. 3: Pajama Party

When Paul Revere rode in, it was midnight, and he woke up the town! Surprise your kids with a pajama party as you tell them this story. Maybe add some cookies and milk or other snack to spice it up.

---

9 "Paul Revere's Ride," Henry Wadsworth Longfellow, *English Poetry III: From Tennyson to Whitman, The Harvard Classics, 1909–14,* "http://www.bartleby.com/42/789.html (4/4/16).

Notes: _____

_____

_____

_____

_____

_____

_____

_____

DAY 5: GAME TIME

DON'T BLOW IT!

Suggested Time: 10 minutes

Memory Verse: We must quickly carry out the tasks assigned us by the one who sent us. —John 9:4a

Teacher Tip: Make this game work for your space and number of players. For 1 player, explain the game instructions, then time him/her. Feel free to adjust the lengths of the relays and/or exercises to match your space and number of players.

Supplies: ☐ 2 Hula hoops, ☐ 2 Jump-ropes, ☐ 2 Baseball bats (can be plastic), ☐ 1 Whistle

Game Instructions:

Divide your players into 2 teams. You will be the referee. Set up your relay in stations, several feet apart. Here are the relays:

1. Hula-hoop—10 times

2. Jump-rope—forward and backward, 10 times each

3. Jumping jacks—10 sets of in and out

4. Baseball bat—Position the bat in an upright position, with the hitting end on the floor. Player must place his/her forehead on the base of the handle, and spin in a circle 5 times. (The base of the bat must remain on the floor at all times. The player must drop the bat before exiting the station.)

When a player completes all 4 stations, he/she must run back and tag the next player in line. Let the children know that it is important to listen because the instructions and what to do at each station will only be given 1 TIME. After the game has started, if a player doesn't follow the instructions for each station perfectly, the referee will blow the whistle and send the player to the back of the line.

Game Goal:

The first team to have every member complete 1 round without the referee blowing the whistle, wins!

Final Word:

To win any race in life, we must listen and quickly obey God's instructions. This week, practice listening to God's voice and obeying what He says, the first time!

ACTIVITY PAGE   JONAH AND THE BIG FISH

Memory Verse: We must quickly carry out the tasks assigned us by the one who sent us.
—John 9:4a

Name: _____

Notes: _____

_____

_____

_____

_____

_____

_____

_____

_____

_____

_____

_____

_____

_____

_____

_____

_____

_____

_____

_____

_____

_____

_____

_____

_____

_____

_____

_____

_____

_____

_____

_____

_____

_____

_____

_____

WEEK 10: I LIVE AND WALK BY FAITH, NOT BY WHAT I SEE

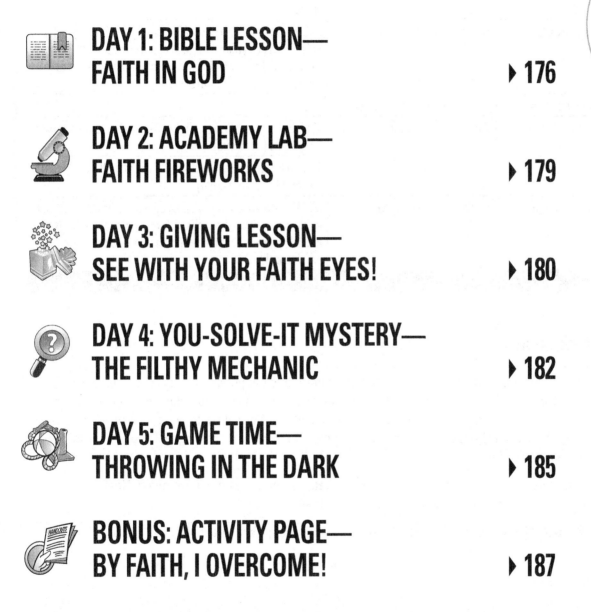

Memory Verse: *We live by faith, not by sight.* —2 Corinthians 5:7 NIV

WEEK 10: SNAPSHOT — I LIVE AND WALK BY FAITH, NOT BY WHAT I SEE

DAY	TYPE OF LESSON	LESSON TITLE	SUPPLIES
Day 1	Bible Lesson	Faith in God	None
Day 2	Academy Lab	Faith Fireworks	2 Lab coats, 2 Pairs of safety goggles, Milk, Food coloring: red, yellow, blue, green, Dish soap, 1 Plate (or plates for each child) deep enough to hold a small amount of milk, Cotton swabs
Day 3	Giving Lesson	See With Your Faith Eyes!	None
Day 4	You-Solve-It Mystery	The Filthy Mechanic	"CLUE!" sign or flashing light, Superkid Academy polo or T-shirt (optional)
Day 5	Game Time	Throwing in the Dark	2 Hula hoops, 2 Blindfolds, 2 Buckets filled with balls, Timer, Music (optional)
Bonus	Activity Page	By Faith, I Overcome!	Markers/colored pencils/OR crayons, Safety scissors, Ribbon (curly works well), 1 Copy for each child (Note: For a longer-lasting mask, print on thicker paper, like card stock)

Lesson Introduction:

The word *FAITH* has been watered down until people don't understand the power of it. It is used many times to mean your religion. No! It is a powerful force inside all of us—especially in our Superkids! We've been given the God kind of faith. He has put in us the ability to trust in Him and His Word, despite what we see. Kids have an advantage over adults in this because life hasn't caused them to become discouraged. Feed their faith now, and faith will be their way of life.

One teaching tip for this week: When teaching, don't try to read the scriptures about Abraham, Noah and Thomas. It is best to summarize—especially the ones about Noah.

Remember, Jesus said, "Have faith in God." That's not just a good idea; it's the best offer you'll find!

Love,

Commander Kellie

Commander Kellie

Lesson Outline:

This week, your children will learn about the strong force of FAITH. How do you live by faith in a world full of obstacles and discouragement? The Answer: FAITH IN GOD!

I. GOD'S WORD WILL CHANGE ANY CIRCUMSTANCE

a. *Circumstance*—a condition or state of being; the way things are; what we see

b. What you see is a fact—God's Word is the truth.

c. If you look at and believe the Word instead of what you see, things will change. 2 Corinthians 4:18

II. LIVE BY FAITH, NOT BY SIGHT 2 Corinthians 5:7 NIV

a. Do you believe what God says?

    1. Abraham believed God. Romans 4:18-21

    2. Noah believed God. Genesis 6:9-7:5

    3. What did Thomas do? John 20:24-29

b. Jesus said, "Blessed are those who believe without seeing me." John 20:29

    1. Are you one of them?

    2. It's your choice.

c. Jesus told His disciples: "Have faith in God." Mark 11:22-24

III. DON'T THROW AWAY YOUR FAITH BECAUSE OF WHAT YOU SEE Hebrews 10:35

a. Faith is confidence in what God says, though you can't see it. Hebrews 11:1

b. Hebrews 11:4-38 is a list of people who chose to believe what God said instead of what they saw.

c. They pleased God! Hebrews 11:6

d. We can be part of this group, too. Hebrews 11:39-40

e. They are watching and cheering us on as we keep our eyes on Jesus (that's faith!), not on what we can see. Hebrews 12:1-2

Notes: _____

_____

_____

DAY 1: BIBLE LESSON

FAITH IN GOD

Memory Verse: *We live by faith, not by sight.* —2 Corinthians 5:7 NIV

Noah is a great example of someone who had faith in God that rain would flood the earth when he'd never even seen rain fall from the sky before. He put his faith to work, and his obedience saved his family, the animals and our lives, too!

Read Genesis 6:9-22, 7:
Noah Believes God

This is the account of Noah and his family. Noah was a righteous man, the only blameless person living on earth at the time, and he walked in close fellowship with God. Noah was the father of three sons: Shem, Ham, and Japheth.

Now God saw that the earth had become corrupt and was filled with violence. God observed all this corruption in the world, for everyone on earth was corrupt. So God said to Noah, "I have decided to destroy all living creatures, for they have filled the earth with violence. Yes, I will wipe them all out along with the earth!

"Build a large boat from cypress wood and waterproof it with tar, inside and out. Then construct decks and stalls throughout its interior. Make the boat 450 feet long, 75 feet wide, and 45 feet high. Leave an 18-inch opening below the roof all the way around the boat. Put the door on the side, and build three decks inside the boat—lower, middle, and upper.

"Look! I am about to cover the earth with a flood that will destroy every living thing that breathes. Everything on earth will die. But I will confirm my covenant with you. So enter the boat—you and your wife and your sons and their wives. Bring a pair of every kind of animal—a male and a female—into the boat with you to keep them alive during the flood. Pairs of every kind of bird, and every kind of animal, and every kind of small animal that scurries along the ground, will come to you to be kept alive. And be sure to take on board enough food for your family and for all the animals."

So Noah did everything exactly as God had commanded him.

When everything was ready, the Lord said to Noah, "Go into the boat with all your family, for among all the people of the earth, I can see that you alone are righteous. Take with you seven pairs—male and female—of each animal I have approved for eating and for sacrifice, and take one pair of each of the others. Also take seven pairs of every kind of bird. There must be a male and a female in each pair to ensure that all life will survive on the earth after the flood. Seven days from now I will make the rains pour down on the earth. And it will rain for forty days and forty nights, until I have wiped from the earth all the living things I have created."

So Noah did everything as the Lord commanded him.

Noah was 600 years old when the flood covered the earth. He went on board the boat to escape the flood—he and his wife and his sons and their wives. With them were all the various kinds of animals—those approved for eating and for sacrifice and those that were not—along with all the birds and the small animals that scurry along the ground. They entered the boat in pairs, male and female, just as God had commanded Noah. After seven days, the waters of the flood came and covered the earth.

When Noah was 600 years old, on the seventeenth day of the second month, all the underground waters erupted from the earth, and the rain fell in mighty torrents from the sky. The rain continued to fall for forty days and forty nights.

That very day Noah had gone into the boat with his wife and his sons—Shem, Ham, and Japheth—and their wives. With them in the boat were pairs of every kind of animal—domestic and wild, large and small—along with birds of every kind. Two by two they came into the boat, representing every living thing that breathes. A male and female of each kind entered, just as God had commanded Noah. Then the Lord closed the door behind them.

For forty days the floodwaters grew deeper, covering the ground and lifting the boat high above the earth. As the waters rose higher and higher above the ground, the boat floated safely on the surface. Finally, the water covered even the highest mountains on the earth, rising more than twenty-two feet above the highest peaks. All the living things on earth died—birds, domestic animals, wild animals, small animals that scurry along the ground, and all the people. Everything that breathed and lived on dry land died. God wiped out every living thing on the earth—people, livestock, small animals that scurry along the ground, and the birds of the sky. All were destroyed. The only people who survived were Noah and those with him in the boat. And the floodwaters covered the earth for 150 days.

Discussion Questions:

3. **What are three things that happened in this passage?**

    Answers will vary, but make sure your children understand the passage.

4. **Last week, we discussed swift obedience to God. How did Noah react when God gave him the measurements to build the ark?**

    He quickly began building. He did exactly as the Lord told him to.

5. **Some would say that faith is something you can't see, but the Bible says that it is the SUBSTANCE of things hoped for and EVIDENCE of the unseen. Think like a detective: What was the EVIDENCE that Noah had faith in God?**

    He built the ark! Also, because the animals and the people were spared, we have both on the earth today.

6. **Just as Jonah's disobedience to God affected other people, Noah's faith and obedience to God is still affecting people today. Discuss how we can affect others through our faith and by putting action to it.**

    Answers will vary, but make sure that your Superkids are inspired to be a good influence and example to others.

7. **Fill in the blanks from James 2:26: Faith without works is _____.**

    Dead

8. Hebrews 11:6 says, "And it is impossible to please God without faith." Discuss ways that you and your Superkids can begin to put **ACTION** to your faith, so there is **EVIDENCE** in your life that you have faith in God. Hint: These are also actions that are pleasing to God!

Answers may vary.

- Sharing Jesus with other people so they can receive Him as their Savior and Lord

- Sharing Jesus's love with other people by praying for them when they are sick or have a need, giving to them, etc.

- Speaking what you believe God is going to do before you see it in the natural—confessing your faith

- Sowing a seed (gift) and believing God for your harvest

- Praying in tongues

- Walking in love toward your enemies, like doing something kind for them

- Receiving God's help to forgive someone who hurt you by praying for them

9. Hebrews 11:7 says, "It was by faith that Noah built a large boat to save his family from the flood. He obeyed God, who warned him about things that had never happened before. By his faith Noah condemned the rest of the world, and he received the righteousness that comes by faith." Do you think others told Noah he was crazy or made fun of him for building an ark (big boat) on dry land in anticipation of an event that had *never* before occurred? Discuss how you think Noah felt when people pressured him not to build the ark, and how you, too, can overcome obstacles and others' opinions when you begin to step out in faith.

Noah was most likely mocked and told that he was crazy, but thank God, he listened to what God said instead of other people. Refer your children back to question 6 examples. What are some things people might say and do if they see you sharing the good news of Jesus, praying for the sick or for people who have hurt you, etc.?

Notes: _____

_____

_____

_____

_____

_____

_____

_____

_____

_____

_____

_____

_____

_____

DAY 2: ACADEMY LAB | FAITH FIREWORKS

Suggested Time: 10 minutes

Memory Verse: *We live by faith, not by sight.* —2 Corinthians 5:7 NIV

Supplies: ■2 Lab coats (1 for the scientist, 1 for the helper), ■2 Pairs of safety goggles, ■Milk, ■Food coloring: red, yellow, blue, green, ■Dish soap, ■1 Plate (or plates for each child) deep enough to hold a small amount of milk, ■Cotton swabs

Prior to Lesson:

Pour enough milk on a plate (and/or plates for each child) to completely cover the bottom, and then allow the milk to settle.

Lesson Instructions:

How many of you enjoy Independence Day—the Fourth of July? Isn't it fun to wait until after it gets dark and watch the fireworks displays? They can be spectacular with all their bright colors, can't they?

Well, today, we're going to make our own fireworks displays! Let's gather around our plates of milk. *(Or, you may decide to have your children just watch you do the experiment.)*

We're going to add one drop each of these four food colorings into the center of the milk. *(Add the drops close together into the center of yours and each child's milk, if you're allowing each to have his/her own.)* Now, let's place the tip of the cotton swab in the center of the food-coloring droplets. *(Nothing will happen.)* Nothing happened, did it?

Now, let's see what will happen when we place a drop of liquid dish soap on the *other* end of our cotton swabs, touch the tip with the soap on it into the middle of the milk, and hold it there. Wow, look at that! The colors are exploding. It's like the Fourth of July in a plate of milk! By using other cotton swabs with more soap on them, we can experiment with the effects of placing the cotton swab at different places in the milk to see what happens.

Did you notice that the colors in the milk continue to move even when the cotton swab is removed?

Final Word:

So, let's think about this for a moment. When we used the end of the cotton swab that didn't have soap on it, nothing happened. But, when we added soap to the end of it, something changed in the milk. It's the same with our faith. When we release our faith, circumstances begin to change. And, just as the milk kept moving after the cotton swab was removed, your faith is still in action!

DAY 3: GIVING LESSON

SEE WITH YOUR FAITH EYES!

Suggested Time: 10 minutes

Offering Scripture: Faith is the confidence that what we hope for will actually happen; it gives us assurance about things we cannot see. —Hebrews 11:1 NLT-96

Lesson Instructions:

Does anyone have anything you're believing God for? *(Allow children to share.)* You know, God delights to give us the desires of our hearts because we are His kids, and He loves us! Have any of you ever sown seed for the things you're believing for?

Did you know that Commander Kellie was about your age when she learned how to use her faith? Her first faith project, along with her brother, was a boat—the big kind, not a toy boat! Commander Kellie was 7 years old and her brother was 5 years old when they started on their faith project with God!

First, they wrote out an agreement with the Lord, standing on Matthew 18:19, which says that if two people agree in faith, they can have what they ask for.

In their agreement, they asked the Lord for the PERFECT boat. Then, John, Kellie and their mom and dad prayed, agreed and signed the agreement.

Then they put their agreement on the refrigerator, and every time they passed by, they touched it and said, "Thank God for the boat!" They were thanking Jesus because they knew that it was ALREADY theirs and on its way to them!

Not long after that, they got <u>two</u> boats that were EXACTLY what they had asked for!

But that wasn't the last time Commander Kellie used her faith. She said: "When I was about 10, I wanted a new bicycle. Daddy asked me if I knew what I wanted, and if I had a picture of it. I told him that I wanted a Schwinn 10-speed. He asked me if I had my seed to sow for it. I remember bringing him my money that I had saved. And, not long afterward, I remember going to the store and getting to pick out the exact bike I wanted!"

Another time, Commander Kellie was believing God for a horse! By the time she was 12, she was already a practiced believer. She asked her dad first if it was OK for her to believe for a horse. Well, of course her dad was always wise enough to never put down his children's faith. But, he thought to himself, *What am I going to do with a horse? We don't have any place for a horse!*

But, he went ahead and told her that she could have whatever she believed for. Not long after, a lady they had never met called from California to say that the Lord had told her that she knew her horse was to be Kellie Copeland's horse! Commander Kellie and her dad rejoiced, but he thought again: *Where am I going to put this horse?*

But just a day later, someone else called and asked her dad if he needed a place to keep a horse. Isn't God good? No one outside Commander Kellie's family even knew she wanted a horse! God gave her a *thoroughbred racehorse* AND provided a place to keep it!

So, do you think God knows how to take care of His kids? He sure does! And remember, He is no respecter of persons. But He always responds to our faith! That means your faith is just as good as Commander Kellie's but, just like she did, you have to start using it, and believe that God is your wonderful heavenly Father who loves to do good things for you!

Notes: _____

_____

_____

_____

_____

_____

_____

_____

_____

_____

_____

_____

_____

_____

_____

_____

_____

_____

_____

_____

_____

_____

_____

_____

_____

_____

_____

_____

_____

_____

DAY 4: YOU-SOLVE-IT MYSTERY **THE FILTHY MECHANIC**

 Suggested Time: 10 minutes

 Memory Verse: We live by faith, not by sight. —2 Corinthians 5:7 NIV

 Teacher Tip: Punch it up by dressing up as Superkid James, and telling the story in character, changing your voice and having fun with it.

Optional Costume: ■ Superkid James could wear Superkid Academy polo or T-shirt
Supplies: ■ "CLUE!" sign or flashing light

Background:

Today, your children will hear a mystery story that they can solve themselves! Before reading this story, ask them to listen closely for clues and try to figure it out before you get to the end. **Bolded words** are slightly stressed because they help solve the mystery. For younger kids, you could hold up a "CLUE!" sign, or flash a light when a clue is revealed.

Story: The Filthy Mechanic

(Superkid James begins telling the story that takes place near Superkid Academy):

"Hey, kids!"

My friend Chad and I jumped, as a mechanic with a nametag that read "Slick" popped out from under a Super-Copter panel. The SuperCopter was in for a few repairs and we had arrived to pick it up. Slick slammed the panel closed and clapped his hands together twice.

"There ya go!" he chimed. **"I just finished. Been working on it all mornin', you know, nonstop."** He smiled. He was about 6 feet tall with peppered hair and a smile that hid his teeth. His clothes were covered with globs of grease and **he was wiping his hands on a towel, carefully wiping around a gold ring on his right hand, which spelled his name in shiny grooves.** Apparently this guy was real proud to be called "SLICK." He reached over and gulped some coffee from a **clean, white cup.**

"So," I asked, "did you get the approximator fixed?"

"Well...yes..." Slick stammered, **"but I had to give it a grease job, too.** I wouldn't have, but once I got to looking at the SuperCopter, I knew I had to. You wouldn't have flown this puppy much longer without a good grease job. You wouldn't want that now, would ya?"

"An ungreased chopper would make me nervous," Chad said. "But how much you gonna charge us for *extra* service?"

Slick closed one eye and scratched his neck. "Only $75."

I thought Chad's eyes were going to pop straight out of their sockets.

"$75! Whoa!" was all he could say.

"Wait," I said, wanting to clarify. "So you've fixed the approximator and given it a grease job for a *total* of $75—correct?"

Slick bit his lower lip, showing his teeth for the first time. "Well, now, **the approximator was $100—which I fixed last night—plus $75 for the grease job I gave it this morning.** That total is...." He looked at the ceiling for a moment and then announced, "$175."

"$175! Whoa!" Chad exclaimed. "We don't have that kind of money!"

I shook my head. "Don't forget we live by faith, not by sight," I said to Chad. "Don't let bad news shake you. Our faith is in God and He will supply our needs!"*

"Well, that's the breaks, boys," Slick said, licking his lips. "You understand: **I have to charge extra for working nonstop this morning in order to get the grease job done on time.** If I didn't put in the extra time, it would have been much less." Slick smiled again. **"It's a dirty job,** but someone has to do it!" He laughed at his own joke.

A door suddenly slammed behind us as the store manager walked in. "Hello, James, Chad. Have you met our new mechanic, Slick?"

"They have," Slick interjected. "They were just gettin' ready to pay me for fine service and be on their way."

"Except," I interrupted, "your new mechanic is charging us extra for working this morning...but he *didn't* work." Chad's mouth dropped open at my accusation.

"Is this true?" the manager asked Slick. "Did you lie to these boys?"

"Naw!" Slick rebutted. "I just finished greasin' when they walked in. I've been working all morning."

But he hadn't...and I can prove it.

*2 Corinthians 5:7; Hebrews 10:35; Philippians 4:19

So, Superkids, have you solved the mystery? Can you think of how James knew the mechanic wasn't telling the truth? Does anyone know what some of the clues were? *(Allow time for the kids to take turns guessing. If no one gets the answer, suggest the clues to them again. Finally, reveal the answer by reading the Solution, and remind the kids how James used today's memory verse in the story.)*

Solution:

"I know he didn't work this morning," I told the manager, "because he said he had to work *nonstop* on the grease job until we got here. And anyone who works with grease is going to get it all over their hands."

"I've got grease on my hands!" the mechanic exclaimed, thrusting his filthy hands at the boys. I snatched the greasy rag out of Slick's right hand.

"Right," I said, "but the grooves in your ring are shiny. And if you had *really* been working with grease non-stop, there would be grease in those grooves. Besides," I added, "that white cup you drank from had no dark smudges on it at all...unlikely if your hands had been greasy this morning."

Slick just stood speechless as Chad offered an, "All right, James!" The manager grabbed Slick by the arm.

"Well, this job is on us," the manager said, then turning to Slick, "and you and I are going to have a *long* talk."

The mechanic didn't say a word...he just kept staring at his shiny, telltale gold ring.

Notes: _____

_____

_____

_____

_____

_____

_____

_____

_____

_____

_____

_____

_____

_____

_____

_____

_____

_____

_____

_____

_____

_____

_____

_____

_____

_____

_____

DAY 5: GAME TIME — THROWING IN THE DARK

Suggested Time: 10 minutes

Memory Verse: We live by faith, not by sight. —2 Corinthians 5:7 NIV

Teacher Tip: Depending on the age of your group, you can add to each team someone holding a wastebasket to catch the balls as they pass through the hula hoop or help them hold it yourself.

Supplies: ■ 2 Hula hoops, ■ 2 Blindfolds, ■ 2 Buckets filled with balls, ■ Timer, ■ Music (optional)

Game Instructions:

Divide your children into 2 teams, with a team captain for each. If you are limited in numbers of players, feel free to adapt the game to make it fit your needs, or see Variation No. 2.

Explain to the children that this is a competition to see how many balls can successfully make it through the hoop. Demonstrate how easy it is to throw a ball through one of the hoops. Ask the throwers to come and practice a few times to gain confidence in their ability to throw the ball through the hoop. Have the team captains hold the hula hoop at different distances, and now tell the children that there is a slight catch in this game: ALL THROWERS WILL BE BLINDFOLDED! Now, blindfold the throwers and start the music or blow a whistle to signal the start of the round. Have the blindfolded throwers attempt to throw the balls through the hoops while being guided by their captains' voices on where and how to throw.

Game Goal:

The team with the most balls thrown through its hoop in the time allotted, wins!

Final Word:

Just as the captains guided the throwers when they couldn't see, God's Word will guide you and change the outcome of any circumstance you face. Learning to tune out everything else and just listen to Him will help you be able to know God's plan for you during even the toughest times!

Variation No. 1:

Many players. Do the game as directed, two teams against each other. Everyone should get a chance to throw or guide people. If you have time, feel free to let people switch between being the captain who guides, and the thrower. If you have a lot of people, feel free to hold up more than 1 hula hoop per team.

Variation No. 2:

1-3 players. Give everyone the same amount of time, and you can guide them as they throw.

Notes: _____

_____

_____

_____

_____

_____

_____

_____

_____

_____

_____

_____

_____

_____

_____

_____

_____

_____

_____

_____

_____

_____

_____

_____

_____

_____

_____

ACTIVITY PAGE · BY FAITH, I OVERCOME!

Memory Verse: *We live by faith, not by sight.* —2 Corinthians 5:7 NIV

Supplies: ☐ Markers/colored pencils/OR crayons, ☐ Safety scissors, ☐ Ribbon (curly works well) to attach your mask to wear, ☐ 1 Copy for each child (Note: For a longer-lasting mask, print on thicker paper like card stock.)

By Faith, I Overcome!

Everything looks different when we see our lives through the eyes of faith.

Instructions:

1. Have children decorate their faith masks.

2. In the blanks on the eyes, have them write what faith has helped them overcome. Examples: fear, bullying, peer pressure, monsters under my bed, etc.

3. With help/safety scissors, have children cut the eyes out of their masks, and leave those evil things in the trash.

4. Attach string or ribbon to the ends, and wear it!

Notes: _____

_____

_____

_____

_____

_____

_____

_____

_____

_____

_____

_____

_____

BY FAITH,
I OVERCOME!

WEEK 11: I WALK IN THE POWER OF MY STRONG SPIRIT

 Memory Verse: *Since we are living by the Spirit, let us follow the Spirit's leading in every part of our lives.*
—Galatians 5:25

189

WEEK 11: SNAPSHOT — I WALK IN THE POWER OF MY STRONG SPIRIT

DAY	TYPE OF LESSON	LESSON TITLE	SUPPLIES
Day 1	Bible Lesson	A Strong and Mighty Spirit	None
Day 2	Food Fun	Ginger: The Strong Spice	Oven or toaster oven, Cookie sheet, Hand mixer, Large mixing bowl, Medium-sized bowl, Sturdy spatula, Measuring utensils, Plate, ¾ Cup shortening, 1 Cup granulated sugar plus extra sugar, 4 Tablespoons molasses, 1 Egg, 2 Cups flour, 3 Teaspoons baking soda (fresh), 1 Teaspoon cinnamon, 1 Teaspoon ginger, ½ Teaspoon cloves, ¼ Teaspoon salt
Day 3	Giving Lesson	Don't Let the Devil Steal Your Seed	Hot, grilled-cheese sandwich
Day 4	Read-Aloud	The Right Stuff	None
Day 5	Game Time	Power Up	List of scriptures, Your Superkids' Bibles, Superhero attire (cape, mask, etc.), Penny prizes
Bonus	Activity Page	David's Differences	1 Copy for each child

Lesson Introduction:

Again, we're doing the choosing thing! This week's message makes me think of our fruit of the spirit lesson in Volume 2. Remember the battle between Flesh Guy and Spirit Guy? Our spirits are filled with life, filled with the fruit of the spirit. We must choose to allow the Holy Spirit to guide us. It's good for you, as their commander, to see the big picture. Connect these lessons as the Holy Spirit reminds you of them—The Sweet Life, choices, obedience—in fact last week's lesson on walking by faith is perfect to connect here. You are connecting the dots to build a Superkid picture!

One thing that keeps coming back to me to mention is "bullying." You'll know from the Spirit if this is something your kids need help with. If so, this is a good week to address it. Lesson Outline point No.1 talks about being controlled by your own ability or someone else's. This could address the bully or the victim. If our Superkids let their spirits control their actions, they won't try to control others, nor will they allow others to control them. Just be led in this. You are anointed to pull it all together, Commander!

Love,

Commander Kellie

Commander Kellie

Lesson Outline:

This week your children will learn about how to choose the spirit man's response over the flesh man's response. When we allow the Holy Spirit to lead, and say NO to our flesh, the Lord's battle in us is WON! God's guidance = God's power to be victorious!

I. WE CAN CHOOSE WHAT EMPOWERS AND CONTROLS US

a. To *empower* means to "give authority, control or influence to."

b. What do you allow to control you?

    1. Circumstances (what you see, hear, etc.) 2 Corinthians 5:7

    2. Your human nature (emotions, feelings, flesh) Romans 8:5-11

    3. Your own ability or inability Habakkuk 2:4

    4. Others' ability Jeremiah 17:5
    This can lead to becoming a bully or the victim of a bully.

c. Rely on the Spirit of God inside you. Galatians 5:16

II. DAVID WAS FACED WITH ALL THESE OPTIONS
1 Samuel 17:1-54 MSG

a. His brothers, the king and all Israel were afraid of Goliath.

b. David had faced and overcome the lion and the bear by trusting in the power of God.

c. His brother tried to bully him and put him down, but David only thought of God's ability.

d. David had a choice of weapons and the king's armor, but chose a slingshot and the power of God!

III. GOD WANTS TO EMPOWER US FROM THE INSIDE
Ephesians 3:16-20

a. Greater is He who is in you! 1 John 4:4

b. Let Him guide and empower you. Galatians 5:25

c. Your spirit becomes stronger every time you choose to let Him lead you.

d. Just as David practiced on the lion and the bear, you should practice on little, everyday things, to let the Holy Spirit guide you. Then, when a giant problem comes against you, you'll defeat it, too!

Notes: _____

_____

DAY 1: BIBLE LESSON

A STRONG AND MIGHTY SPIRIT

Memory Verse: *Since we are living by the Spirit, let us follow the Spirit's leading in every part of our lives.* —Galatians 5:25

A young teenage boy becomes STRONGER than a huge warrior giant because his spirit is fixed and steady, trusting in God. See how David walked in the power of his strong spirit when he slew Goliath.

Read 1 Samuel 17:1-54 MSG:
David & Goliath

The Philistines drew up their troops for battle. They deployed them at Socoh in Judah, and set up camp between Socoh and Azekah at Ephes Dammim. Saul and the Israelites came together, camped at Oak Valley, and spread out their troops in battle readiness for the Philistines. The Philistines were on one hill, the Israelites on the opposing hill, with the valley between them.

A giant **nearly ten feet tall** stepped out from the Philistine line into the open, Goliath from Gath. He had a bronze helmet on his head and was dressed in armor—**126 pounds** of it! He wore bronze shin guards and carried a bronze sword. His spear was like a fence rail—the spear tip alone weighed over fifteen pounds. His shield bearer walked ahead of him.

Goliath stood there and called out to the Israelite troops, "Why bother using your whole army? Am I not Philistine enough for you? And you're all committed to Saul, aren't you? So pick your best fighter and pit him against me. If he gets the upper hand and kills me, the Philistines will all become your slaves. But if I get the upper hand and kill him, you'll all become our slaves and serve us. I challenge the troops of Israel this day. Give me a man. Let us fight it out together!"

When Saul and his troops heard the Philistine's challenge, they were terrified and lost all hope.

Enter David. He was the son of Jesse the Ephrathite from Bethlehem in Judah. Jesse, the father of eight sons, was himself too old to join Saul's army. Jesse's three oldest sons had followed Saul to war. The names of the three sons who had joined up with Saul were Eliab, the firstborn; next, Abinadab; and third, Shammah. David was the youngest son. While his three oldest brothers went to war with Saul, David went back and forth from attending to Saul to tending his father's sheep in Bethlehem.

Each morning and evening for forty days, Goliath took his stand and made his speech.

One day, Jesse told David his son, "Take this sack of cracked wheat and these ten loaves of bread and run them down to your brothers in the camp. And take these ten wedges of cheese to the captain of their division. Check in on your brothers to see whether they are getting along all right, and let me know how they're doing—Saul and your brothers, and all the Israelites in their war with the Philistines in the Oak Valley."

David was up at the crack of dawn and, having arranged for someone to tend his flock, took the food and was on his way just as Jesse had directed him. He arrived at the camp just as the army was moving into battle formation, shouting the war cry. Israel and the Philistines moved into position, facing each other, battle-ready. David left his bundles of food in the care of a sentry, ran to the troops who were deployed, and greeted his brothers. While they were talking together, the Philistine champion, Goliath of Gath, stepped out from the front lines of the Philistines, and gave his usual challenge. David heard him.

The Israelites, to a man, fell back the moment they saw the giant—totally frightened. The talk among the troops was, "Have you ever seen anything like this, this man openly and defiantly challenging Israel? The man who kills the giant will have it made. The king will give him a huge reward, offer his daughter as a bride, and give his entire family a free ride."

David, who was talking to the men standing around him, asked, "What's in it for the man who kills that Philistine and gets rid of this ugly blot on Israel's honor? Who does he think he is, anyway, this uncircumcised Philistine, taunting the armies of God-Alive?"

They told him what everyone was saying about what the king would do for the man who killed the Philistine.

Eliab, his older brother, heard David fraternizing with the men and lost his temper: "What are you doing here! Why aren't you minding your own business, tending that scrawny flock of sheep? I know what you're up to. You've come down here to see the sights, hoping for a ringside seat at a bloody battle!"

"What is it with you?" replied David. "All I did was ask a question." Ignoring his brother, he turned to someone else, asked the same question, and got the same answer as before.

The things David was saying were picked up and reported to Saul. Saul sent for him.

"Master," said David, "don't give up hope. I'm ready to go and fight this Philistine."

Saul answered David, "You can't go and fight this Philistine. **You're too young and inexperienced**—and he's been at this fighting business since before you were born."

David said, "I've been a shepherd, tending sheep for my father. Whenever a **lion or bear** came and took a lamb from the flock, I'd go after it, knock it down, and rescue the lamb. If it turned on me, I'd grab it by the throat, wring its neck, and kill it. Lion or bear, it made no difference—I killed it. And I'll do the same to this Philistine pig who is taunting the troops of God-Alive. **God, who delivered me from the teeth of the lion and the claws of the bear, will deliver me from this Philistine.**"

Saul said, "Go. And God help you!"

Then Saul outfitted David as a soldier in armor. He put his bronze helmet on his head and belted his sword on him over the armor. David tried to walk but he could hardly budge.

David told Saul, "I can't even move with all this stuff on me. I'm not used to this." **And he took it all off.**

Then David took his shepherd's staff, selected **five smooth stones** from the brook, and put them in the pocket of his shepherd's pack, and with his **sling** in his hand approached Goliath.

As the Philistine paced back and forth, his shield bearer in front of him, he noticed David. He took one look down on him and sneered—a mere youngster, apple-cheeked and peach-fuzzed.

The Philistine ridiculed David. "Am I a dog that you come after me with a stick?" And he cursed him by his gods.

"Come on," said the Philistine. "I'll make roadkill of you for the buzzards. I'll turn you into a tasty morsel for the field mice."

David answered, "You come at me with **sword and spear and battle-ax. I come at you in the name of God-of-the-Angel-Armies, the God of Israel's troops,** whom you curse and mock. This very day God is handing you over to me. I'm about to kill you, cut off your head, and serve up your body and the bodies of your Philistine buddies to the crows and coyotes. The whole earth will know that there's an extraordinary God in Israel. And everyone gathered here will learn that **God doesn't save by means of sword or spear.** The battle belongs to God—he's handing you to us on a platter!"

That roused the Philistine, and he started toward David. David took off from the front line, running toward the Philistine. David reached into his pocket for a stone, slung it, and hit the Philistine hard in the **forehead,** embedding the stone deeply. **The Philistine crashed, facedown in the dirt.**

That's how David beat the Philistine—with a sling and a stone. He hit him and killed him. No sword for David!

Then David ran up to the Philistine and stood over him, pulled the giant's sword from its sheath, and finished the job by cutting off his head. When the Philistines saw that their great champion was dead, they scattered, running for their lives.

The men of Israel and Judah were up on their feet, shouting! They chased the Philistines all the way to the outskirts of Gath and the gates of Ekron. Wounded Philistines were strewn along the Shaaraim road all the way to Gath and Ekron. After chasing the Philistines, the Israelites came back and looted their camp. David took the Philistine's head and brought it to Jerusalem. But the giant's weapons he placed in his own tent.

Discussion Questions:

1. **How tall was Goliath?**

   Almost 10 feet tall

2. **David was believed to be about 15 years old when Goliath challenged the Israelite soldiers. What did David do while his older brothers were fighting in the king's army?**

   He was watching his father's sheep.

3. **How heavy was Goliath's armor?**

   a. **about 2 pounds (the weight of a pack of bananas)**

   b. **about 15 pounds (the weight of a big watermelon)**

   c. **about 60 pounds (the weight of a medium-sized dog)**

   d. **about 125 pounds (the weight of a thin, teenage boy, possibly the same weight as David)**

   Answer: d

4. **What kind of armor was David wearing to fight Goliath?**

   None

5. **Who did David believe was going to protect him in the fight with Goliath? Why?**

   The living God. Because he had a covenant with God, and Goliath didn't.

6. **How did David end up being summoned by King Saul?**

   He was the only one in the camp talking faith and covenant. He was rare because he trusted in his covenant with God more than the words of the giant Philistine.

7. **When David volunteered to fight Goliath, King Saul said he was too _____ and _____ to fight the giant warrior.**

young, inexperienced

8. **Before David fought Goliath, what else had he fought to save his father's sheep?**

A lion and a bear

9. **What weapon did David bring to fight Goliath, and who did he say was with him?**

5 smooth stones, his slingshot, and God, the Lord of heaven's armies

10. **David said about Goliath's weapons, "God doesn't save by means of _____ or _____."**

sword, spear

11. **When the angry Goliath charged David, how did David respond?**

   a. **ran away, scared**

   b. **charged toward Goliath to attack him**

   c. **stood still**

   Answer: b

12. **Where did David hit Goliath with the stone from his sling, and what happened to the giant?**

David's stone hit the giant and sank deeply into his forehead. Goliath crashed, facedown into the dirt.

13. **When the Philistines saw their warrior had been defeated and killed, what did they do?**

   a. **ran away, scared**

   b. **charged to attack the Israelites**

   c. **stood still**

   Answer: a

14. **Many times, God calls us to respond to smaller bullies (like the lion and the bear) to teach us how to handle the big ones (like Goliath). Who are the bullies in your life? Discuss any bullying you've seen, and how to stand up to it. How can you get to the place where you can stand against bullying to save others, not just yourself (like David did)?**

Sometimes, it's easier to point out bullying in others' lives—but this is a great place to admit to your children how you may have had to stand up to a bully at work or dealt with one when you were growing up. Did anyone ever stand up for you? Your Superkids may be more apt to open up once they've heard a story from your own life.

Notes: _____

_____

_____

_____

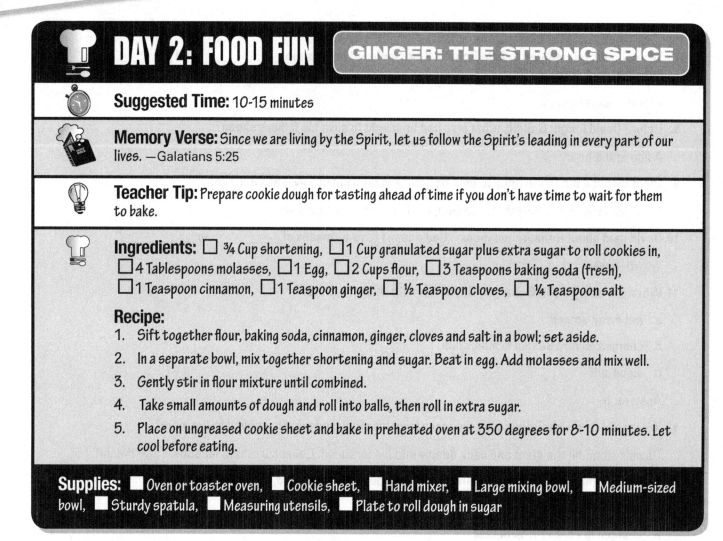

DAY 2: FOOD FUN | GINGER: THE STRONG SPICE

Suggested Time: 10-15 minutes

Memory Verse: Since we are living by the Spirit, let us follow the Spirit's leading in every part of our lives. —Galatians 5:25

Teacher Tip: Prepare cookie dough for tasting ahead of time if you don't have time to wait for them to bake.

Ingredients: ☐ ¾ Cup shortening, ☐ 1 Cup granulated sugar plus extra sugar to roll cookies in, ☐ 4 Tablespoons molasses, ☐ 1 Egg, ☐ 2 Cups flour, ☐ 3 Teaspoons baking soda (fresh), ☐ 1 Teaspoon cinnamon, ☐ 1 Teaspoon ginger, ☐ ½ Teaspoon cloves, ☐ ¼ Teaspoon salt

Recipe:
1. Sift together flour, baking soda, cinnamon, ginger, cloves and salt in a bowl; set aside.
2. In a separate bowl, mix together shortening and sugar. Beat in egg. Add molasses and mix well.
3. Gently stir in flour mixture until combined.
4. Take small amounts of dough and roll into balls, then roll in extra sugar.
5. Place on ungreased cookie sheet and bake in preheated oven at 350 degrees for 8-10 minutes. Let cool before eating.

Supplies: ☐ Oven or toaster oven, ☐ Cookie sheet, ☐ Hand mixer, ☐ Large mixing bowl, ☐ Medium-sized bowl, ☐ Sturdy spatula, ☐ Measuring utensils, ☐ Plate to roll dough in sugar

Prior to Lesson:

Prepare the cookie dough before you teach the lesson if there will not be enough time to wait for them to bake. Be sure to keep a close watch on the cookies since many ovens can vary in temperature and evenness of cooking. To save time, measure out your ingredients (EXCEPT the spices) before beginning the lesson.

Lesson Instructions:

Today, we're going to make some cookies! We all love cookies, don't we? But these cookies aren't just delicious—because they have a special ingredient, they are actually good for helping with an upset stomach! Wow! Most cookies are probably not the best thing to eat when your tummy hurts, but these cookies help digestion and with motion sickness in cars, planes, boats and more.

Can anyone guess what the secret ingredient is, and what kind of cookies we're making? *(Allow children to guess.)* The secret ingredient is *ginger* and the cookies are called gingersnaps! Has anyone ever heard of them?

Did you know that ginger is a root that's originally from parts of South Asia and was possibly first cultivated in India? In ancient times, it was prized for its effects on health and even used as a medicine before it was used in cooking. Ginger was used in ancient Rome, Africa and the Caribbean. In medieval times, ginger was brought to Europe to be used in baked treats.

Gingersnap cookies have a long tradition in Germany and England. Instead of using sugar, because it was so expensive, they used molasses to sweeten the cookies. As the two countries expanded to the Americas, of course, they brought their baking and cooking traditions right along with them. So, the early American settlers from Europe continued to bake gingersnaps with the powdered ginger. Recipes that had been passed down for generations continued to be used, and today, we still bake gingersnaps for holidays.[10]

OK, so let's make some of these amazing cookies! *(Follow the recipe given.)*

After we finish baking these special treats, our gingersnaps should turn out looking like this. *(Hold up a pre-made cookie.)* Don't they look yummy! Mmmm, they smell yummy, too! *(As children are waiting for the gingersnaps to bake, say:)* I was noticing that we only put a small amount of ginger in our cookies. Even though there's more flour, sugar and molasses than ginger in these cookies, they're still called *GINGERSNAPS!* Cinnamon is another wonderful spice we used in the same amount (1 Teaspoon) but they aren't called "cinnamon-ginger cookies," are they? Why do you think that is? *(Allow children to guess.)* Actually, it's because ginger is a very strong spice, and that's the flavor that's the most noticeable in the cookies when you eat them.

Even though you shouldn't eat a lot of sugar that's usually put in cookies because it's not good for you, the ginger in these treats makes them unique from other cookies because ginger is healthy for digestion, too!

When we're led by the Holy Spirit, God can empower us to do great things—just like the ginger in this cookie empowers the cookie to be a BLESSING to our taste buds and our stomachs!

10 "The History of Gingersnaps in Colonial Times," Lindsay Howell, ehow DISCOVER, http://www.ehow.com/info_12020843_history-ginger-snaps-colonial-times.html (4/5/16).

Notes: _____

_____

_____

_____

_____

_____

_____

_____

_____

_____

_____

_____

_____

_____

_____

_____

DAY 3: GIVING LESSON | DON'T LET THE DEVIL STEAL YOUR SEED

 Suggested Time: 10 minutes

 Offering Scripture: You must each decide in your heart how much to give. And don't give reluctantly or in response to pressure. "For God loves a person who gives cheerfully." —2 Corinthians 9:7

Supplies: ☐ Hot, grilled-cheese sandwich

Lesson Instructions:

Superkids, how many of you have realized that the devil is a big bully? If he can steal anything from you, he will. He'd like to steal your seed. Sometimes he even uses other people to put pressure on you to give.

Have you ever had something you really enjoy? Maybe a special toy, or maybe like a hot, delicious, toasty grilled-cheese sandwich? *(Take out the hot, grilled-cheese sandwich for the children to see.)* And then someone puts pressure on you to give it to them—or give them a bite?

I need someone who REALLY likes grilled-cheese sandwiches to eat this. Oh, this looks and smells so good! *(Choose one of the kids, and as he/she is eating it, do your best to put pressure on the Superkid to give you a bite.)*

Wow, you know that looks so delicious. Can I just have one, little bite? It's really not fair that you have that whole sandwich to yourself and I don't have any! I'm just so hungry, and I haven't eaten all day! I could really use a nice, grilled-cheese sandwich. Whoa, look at all that. Just one teensy-weensy bite? You have *so* much! Oh, wow! Is that really for me? Oh, thank you!

Superkids, is it fun to give to someone who is acting like that and not letting us enjoy something they want from us? When people manipulate and put pressure on us, what should we do? Should we give in to their manipulation, or not? What should we do when people get pushy?

Let's read 2 Corinthians 9:7. According to this verse, giving is supposed to be fun! If you aren't able to give cheerfully, something is going wrong!

But then, on the other hand, have you ever given something away that, even though it was your favorite thing, it was so much fun to give because you WANTED to give it? That's the way it should be at church! It's because you're in a place where you aren't being pressured to give, and you can easily ask the Holy Spirit what you're to give in the offering. Maybe that's not always true at home with a family member, or at school with a bully, or even your best friend.

Pray and ask the Holy Spirit before you give to someone like that because no one should put pressure on others to give. You don't have to point them out publicly, but make it a point to begin noticing the difference for yourself! If people are trying to manipulate you, THAT IS NOT OF GOD!

So, how can we tell the difference between being pushed by pressure and manipulation or being led by the Holy Spirit? Sometimes it might be a hard decision when the Holy Spirit asks you to give. But, even if the Lord asks you to give something that's a huge gift, or is special to you, when you obey God, He'll always fill you with JOY as you give, so that you get to be a CHEERFUL giver! When someone is pressuring you to give something away, and there's no joy after you've sown your seed—that's manipulation!

This scripture says God loves a *cheerful* giver! The devil loves to manipulate the giver and steal his/her seed. Sometimes, the person will put a guilt trip on you or beg and pressure, like I just did to get a bite of the grilled-cheese sandwich. But, learning the difference between being led by the Holy Spirit and being pushed by the devil can be a learning process. The Holy Spirit will teach you to know the difference, if you ask Him to!

So, let's pray: "Dear Lord, I ask You to teach me the difference between Your leading and pressure from the devil. Please lead me in my giving today. In Jesus' Name. Amen!"

Note: If you feel that your children have still not understood the lesson, take them through some more examples, or let them ask questions.

Notes: _____

_____

_____

_____

_____

_____

_____

_____

_____

_____

_____

_____

_____

_____

_____

_____

_____

_____

_____

_____

_____

_____

DAY 4: READ-ALOUD   **THE RIGHT STUFF**

Suggested Time: 10 minutes

 Memory Verse: Since we are living by the Spirit, let us follow the Spirit's leading in every part of our lives. —Galatians 5:25

Story:

It was early morning—before daybreak—at the boat docks of the Bay Marina. Outside, a light fog covered the sign for "Big Daddy's Fishing Tours." The only people up at this hour were the professional fishermen, so of course this included the young cabin boy, Jack, and his father, Big Jack, also known as Big Daddy.

Inside the tour company, Jack was loading the boat for a big fishing day, when in came one of their first customers: Tom.

Tom loved the smell of the ocean in the morning. He shrugged his bag back over his shoulders in excitement as he heard the sound of foghorns in the distance. Seeing Jack, Tom smiled, "Good morning, young man."

Jack sighed as he gave Tom a good looking-over.

Tom continued, "Are you going on the fishing trip this morning?"

"Yep," Jack responded quickly, as he went back to loading gear.

"Boy, I bet you're excited!" Tom said.

"Nope," Jack replied.

"For real, you can go fishing on the ocean and not be excited?" Tom couldn't believe his ears.

"Yep." Jack kept working.

Tom laughed. "Do you say anything besides yep and nope?" he asked.

Jack paused and looked straight at Tom, like he was a big nuisance. "Uh-huh," he answered, and went straight back to work.

Tom was not to be put off. "Then tell me something. Why aren't you excited about going fishing?" he asked.

"Well, first off," Jack began, "it's foggy this morning, which means we may not get going for another hour or so. Mister, do you *like* waiting around for hours?"

Tom shook his head and said, "Nope."

Jack continued, "Second, if we leave late, that means we'll get back late, and I have a birthday party to go to. Do you like birthday parties, mister?"

"Yep."

"Me too," said Jack. "And third, I work for Big Daddy's Fishing Tours, and I do this five days a week, so it's not like it's a big surprise or anything. Now, don't get me wrong, I enjoy working for Big Daddy's Tours. They're the best, but I don't get excited like I did the first time I was on the ocean. You know what I mean?"

"Yep," was all Tom could reply.

"Say, mister, are you making fun of me?" Jack asked.

"Uh-uh." Tom truly wasn't trying to pick a fight. "I was just agreeing with you. Since I got all this stuff ready, I don't want to leave late, either."

Jack looked around. "Stuff ready? What stuff?" he asked.

Tom pulled out his lunch sack. "All this stuff in my bag," he said. "Look, I have my lunch. I made a peanut butter sandwich."

Jack couldn't help but laugh. "Don't you know anything, mister? Big Daddy always provides lunch. That's the highlight of the trip when Big Daddy starts grilling those steaks and baking those potatoes. What else you got in that sack?"

"Well, I have a blow-up toy in case I fall in the water," Tom said.

Jack's hand went straight to his forehead. "A blow-up toy doesn't work for saving lives!" Big Daddy has Coast Guard-approved life jackets for everyone. What else you got in that sack?" Jack was almost too afraid to ask again.

"Well, I have my fishing equipment," Tom said.

Jack breathed easier and thought *Yes! Finally, something useful!*

Tom pulled out his fishing rod that looked like it was meant for a little kid. "See, I brought my Snoopy rod and reel from the last time I went fishing."

Jack looked at what Tom called his "fishing equipment" with disgust. "Was that when you were 3?" he asked.

"Hey!"

"Look, mister, that rod may be good for catching minnows in a lake, but in the ocean, you have to use strong equipment for catching big fish. Some of the fish out there are bigger than you."

"But I don't have a strong fishing rod!" Tom said sadly.

Jack shook his head. "Didn't you read the pamphlet? Big Daddy provides everything you need for these trips: food, safety equipment, AND strong, ocean-tested rods and reels. He even hired me to bait your hook and serve your lunch. All you have to do is fish and have a good time."

Tom was amazed. He had no idea all of that was included. "Wow, that's great! I've never been fishing on the ocean before, and I'm so excited, I'm about to pop!"

"Don't do it here, mister, because I would have to clean it up," Jack joked.

As Tom laughed, he noticed the fog was clearing and daylight breaking through. His excitement escalated as he heard the sound of a ship's motor starting.

Jack noticed too. "Hey, it looks like the fog cleared up, just in time! You're going fishing, and I'm not going to miss that birthday party," Jack said happily.

"Great!" Tom replied.

"Grab the other end of this cooler, and let's go!" Jack said.

"Hey, whose birthday is it, anyway?" Tom asked.

"Mine," Jack said with a shrug.

Tom had no idea. "Well, happy birthday! Maybe I'll catch a big fish for your birthday."

"Thanks, but I prefer ice cream and cake," Jack said, with a smile. But secretly, he really did hope that Tom would catch at least one fish. After all, he'd paid for it!

Discussion Questions:

Use these questions as conversation starters, but feel free to ask your own questions.

1. How did Jack know what equipment they would need for the fishing trip?

He was an experienced fisherman and boater.

2. What did Tom get when he bought the all-inclusive fishing trip?

A nice lunch, protective gear, good-quality equipment to use, and help in catching fish

3. What would Tom's fishing trip have been like without Jack and Big Daddy's company?

Not very good. He could have gotten lost, wouldn't have had a good lunch, maybe have drowned had he fallen into the ocean with his little, inflatable toy—and without the right equipment, he wouldn't have caught any fish!

Notes: _____

_____

_____

_____

_____

_____

_____

_____

_____

_____

_____

_____

DAY 5: GAME TIME

POWER UP

Suggested Time: 10-15 minutes

Memory Verse: Since we are living by the Spirit, let us follow the Spirit's leading in every part of our lives. —Galatians 5:25

Scripture References: Exodus 15:2; Mark 12:30; 2 Samuel 22:30; Luke 22:43; Isaiah 40:29; Acts 16:5; Philippians 4:13; Psalm 8:2; 2 Thessalonians 3:3; Psalm 59:9; Romans 5:4; Psalm 18:32; Ephesians 3:16

Supplies: ■ List of scriptures, ■ Your Superkids' Bibles, ■ Superhero attire (cape, mask, etc.), ■ Penny prizes

Prior to Game:

Plan how you will dress as Spirit Man and how you will sound. Think about what superhero, over-exaggerated actions you will do. It may be a good exercise to get you outside your comfort zone. Remember, your kids love you, so the more you put into the character, the more they'll enjoy it! Have prizes ready, and have your kids bring their Bibles for the game.

Game Instructions:

SPIRIT MAN

I am SPIRIT MAN! Unlike other superheroes,

my power comes from the greatest

and most powerful source of all!

I have been sent today to teach you

how to walk in the power of your strong spirit!

Some of you have your power source with you today!

If you brought your Bible, stand at attention

and place your Bible over your heart.

(SPIRIT MAN stands at attention, holding Bible to heart. Make sure your Superkids brought their Bibles with them. Say to the ones who have their Bibles, "Way to go!" or "Good job!")

SPIRIT MAN

God wants to empower us today.

This is how we do it!

Hold your Bible above your head.

I will announce a scripture,

and it's your job to find out where it is in your power source.

The first Superkid who locates it and comes to the front

will be given the opportunity to unlock the code

of where our power comes from.

POWER UP!

(SPIRIT MAN and Superkids hold their Bibles over their heads. This ensures all kids start from the same point.)

SPIRIT MAN:

Are you ready? Time to download

_____.

(Announce the Scripture reference as you are lowering your Bible and opening to the reference.)

SPIRIT MAN:

Way to go, _____ (child's name)!

(After the Superkid reads the verse, SPIRIT MAN gives them a prize and will lead all Superkids in repeating the verse.)

SPIRIT MAN:

Bibles closed, POWER UP!!!!

(SPIRIT MAN and Superkids hold their Bibles over their heads.)

Time to download _____.

*(Announce the scripture reference as you are lowering your Bibles and opening to the reference. **Repeat the steps until all verses have been read.**)*

Final Word:

SPIRIT MAN:

What was the one word that showed up in every scripture?

You're right! It's STRENGTH.

REAL strength and power comes from God.

He empowers us to do His work.

When we download His Word into our hearts,

His strength makes US strong just like a superhero!

(SPIRIT MAN salutes and stands at attention, holding the Bible to his heart.)

SPIRIT MAN:

Take time to power up every day!

(SPIRIT MAN lowers his hand from his salute and flies off.)

Notes: _____

_____

_____

_____

_____

_____

_____

_____

_____

_____

_____

_____

_____

_____

_____

_____

_____

_____

_____

_____

ACTIVITY PAGE

DAVID'S DIFFERENCES

Memory Verse: *Since we are living by the Spirit, let us follow the Spirit's leading in every part of our lives.* —Galatians 5:25

ANSWER KEY:

Photo # 1 is correct!

Name:_____

This week, we learned how David walked in the power of his strong spirit and defeated Goliath.
Can you see the 12 differences between the photos below? Which one is correct?

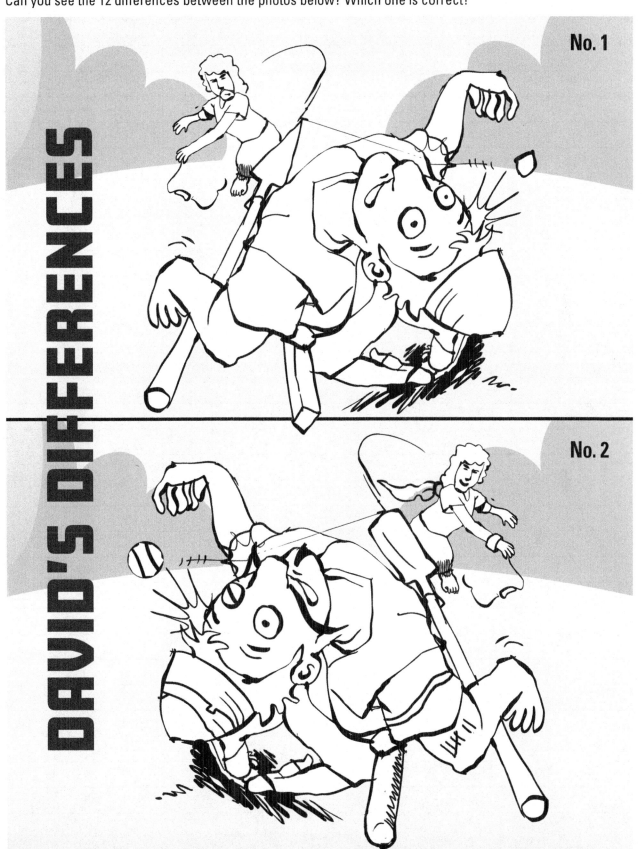

DAVID'S DIFFERENCES

No. 1

No. 2

Notes: _____

_____

_____

_____

_____

_____

_____

_____

_____

_____

_____

_____

_____

_____

_____

_____

_____

_____

_____

_____

_____

_____

_____

_____

_____

_____

_____

_____

_____

_____

_____

_____

_____

_____

_____

WEEK 12: I AM FULL OF WISDOM AND UNDERSTANDING

 Memory Verse: Wisdom is supreme; therefore get wisdom. Though it cost all you have, get understanding.
—Proverbs 4:7 NIV-84

WEEK 12: SNAPSHOT — I AM FULL OF WISDOM AND UNDERSTANDING

DAY	TYPE OF LESSON	LESSON TITLE	SUPPLIES
Day 1	Bible Lesson	Solomon: The Wise Guy	Optional Supplies: Pen and paper
Day 2	Storybook Theater	Who's the Wisest One of All?	Optional Costumes, Props, Art supplies
Day 3	Giving Lesson	Seed Faith	Pictures of Oral Roberts and his ministry
Day 4	Real Deal	George Washington Carver	Supplies: Photos of George Washington Carver (early and later), Sweet-potato fries and/or peanuts (optional), Optional costume: Button-down shirt with a real flower in the pocket, slacks
Day 5	Game Time	Locked Away	Inflatable pool/tub or bucket (something big enough for 2 children to dig in), 2 Bags of sand; more or less depending on tub size you choose, "Treasure chest," Lock with key, Tarp, 2 Blindfolds, Prizes, 10-20 Keys (see Variations to cut down on supplies)
Bonus	Activity Page	Keys to Wisdom	1 Copy for each child, Bible

Lesson Introduction:

Another great opportunity to help Mom and Dad! Developing an understanding of wisdom vs. foolishness will help our Superkids receive correction when it comes. Challenge them today: "How do you respond when wisdom comes to you from Mom and Dad? Do you value it? Do you hide things from them or do you <u>want</u> them to correct you when you are wrong?" *(Pssst…*that's wisdom!) A wise Superkid would say, "Mom, Dad, we need to talk. I need wisdom. Here's what I've done wrong."

Yeah, that's a challenging thought to a kid—asking for correction. But if they understand that foolishness is resisting wisdom and they learn to value wisdom above all else, they'll quickly become more mature in their thinking and judgment processes. As their Commander, my goal is always to graduate sixth-graders who can make wise adult decisions. This is understanding. What a powerful concept!

Love,

Commander Kellie

Commander Kellie

Lesson Outline:

This week, your children will learn about how to be truly WISE. Don't just wait for it to call out to you—YOU call out for IT! Desire not just wisdom, but also understanding, like Solomon did.

I. WISDOM VS. FOOLISHNESS

a. *Wisdom*—knowledge of what is true or right, along with knowing what to do

b. *Foolishness*—pushing away or turning your back on wisdom

c. Wisdom is like a porch light—the closer you get, the more you can see. Proverbs 4:18

d. Foolishness is like turning your back on the light—the wicked (disobedient) don't know what they stumble over. Proverbs 4:19

II. WISDOM IS A CHOICE YOU MAKE Proverbs 1:20-33

a. You can be wise or simple-minded—rely on God for wisdom, or yourself (self-confident fool). Verse 22

b. If you choose to be foolish, you are stuck with the results of doing things your way. Verse 31

c. Decide to recognize and value wisdom that comes from the Word of God, the Holy Spirit, parents, pastors and teachers. Proverbs 4:7 NIV-84

d. You'll be blessed! Proverbs 1:33

III. KEYS TO WISDOM: VALUE IT, ASK FOR IT, LISTEN TO IT, OBEY IT

a. Solomon valued wisdom above riches, so God gave him both! 1 Kings 3:5, 13-14, 4:29-34

b. Ask our generous Father for wisdom—He will give it. James 1:5

c. Listen to wisdom (and treasure, or value it). Proverbs 2:1-6

d. Obey God's wisdom. Proverbs 4:10

Notes: _____

_____

_____

_____

_____

_____

_____

DAY 1: BIBLE LESSON

SOLOMON: THE WISE GUY

Memory Verse: *Wisdom is supreme; therefore get wisdom. Though it cost all you have, get understanding.* —Proverbs 4:7 NIV-84

Optional Supplies: ☐ Pen and paper

Being wise begins with valuing wisdom and seeking it as King Solomon did. When he asked God for wisdom, God granted him riches and long life as well.

Read 1 Kings 3:3-28:
A Very Wise King

Solomon loved the Lord and followed all the decrees of his father, David, except that Solomon, too, offered sacrifices and burned incense at the local places of worship. The most important of these places of worship was at Gibeon, so the king went there and sacrificed 1,000 burnt offerings. That night the Lord appeared to Solomon in a dream, and God said, "What do you want? Ask, and I will give it to you!"

Solomon replied, "You showed great and faithful love to your servant my father, David, because he was honest and true and faithful to you. And you have continued to show this great and faithful love to him today by giving him a son to sit on his throne.

"Now, O Lord my God, you have made me king instead of my father, David, but I am like a little child who doesn't know his way around. And here I am in the midst of your own chosen people, a nation so great and numerous they cannot be counted! Give me an understanding heart so that I can govern your people well and know the difference between right and wrong. For who by himself is able to govern this great people of yours?"

The Lord was pleased that Solomon had asked for wisdom. So God replied, "Because you have asked for wisdom in governing my people with justice and have not asked for a long life or wealth or the death of your enemies— I will give you what you asked for! I will give you a wise and understanding heart such as no one else has had or ever will have! And I will also give you what you did not ask for—riches and fame! No other king in all the world will be compared to you for the rest of your life! And if you follow me and obey my decrees and my commands as your father, David, did, I will give you a long life."

Then Solomon woke up and realized it had been a dream. He returned to Jerusalem and stood before the Ark of the Lord's Covenant, where he sacrificed burnt offerings and peace offerings. Then he invited all his officials to a great banquet.

Sometime later two [women] came to the king to have an argument settled. "Please, my lord," one of them began, "this woman and I live in the same house. I gave birth to a baby while she was with me in the house. Three days later this woman also had a baby. We were alone; there were only two of us in the house.

"But her baby died during the night when she rolled over on it. Then she got up in the night and took my son from beside me while I was asleep. She laid her dead child in my arms and took mine to sleep beside her. And in the morning when I tried to nurse my son, he was dead! But when I looked more closely in the morning light, I saw that it wasn't my son at all."

Then the other woman interrupted, "It certainly was your son, and the living child is mine."

"No," the first woman said, "the living child is mine, and the dead one is yours." And so they argued back and forth before the king.

Then the king said, "Let's get the facts straight. Both of you claim the living child is yours, and each says that the dead one belongs to the other. All right, bring me a sword." So a sword was brought to the king.

Then he said, "Cut the living child in two, and give half to one woman and half to the other!"

Then the woman who was the real mother of the living child, and who loved him very much, cried out, "Oh no, my lord! Give her the child—please do not kill him!"

But the other woman said, "All right, he will be neither yours nor mine; divide him between us!"

Then the king said, "Do not kill the child, but give him to the woman who wants him to live, for she is his mother!"

When all Israel heard the king's decision, the people were in awe of the king, for they saw the wisdom God had given him for rendering justice.

Discussion Questions:

1. **What are three things that happened in this passage?**

   Answers will vary, but make sure your children understand the passage.

2. **When God told Solomon He would grant him anything he wanted, what did Solomon ask for?**

   A wise and understanding heart

3. **Why did King Solomon ask for wisdom?**

   He wanted wisdom so he could govern God's people well and know the difference between right and wrong. He admitted to God that he felt the pressure of being in charge of such a great kingdom.

4. **What did God give King Solomon, as well as wisdom? Why?**

   God also gave him riches and fame—and promised him long life, if he followed God's decrees. God did this because He was pleased that Solomon asked for and valued wisdom.

5. **How did King Solomon figure out who the baby's real mother was?**

   He knew that the baby's real mother would cry out to save the life of her baby.

6. **King Solomon valued wisdom. Can you think of certain areas in your life you could learn to value wisdom more?**

   Answers may vary. But this a great place to talk about the blessings that we sometimes take for granted in a good education (history, math, English or language classes) or being able to learn the Word of God in church.

7. **When it comes to school or life lessons we don't enjoy, most people choose to avoid them. But with God's help, a Superkid's worst subject can become a great victory! Is there a specific part of your education in which you need God's help?**

   Try to relate something in your own lives, maybe from work, parenting, household projects, cooking or other things you've struggled with and needed God's wisdom.

8. **A prayer for God's wisdom. Read Psalm 119:97-100, and pray it over your area of struggle in school. (See question 7.) Pray together, and feel free to have your kids write out this psalm. Instruct them to keep it in front of their eyes when they have to work on the subject for which they need God's wisdom. (Ex: Tape it to the front of their history book or on the refrigerator, if cooking is an area of struggle.)**

   Oh, how I love your instructions!
   I think about them all day long.
   Your commands make me wiser than my enemies,
   for they are my constant guide.
   Yes, I have more insight than my teachers,
   for I am always thinking of your laws.
   I am even wiser than my elders,
   for I have kept your commandments.

   Notes: _____

   _____

   _____

   _____

   _____

   _____

   _____

   _____

   _____

   _____

   _____

   _____

   _____

   _____

   _____

   _____

   _____

   _____

   _____

   _____

DAY 2: STORYBOOK THEATER

WHO'S THE WISEST ONE OF ALL?

 Suggested Time: 10-15 minutes

 Memory Verse: Wisdom is supreme; therefore get wisdom. Though it cost all you have, get understanding. —Proverbs 4:7 NIV-84

List of Characters and Costumes:

- Announcer: Suit or black pants, collared shirt and tie
- Dumbbell Dorothy: Workout outfit, bright colors
- Spick-and-Span Sam: Janitor, one-piece or blue button-down shirt with jeans and a utility belt full of cleaning supplies
- Techstar Thomas: Hipster outfit with laptop, headphones, tons of techie gear
- Edie Encyclopedia (also can be Eddie to change to male): Glasses, chess club-type of outfit like an argyle sweater, tall socks and skirt, (or slacks if male) and a huge encyclopedia
- Cue Card Holder (optional): wears black and holds cue cards

Optional Props: ☐Cue cards, ☐Dumbbells, ☐Wagon/dolly or suitcase to roll the dumbbells, ☐Lots of cleaning supplies, ☐Tech gear (laptop), ☐Phone, ☐Wires, ☐Large encyclopedia, ☐Pageant sash that reads: "Wisest of All," ☐Crown or hat for the winner, ☐Confetti

Supplies: ■Whiteboard, chalkboard or easel with paper, ■Dry-erase markers if using whiteboard, colored chalks if using chalkboard, or pencil (art pencils work best) and eraser, ■Black marker and rags (to blend chalks) if using paper, ■Art smock (to keep your artist's clothes clean)

Variation No. 1:

Read the story as part of your read-aloud time. Remember: Reading the story beforehand and giving different voices to each character will help bring life to the story.

Variation No. 2:

Read the story as an old-time radio skit, complete with different actors for each part. If you are limited on participants, then assign more than one part per person, and change the voice. Make copies of the skit and have each actor highlight his/her lines. Great for a large family, Bible study group or co-op.

Variation No. 3:

Act out the story as a fun skit. Perhaps your children can practice during the day (even creating costumes from everyday items) and then perform it in the evening before the whole family. Before beginning your skit, remember to introduce your cast! Great for a large family, Bible study group or co-op.

Variation No. 4:

Create a storybook theater where one or more family members sketch the story on a whiteboard, chalkboard or artist's easel as another member reads the story. Initially, there will be a few supplies to purchase but don't let this be a deterrent from using the illustrated story option! Once the supplies have been purchased, they'll be long-lasting and reusable.

To make your presentation easier, lightly sketch the drawing with a pencil prior to presentation. Time may not allow the picture to be completely drawn and colored at the time of the lesson. Erase pencil lines, so light lines are visible to the artist but not visible to your children. Review the story ahead of time to determine the amount of time needed to complete the illustration while telling the story. When the story begins, use black markers to "draw" the picture, following the sketched pencil lines. Next, apply color using the pastel chalk. Then, blend the color with the rags. Finally, cut the illustration from the board, roll it up, secure it with rubber bands, and share it with one of your children!

Story:

"Good day, and welcome to the 45th Annual Wisdom Pageant! Applause, please," the announcer, Alex Amillion said, as the crowd went wild.

(Hold up Cue Card: APPLAUSE!)

"Mirror, mirror on the wall, who is the wisest one of all? It's been a tough competition but we're down to our final four! First, we have Dumbbell Dorothy."

Again, the people cheered. Dorothy entered the stage with her dumbbell weights, but instead of working out with them, she was rolling them in a wagon! Alex continued, "Dorothy knows that using the heaviest weights will make her stronger, faster. So she carries them with her wherever she goes! Just look at those, uh... muscles?"

As Alex looked at Dorothy, there weren't many muscles to be seen—Dorothy was getting winded just from the walk around the stage!

Hopeful, Alex Amillion continued: "Next up is Spick-and-Span Sam." Sam entered the stage with a broom, mop bucket, rags, lots of cleaning supplies and a feather duster. He looked ready to clean any big spill.

"Sam is never without his cleaning products," Alex said. "He knows that you have to have the right stuff to make the floor shine." Alex watched proudly as Sam sprayed a washcloth with cleaner. But, instead of rubbing the washcloth on the floor, Sam began rubbing the cleaner *bottle* on the floor.

Alex Amillion scratched his head as Sam scrubbed away with the cleaner bottle. "That's OK, Sam," Alex said. "You don't have to... uh... scrub the whole floor." Sam scrubbed some more, but finally stood up and took his place, looking a little defeated.

Alex Amillion was thrilled to announce, "Our third contestant is Techstar Tom."

Wow! Tom looked so cool. Alex had high hopes that this could be the next Wise Guy of the Year. Tom came out in sweet spyglasses, a brand-new laptop and phone, plus so many gadgets in his ears and on his wrists that Alex didn't know what to make of it all.

"Tom knows that being a Techie star is not as easy as it looks," Alex said excitedly. Tom's gadgets swirled and buzzed with excitement. Alex continued, "You need some serious equipment to stay up to speed on the latest and greatest gadgets!"

Suddenly, Tom's phone rang. The audience was excited to see how Tom would answer it, but poor Techstar Tom was trying to talk into his laptop's keyboard: "Yeah, Mom, I can't hear you, but I'll be home in time for dinner," Techstar Tom said, with his ear to his laptop keys.

Unsure, Alex tried to cover for him with a jovial laugh, but the phone rang and rang, unanswered.

Tom still tried to speak through the laptop, putting the keyboard up to his ear, "Mom, I can't hear you, but you know my answer is always spaghetti WITHOUT meat sauce!"

Alex coughed. "Ahem." It was time to get back to the program.

"Gotta go, Mom," Tom said as he closed the laptop and strutted his stuff to stand next to Sam.

Well, Alex Amillion didn't have much hope left, but with a cheery voice, he announced the last contestant: "And last, but not least, Edie Encyclopedia!"

As Edie entered, she looked a lot nerdier than the rest and brought only one thing with her: a HUGE book—the encyclopedia she was reading.

Curious, Alex continued, "Edie has read her encyclopedia 415 times. She has committed to carry it with her until she has memorized every page."

Edie walked slowly to stand next to Tom. She was so engrossed in her book, she didn't even look up.

With fervor, Alex addressed the crowd: "Who will be this year's ruling Wise Guy? Is it... Drumroll, please."

(Cue Card: Drum Roll)

At Alex's request, the audience drummed in suspense. This was Alex's favorite part: to announce a winner. But Alex was sweating like never before. None of these contestants had truly outshone the others. "Is it..." Alex stalled, "Dumbbell Dorothy...?" Alex gestured to Dorothy as she rolled her cart of weights back and forth, as if she were really working out.

"Spick-and-Span Sam...?" Alex said in Sam's direction. Sam pushed his cleaning bottle back and forth over the floor.

"Techstar Thomas...?" Alex continued, as Thomas opened his laptop like a phone again.

"Or...is it Edie Encyclopedia"? Edie looked up from her book as she heard Alex announce her name.

Edie looked around, and it was then that she noticed everyone else. "Wait!" she shouted. "Do you guys know you are all using these the wrong way?" Her shout stopped the other three contestants in their tasks.

Edie walked over to Dorothy. "Dorothy, you have to lift those with your arms to get results," she said, as she showed Dorothy how to lift her weights.

Edie went to Sam next. "Sam, you can't rub the bottle on the floor. You have to spray the cloth with cleaner, and then scrub the floor *with the cloth,*" she said kindly as she demonstrated to Sam how to properly clean the floor.

Sam tried it himself with much better results. He smiled, and Edie went to Tom.

"And Tom, you're using your laptop like a phone," Edie said as she pulled his phone out of his pocket and helped him put it to his ear. "This is your phone—it goes on your ear." Tom was in awe.

Impressed, Alex Amillion asked, "Edie, how did you come by such wisdom?"

Alex really hoped she had the right answer, and her knowledge was not just a fluke.

Edie answered, "In my encyclopedia...and also just common sense."

And her answer was good enough for Alex Amillion to call it: "Well, there it is, folks," Alex announced proudly. "It looks like the wise guy of the year goes to...Edie Encyclopedia!"

(Cue Card: APPLAUSE!)

The crowd went wild, and confetti fell from the ceiling. Edie stepped forward as Alex proudly presented her with a sash and crown. "Take your walk, Edie!" Alex said while guiding her in her wisdom walk around the stage. Edie waved and blushed, all the time knowing, from her reading, that it was paper confetti and not metallic confetti that was being tossed from the ceiling.

Alex Amillion stood proudly and waited center stage. "Only *you* have understood how to apply the wisdom that you have learned, Edie." Alex raised Edie's hand in the air. "Give it up one last time for Edie Encyclopedia!"

Even the other contestants clapped exuberantly. Edie truly had shown she was the wisest of them all.

(Cue Card: APPLAUSE!)

THE END

Notes: _____

_____

_____

_____

_____

_____

_____

_____

_____

_____

_____

_____

_____

_____

_____

_____

_____

_____

DAY 3: GIVING LESSON

SEED FAITH

 Suggested Time: 10 minutes

 Offering Scripture: Don't be misled—you cannot mock the justice of God. You will always harvest what you plant. —Galatians 6:7

 Teacher Tip: Bringing in pictures of Oral Roberts and some of his accomplishments is a fun way to make this Giving Lesson more exciting.

Supplies: ■ Pictures of Oral Roberts and his ministry

Lesson Instructions:

Has anyone ever heard of *seed faith?* Everything in life begins with a seed, even the things we receive by faith. Genesis 8:22 says, "While the earth remains, seedtime and harvest...shall not cease" (KJV). You can see from this scripture that the law of seedtime and harvest, planting and reaping, giving and receiving won't change as long as there is an earth.[11] So, when you sow a seed, you'll always reap a harvest of what you've sown.

Does anyone know which man in the last 100 years, has brought the principle of seedtime and harvest to people's attention? I'm going to give you some hints, and let's see if you can tell me who you think it might be.

This man was persecuted (treated really badly) for saying "God is a good God." He was also known for saying, "Something GOOD is going to happen to you," and, "Expect a miracle." He was a man of great faith who had a worldwide ministry, and he used the principle of seed faith to build a university in Tulsa, Oklahoma.

Can anyone guess who this man is? *(Give children time to guess.)*

The man's name is Oral Roberts.

When he began his ministry, he had nothing. He didn't even have enough money to pay rent for a house. He, along with his wife and children, were living with a family from their church that was nice enough to let them live there for free. But it was very squished and miserable with two families in one small, two-bedroom house. Yikes!

It got so bad, Oral's wife said that if he didn't get them a house by the next day, she was going to take the kids home to her parents' house until he got them a place to live.

So, Oral Roberts was under great pressure to find an answer. That night, in their church service, he preached like never before. When it came time for the offering, God led him to take an offering for a parsonage (a place for a church's minister to live).

God also told him to begin the offering by giving his entire week's paycheck in the offering! This was all the money that he had for his family for the next week. But he knew that if he obeyed God, he would be blessed. So, Oral Roberts gave his whole paycheck, which was $55.

Then, something amazing happened! People in his congregation began to give and give. When the offering time was over, there was enough money in the offering for a down payment on a house!

When Oral got home, his wife was excited about the news of having a parsonage, but when he told her that he had given his entire week's paycheck, she was upset. She didn't know how they were going to feed their family the next week without grocery money.

They went to sleep that night, but his wife was very angry with him. Then, at about 4 a.m., there was a knock on the door, and when Oral opened the door, there was a farmer standing outside. He told Oral that the Lord instructed him to dig some money up from his yard and give it to Oral. Then, the farmer handed Oral four $100 bills. That was more than seven times what Oral had given in the offering!

Then, the farmer said something to Oral that changed his life forever because it revealed to him the principle of SEED FAITH. The farmer said, "I want to tell you why I gave you this money. I'm a wheat farmer, and I know I have to plant a seed to get a harvest in my wheat field. This $400 is not just money. It's a seed of my faith I am sowing to the Lord to get my own needs met."[12]

Oral's faith rose up when he heard the farmer's words, and he realized that the man had caught on to a powerful biblical principle: **You have to sow a seed to expect a harvest.**

Oral began to understand that this principle applied to everything he was believing God for.

Galatians 6:7 says, "Don't be misled—you cannot mock the justice of God. You will always harvest what you plant."

Oral began to share this principle of seed faith with the world. In fact, the principle of seed faith is so widely known today because of Oral Roberts' teaching about it. At the time, he was persecuted for sharing this message that you can reap a harvest of what you sow. But, of course, he continued to share it because it was not his truth, but God's!

---

11 "Seed Faith," Richard Roberts, Oral Roberts Ministries, 2016, http://oralroberts.com/teaching/seed-faith/ (4/6/16).

12 *Seed Faith 2000,* Oral Roberts (Tulsa: Oral Roberts Ministries) p. 17.

Notes: _____

_____

_____

_____

_____

_____

_____

_____

_____

_____

_____

_____

_____

DAY 4: REAL DEAL

GEORGE WASHINGTON CARVER

 Memory Verse: Wisdom is supreme; therefore get wisdom. Though it cost all you have, get understanding. —Proverbs 4:7 NIV-84

 Concept: Highlighting an interesting historical place, figure, or event that illustrates the theme of the day. The theme of the day is wisdom and understanding.

 Teacher Tip: This segment has many possible variations. Choose the best that fits your family and have fun! Become as familiar with the script as possible, prior to instructing this lesson.

Supplies: ☐ Photos of George Washington Carver (early and later), ☐ Sweet-potato fries and/or peanuts to eat as a snack (optional)

Optional Costume: ☐ Button-down shirt with a real flower in the pocket, slacks

Intro:

Today, we're learning about a great man who one American president called "a great friend of the American farmer. He was a true genius."

Lesson:

Does anyone know what *crop rotation* is? The man we are learning about today perfected this idea and saved the whole part of his country from poverty and ruin.

Crop rotation is the planting of different crops after you have harvested one kind of crop, to allow the soil to replenish. Different crops use different nutrients in the soil. When you keep planting the same crop over and over again, the soil gets depleted and the crops become unhealthy. Planting different crops helps the soil to get better so all the crops grow better.

Isn't that smart? The man we will learn about is also famous for his work with peanuts and sweet potatoes.

Can anyone guess who it is? *(Allow children to guess.)*

His name is George Washington Carver.

About George Washington Carver
Humble Beginnings:

George Washington Carver was born a slave in Diamond Grove, Kansas, in 1864. His owners were Moses and Susan Carver.

When he was just a baby, George and his mom were stolen by slave traders in the night. They found George, but his mom was never found.

The Carvers raised George and his brother James as their own kids. When George was young, the Civil War ended and he was freed, so he grew up as Susan and Moses' foster child.

At a young age, George got a disease called whooping cough, which made him very weak as a growing boy, so, he couldn't do hard, manual labor on the Carvers' farm. He mostly did housework and worked in the garden. Even as a young boy, they called him the "plant doctor" because of his skill in planting and growing his little garden.

George learned to read, write, draw and play music at an early age. He was constantly learning. He valued learning and wisdom a great deal.

At 10 years old, George started formal schooling, but within just ONE year he learned all that the teacher could teach him!

He Highly Valued Wisdom and Knowledge:

There was no one else to teach George in their small town, so at just 12 years old, he moved from home to continue his education. He worked his way through school for the next seven years, doing laundry and housework, just so he could continue his education. Finally, he received his high-school diploma in Minneapolis, Kansas.

This was a big deal for any student, and an EXTRAORDINARY occurrence for an African-American person at that time!

All southern colleges were closed to African-Americans during this period in American history, but George was not deterred! He wrote to a northern university where he was ACCEPTED and received a SCHOLARSHIP!

He used all his savings to get to his new school in the north, but when he got there, he was refused entrance because he had failed to mention in his letter to the school that he was a black man!

George Washington Carver could have become angry and given up. But instead, he believed "nothing just happens." He prayed and God led him to meet a young student from Simpson College in nearby Indianola, Iowa.

He applied to Simpson College and was accepted. George studied music and art there and then transferred to Iowa State College to study botany. There, he received a bachelor of science degree, and a master's degree in agriculture. He began teaching at the university, where he had a huge lab, many students and a greenhouse.

Booker T. Washington, an educator and civil rights activist, asked George to become a teacher at Tuskegee Institute, a smaller college with all African-American students. George said that he would pray about it first with God, and when God said yes, George said yes!

Making a Difference:

When he first started teaching at Tuskegee Institute, George had no lab, and the college didn't have enough money to even buy supplies. But resourceful George made his own supplies! He realized, through his research, that diversified farming was the answer to the South's farming problems.

Here, he started teaching on diversified farming and crop rotation. The South had been dealing with TONS of crop failure in their cotton crops because the soil was exhausted from planting cotton over and over again. George discovered that planting peanuts and sweet potatoes was a way to heal and replenish the soil, so that the farmers could have good cotton crops again. Even when the South had treated him unjustly, George ended up saving their agricultural industry!

Thomas Edison offered him $100,000 to come to work for his company, but George Washington Carver refused. He wanted to continue to make a difference in his students AND continue his work to help Southern farmers recover their crops!

Making History:

George Washington Carver was called to Washington, D.C., because the government was looking for the answer to the farmers' crop failures in the South. THEY thought the answer was to pass a law that would make it harder to trade with other countries.

George spoke last of the 12 agricultural scientists who had been called before the United States Senate to speak. Each speaker had been given 10 minutes, and when Carver first began his speech, the Senate laughed at him because of his poor-looking clothes! But when he began to give the Senate a REAL answer, they begged him to keep talking longer than the allotted 10 minutes.

He spoke for an hour and 45 minutes, sharing his ideas for healing the soil with crop rotation AND new uses for the peanut and sweet potato. He had discovered 300 products from the peanut and more than 100 products from the sweet potato!

After this, he was called to Washington, D.C., many more times during crises. He was called as an advisor to Presidents Theodore Roosevelt, Calvin Coolidge and Franklin Roosevelt on different occasions.

Outro:

George Washington Carver called his lab "God's Little Workshop" and said, "No books are brought in here, and what is the need of books? Here, I talk to the little peanut and it reveals its secrets to me. I lean upon the 29th verse of the first chapter of Genesis: 'Behold, I have given you every herb bearing seed, which is upon the face of all the earth, and every tree, in the which is the fruit of a tree yielding seed; to you it shall be for meat.'" George said, "What other materials do we need than that promise?"[13]

George highly valued the knowledge he received from his formal education in school and college, but he knew that wisdom from God is what gave the ANSWERS he needed!

When someone asked George Washington Carver how he had become so wise and what was the secret to all his discoveries, he put his hand on his BIBLE and said, "The secret lies all in here [the Bible]. Right in the promises of God. Those promises are real, but so few people believe that they are real. They are as real, as solid, yes infinitely more solid and substantial than this table, which the materialist so thoroughly believes in. If you would only believe, O ye of little faith."

Variation No. 1: In Character

Entering in costume is an attention grabber for the Superkids. Feel free to present the information as if you were George Washington Carver himself!

Variation No. 2: Interview

If you are in a co-op and have other teens or adults involved, consider having another person play George Washington Carver, and you can be the interviewer.

Variation No. 3: Field Trip

George Washington Carver worked with plants. Feel free to bring his story to life by taking your children to a garden, a park or even your own backyard. Serving sweet-potato fries and/or peanuts can also be a fun option.

---

13 *The Man Who Talks With the Flowers,* Glenn Clark (St. Paul, Minn.: Macalester Park Publishing Co., 1939).

Notes: _____

_____

_____

_____

_____

_____

_____

_____

_____

_____

_____

_____

_____

_____

_____

_____

_____

_____

_____

_____

_____

DAY 5: GAME TIME

LOCKED AWAY

Suggested Time: 10 minutes

Memory Verse: Wisdom is supreme; therefore get wisdom. Though it cost all you have, get understanding. —Proverbs 4:7 NIV-84

Supplies: ☐ Inflatable pool/tub or bucket (something big enough for 2 children to dig in), ☐ 2 Bags of sand; more or less, depending on size tub you choose, ☐ "Treasure chest," ☐ Lock with key, ☐ Tarp, ☐ 2 Blindfolds, ☐ Prizes, ☐ 10-20 Keys (see Backyard Variation to cut down on supplies)

Prior to Game:

Lay down a tarp and place your inflatable pool, tub or bucket big enough for 2 children to dig in, on top of the tarp. Then, fill the pool with bags of sand. Hide all the keys in the sand, making sure they are well-hidden. Put the prizes in the treasure chest and lock it. Now, place the treasure chest on the opposite side of the room or field. Be ready to help your blindfolded players, so they don't get hurt, and to help unlock the chest.

Game Instructions:

Choose 2 Superkids, or add blindfolds to let all Superkids play. Place the blindfolds over each player's eyes. Then, let the blindfolded children dig in the sand until they discover a key. They may only take 1 key from the sand at a time. Have the player remove the blindfold, run to the chest with the key and hand it to the volunteer. If the key doesn't open the chest, the player must run back to the pool and repeat the process until the correct key is found.

Game Goal:

The first Superkid who finds the correct key to unlock the treasure chest, wins!

Note: The game may be played several times, depending on the size of the group and the time it takes to find the correct key.

Final Word:

God never hides things from us. He has many treasures in His Word that are ready to be unlocked. Keep digging, and you'll find His wisdom.

Variation No. 1: Backyard

Make this game work for you. If you have access to a backyard, hide the keys in the dirt, and set your treasure chest somewhere in the yard.

Variation No. 2: No Sand?

If you can't find sand, use potting soil or even water.

Notes: _____

_____

_____

_____

_____

_____

_____

_____

_____

_____

_____

_____

_____

_____

_____

_____

_____

_____

_____

_____

_____

_____

_____

_____

_____

_____

ACTIVITY PAGE

KEYS TO WISDOM

Memory Verse: Wisdom is supreme; therefore get wisdom. Though it cost all you have, get understanding. —Proverbs 4:7 NIV-84

ANSWER KEY:

KEYS TO WISDOM

KEY: YOU CAN BE WISE OR SIMPLE-MINDED—RELY ON GOD FOR WISDOM OR YOURSELF (SELF-CONFIDENT FOOL).

KEY: GOD GAVE SOLOMON WHAT HE DIDN'T ASK FOR BECAUSE SOLOMON VALUED WISDOM ABOVE RICHES.

JAMES 1:5

PROVERBS 1:33

KEY: LISTEN TO WISDOM TO BE BLESSED AND LIVE IN PEACE.

KEY: GETTING WISDOM IS THE WISEST THING YOU CAN DO! DECIDE TO RECOGNIZE AND VALUE WISDOM THAT COMES FROM THE WORD OF GOD, THE HOLY SPIRIT, PARENTS, PASTORS AND TEACHERS.

PROVERBS 4:7

1 KINGS 3:13

KEY: IF YOU CHOOSE TO BE FOOLISH, YOU ARE STUCK WITH THE RESULTS OF DOING THINGS YOUR WAY AND "CHOKING" ON YOUR OWN SCHEMES.

KEY: IF YOU NEED WISDOM, ASK OUR GENEROUS FATHER FOR IT, AND HE WILL GIVE IT.

PROVERBS 1:22

PROVERBS 1:31

Keys to Wisdom:

King Solomon highly valued wisdom because he was taught to value God's Word by his parents. Can you connect the Key to Wisdom to the right verse?

KEYS TO WISDOM

KEY: YOU CAN BE WISE OR SIMPLE-MINDED— RELY ON GOD FOR WISDOM OR YOURSELF (SELF-CONFIDENT FOOL).

KEY: GOD GAVE SOLOMON WHAT HE DIDN'T ASK FOR BECAUSE SOLOMON VALUED WISDOM ABOVE RICHES.

JAMES 1:5 •

• PROVERBS 1:33

KEY: LISTEN TO WISDOM TO BE BLESSED AND LIVE IN PEACE.

KEY: GETTING WISDOM IS THE WISEST THING YOU CAN DO! DECIDE TO RECOGNIZE AND VALUE WISDOM THAT COMES FROM THE WORD OF GOD, THE HOLY SPIRIT, PARENTS, PASTORS AND TEACHERS.

PROVERBS 4:7 •

• 1 KINGS 3:13

KEY: IF YOU CHOOSE TO BE FOOLISH, YOU ARE STUCK WITH THE RESULTS OF DOING THINGS YOUR WAY AND "CHOKING" ON YOUR OWN SCHEMES.

KEY: IF YOU NEED WISDOM, ASK OUR GENEROUS FATHER FOR IT, AND HE WILL GIVE IT.

PROVERBS 1:22 •

• PROVERBS 1:31

WEEK 13: STAY TRUE TO YOUR CREED

 Memory Verse: But you must remain faithful to the things you have been taught. You know they are true, for you know you can trust those who taught you. —2 Timothy 3:14

WEEK 13: SNAPSHOT — STAY TRUE TO YOUR CREED

DAY	TYPE OF LESSON	LESSON TITLE	SUPPLIES
Day 1	Bible Lesson	Blessings Follow Faithfulness	None
Day 2	You-Solve-It-Mystery	Where Is April?	"CLUE!" sign or flashing light, Colorful skirt and blouse, jewelry, pink camera (optional)
Day 3	Giving Lesson	From Seed to Bread	Tiny seed (preferably wheat), Bread (more fun if it looks like fresh-baked loaf of bread instead of sliced and packaged), Pictures of the steps to making bread (optional)
Day 4	Academy Lab	My Compass, My Creed	Compass, Strong magnet (one with at least a 2-lb. pull), Needle, Thin piece of paper, Scissors, Cup or CD, Bowl (larger than your paper cutout) filled with water
Day 5	Game Time	Tic-Tac-Treat	9 Lunchboxes (fun colors and designs), 9 Lunch-style treats (fruit pies, cupcakes, etc.), Clipboard, Sticky-backed hook and loop fastener (or tape), 5 Large laminated X's and 5 large laminated 0's, Game-show music, Glitzy costume (optional), "Applause!" sign (optional)
Bonus	Activity Page	Ruth	1 Copy for each child

Lesson Introduction:

I have several thoughts and ideas to share with you about this review message. As you encourage your Super-kids to be faithful to the Creed, the Bible story of Ruth will be a great example to them. Get her story down into your heart, and then retell it. I suggest the following verses for you to draw from: *Ruth 1:2, 6-8, 14-22, 2:1-6, 8, 19-23. In Ruth 3, make special note of Ruth's <u>determination</u> to do what Naomi said (v. 5, 18). Chapter 4:1-4, 7-8, 10, 13, 16 and 17 tell the rest of the story. You may want to write the story out ahead of time for the sake of brevity.

This is a great place to encourage your kids to talk to you the way Ruth spoke to her authority. Ruth told Naomi everything at the end of the day! This is a powerful reminder to the Superkids. You can be used of the Lord to bring conversation back to your family!

Time permitting, you might ask how the Creed has changed the way your Superkids think, or the way they do things. Has there ever been a time when they were tempted to let go of the Creed, but held fast? What happened? Have the kids share their testimonies.

In fact, I'd love to hear them! You have amazing Superkids. Second Timothy 2:21-26 lets us know that when we are faithful, we're *useful* to the Lord. Isn't that just a code word for *Superkids on a mission?!*

Love,

Commander Kellie

Commander Kellie

Lesson Outline:

This week, your children will learn about being FAITHFUL! Stay true to the WORD of GOD (your SUPERKID CREED), and you'll stay true to GOD's PLAN!

I. WE LIVE IN DIFFICULT TIMES 2 Timothy 3:1

a. Times are difficult for people because they live like this. 2 Timothy 3:2-5

b. The Bible sounds like it was written today!

c. A creed helps you to remain faithful to the truths you've been taught. 2 Timothy 3:14

II. RUTH'S CREED WAS TO FOLLOW NAOMI AND GOD *Ruth

a. Times were difficult for Ruth, but she made a firm decision to follow Naomi and her God, and she left everything else behind.

b. Ruth listened to and trusted Naomi, and though there were obstacles, the Lord worked them out.

c. The Lord blessed her! She and Boaz got married and became the great-grandparents of King David!

III. REMAIN FAITHFUL TO HIS WORD (THE CREED) 2 Timothy 3:14-17

a. As the Creed gets more detailed and difficult, your decision to be faithful will help you live God's way.

b. Trust the Lord and His faithfulness to His Word (and your Commanders!).

c. The Word (and the Creed) will:

   1. Teach you what is true.

   2. Show you what is wrong in your life.

   3. Correct you when you are wrong.

   4. Teach you to do what is right.

   5. Prepare and equip you to do what He's called you to do. Ephesians 2:10 AMPC—(that good work!)

d. Because we are faithful, we will be useful to the Lord, not useful to the enemy! 2 Timothy 2:21-26

Notes: _____

_____

_____

_____

_____

DAY 1: BIBLE LESSON

BLESSINGS FOLLOW FAITHFULNESS

Memory Verse: But you must remain faithful to the things you have been taught. You know they are true, for you know you can trust those who taught you. —2 Timothy 3:14

This lesson tells the story of Ruth, a woman who chose to be faithful to her mother-in-law, Naomi, and follow her God as well as her instructions. Ruth's wise choices led her to have a happy family and gave her a place in the lineage of Jesus! To cover Ruth's story, the reading lesson is a little longer, so feel free to give your Super-kids a chance to help read it aloud. PLUS, the coloring Activity Page for this week is provided so you can help them stay further engaged by letting let them work on it as you're reading.

Read Ruth 1:1-9, 14b-18, 22, Chapters 2-3, 4:13-17:
Ruth Follows Naomi

In the days when the judges ruled in Israel, a severe famine came upon the land. So a man from Bethlehem in Judah left his home and went to live in the country of Moab, taking his wife and two sons with him. The man's name was Elimelech, and his wife was Naomi. Their two sons were Mahlon and Kilion. They were Ephrathites from Bethlehem in the land of Judah. And when they reached Moab, they settled there.

Then Elimelech died, and Naomi was left with her two sons. The two sons married Moabite women. One married a woman named Orpah, and the other a woman named Ruth. But about ten years later, both Mahlon and Kilion died. This left Naomi alone, without her two sons or her husband.

Then Naomi heard in Moab that the Lord had blessed his people in Judah by giving them good crops again. So Naomi and her daughters-in-law got ready to leave Moab to return to her homeland. With her two daughters-in-law she set out from the place where she had been living, and they took the road that would lead them back to Judah.

But on the way, Naomi said to her two daughters-in-law, "Go back to your mothers' homes. And may the Lord reward you for your kindness to your husbands and to me. May the Lord bless you with the security of another marriage." Then she kissed them good-bye, and they all broke down and wept.

…Orpah kissed her mother-in-law good-bye. But Ruth clung tightly to Naomi. "Look," Naomi said to her, "your sister-in-law has gone back to her people and to her gods. You should do the same."

But Ruth replied, "Don't ask me to leave you and turn back. Wherever you go, I will go; wherever you live, I will live. Your people will be my people, and your God will be my God. Wherever you die, I will die, and there I will be buried. May the Lord punish me severely if I allow anything but death to separate us!" When Naomi saw that Ruth was determined to go with her, she said nothing more.

So Naomi returned from Moab, accompanied by her daughter-in-law Ruth, the young Moabite woman. They arrived in Bethlehem in late spring, at the beginning of the barley harvest.

Ruth Follows Naomi's Instructions

Now there was a wealthy and influential man in Bethlehem named Boaz, who was a relative of Naomi's husband, Elimelech.

One day Ruth the Moabite said to Naomi, "Let me go out into the harvest fields to pick up the stalks of grain left behind by anyone who is kind enough to let me do it."

Naomi replied, "All right, my daughter, go ahead." So Ruth went out to gather grain behind the harvesters. And as it happened, she found herself working in a field that belonged to Boaz, the relative of her father-in-law, Elimelech.

While she was there, Boaz arrived from Bethlehem and greeted the harvesters. "The Lord be with you!" he said.

"The Lord bless you!" the harvesters replied.

Then Boaz asked his foreman, "Who is that young woman over there? Who does she belong to?"

And the foreman replied, "She is the young woman from Moab who came back with Naomi. She asked me this morning if she could gather grain behind the harvesters. She has been hard at work ever since, except for a few minutes' rest in the shelter."

Boaz went over and said to Ruth, "Listen, my daughter. Stay right here with us when you gather grain; don't go to any other fields. Stay right behind the young women working in my field. See which part of the field they are harvesting, and then follow them. I have warned the young men not to treat you roughly. And when you are thirsty, help yourself to the water they have drawn from the well."

Ruth fell at his feet and thanked him warmly. "What have I done to deserve such kindness?" she asked. "I am only a foreigner."

"Yes, I know," Boaz replied. "But I also know about everything you have done for your mother-in-law since the death of your husband. I have heard how you left your father and mother and your own land to live here among complete strangers. May the Lord, the God of Israel, under whose wings you have come to take refuge, reward you fully for what you have done."

"I hope I continue to please you, sir," she replied. "You have comforted me by speaking so kindly to me, even though I am not one of your workers."

At mealtime Boaz called to her, "Come over here, and help yourself to some food. You can dip your bread in the sour wine." So she sat with his harvesters, and Boaz gave her some roasted grain to eat. She ate all she wanted and still had some left over.

When Ruth went back to work again, Boaz ordered his young men, "Let her gather grain right among the sheaves without stopping her. And pull out some heads of barley from the bundles and drop them on purpose for her. Let her pick them up, and don't give her a hard time!"

So Ruth gathered barley there all day, and when she beat out the grain that evening, it filled an entire basket. She carried it back into town and showed it to her mother-in-law. Ruth also gave her the roasted grain that was left over from her meal.

"Where did you gather all this grain today?" Naomi asked. "Where did you work? May the Lord bless the one who helped you!"

So Ruth told her mother-in-law about the man in whose field she had worked. She said, "The man I worked with today is named Boaz."

"May the Lord bless him!" Naomi told her daughter-in-law. "He is showing his kindness to us as well as to your dead husband. That man is one of our closest relatives, one of our family redeemers."

Then Ruth said, "What's more, Boaz even told me to come back and stay with his harvesters until the entire harvest is completed."

"Good!" Naomi exclaimed. "Do as he said, my daughter. Stay with his young women right through the whole harvest. You might be harassed in other fields, but you'll be safe with him."

So Ruth worked alongside the women in Boaz's fields and gathered grain with them until the end of the barley harvest. Then she continued working with them through the wheat harvest in early summer. And all the while she lived with her mother-in-law.

One day Naomi said to Ruth, "My daughter, it's time that I found a permanent home for you, so that you will be provided for. Boaz is a close relative of ours, and he's been very kind by letting you gather grain with his young women. Tonight he will be winnowing barley at the threshing floor. Now do as I tell you—take a bath and put on perfume and dress in your nicest clothes. Then go to the threshing floor, but don't let Boaz see you until he has finished eating and drinking. Be sure to notice where he lies down; then go and uncover his feet and lie down there. He will tell you what to do."

"I will do everything you say," Ruth replied. So she went down to the threshing floor that night and followed the instructions of her mother-in-law.

After Boaz had finished eating and drinking and was in good spirits, he lay down at the far end of the pile of grain and went to sleep. Then Ruth came quietly, uncovered his feet, and lay down. Around midnight Boaz suddenly woke up and turned over. He was surprised to find a woman lying at his feet! "Who are you?" he asked.

"I am your servant Ruth," she replied. "Spread the corner of your covering over me, for you are my family redeemer."

"The Lord bless you, my daughter!" Boaz exclaimed. "You are showing even more family loyalty now than you did before, for you have not gone after a younger man, whether rich or poor. Now don't worry about a thing, my daughter. I will do what is necessary, for everyone in town knows you are a virtuous woman. But while it's true that I am one of your family redeemers, there is another man who is more closely related to you than I am. Stay here tonight, and in the morning I will talk to him. If he is willing to redeem you, very well. Let him marry you. But if he is not willing, then as surely as the Lord lives, I will redeem you myself! Now lie down here until morning."

So Ruth lay at Boaz's feet until the morning, but she got up before it was light enough for people to recognize each other. For Boaz had said, "No one must know that a woman was here at the threshing floor." Then Boaz said to her, "Bring your cloak and spread it out." He measured six scoops of barley into the cloak and placed it on her back. Then he returned to the town.

When Ruth went back to her mother-in-law, Naomi asked, "What happened, my daughter?"

Ruth told Naomi everything Boaz had done for her, and she added, "He gave me these six scoops of barley and said, 'Don't go back to your mother-in-law empty-handed.'"

Then Naomi said to her, "Just be patient, my daughter, until we hear what happens. The man won't rest until he has settled things today."

Ruth Marries Boaz

So Boaz took Ruth into his home, and she became his wife. When he slept with her, the Lord enabled her to become pregnant, and she gave birth to a son. Then the women of the town said to Naomi, "Praise the Lord, who has now provided a redeemer for your family! May this child be famous in Israel. May he restore your youth and care for you in your old age. For he is the son of your daughter-in-law who loves you and has been better to you than seven sons!"

Naomi took the baby and cuddled him to her breast. And she cared for him as if he were her own. The neighbor women said, "Now at last Naomi has a son again!" And they named him Obed. He became the father of Jesse and the grandfather of David.

Discussion Questions:

1. **What are three things that happened in this passage?**

   Answers will vary, but make sure your children understand the passage.

2. **How did Ruth commit to her mother-in-law, Naomi?**

   She committed to stay with her until death and share in Naomi's people and home, and follow her God.

3. **How did Ruth help provide for Naomi's food?**

   She worked in Boaz's field, gleaning wheat.

4. **Instead of expecting Naomi to provide for her, Ruth wanted to be a blessing. Can you think of ways you can be a blessing to *your* parents? (Examples below)**

   • Obey quickly without arguing.

   • Do the dishes/help clean.

   • Do your homework without being asked.

   • Pray for them.

   • Give/make something for them.

   • Listen to their instruction.

5. **Why was it so important for Ruth to listen to Naomi?**

   Because Ruth didn't know the customs of Naomi's people. She needed Naomi's wisdom.

6. **How does this story relate to our own lives?**

   Ruth made wise choices. She chose to stay with her mother-in-law, Naomi, who had taught her faith in the one, true God. And, she was faithful to that decision, but also strove to be a blessing to her. In return, Naomi saw to it that she shared her wisdom with Ruth. When Ruth valued and obeyed Naomi's instructions, she was very blessed with a kind husband, a large household, and a sweet baby who became grandfather to King David and part of Jesus' lineage.

   We can learn from Ruth's example by making wise choices based on the Word of God and our Creed. Like her, we can stay faithful to God, be obedient to our parents, and strive to be a blessing to them and others. God will always reward our faithfulness to obey and please Him, and to be a blessing.

Notes: _____

_____

_____

_____

_____

_____

_____

_____

_____

_____

_____

_____

_____

_____

_____

_____

_____

_____

_____

_____

_____

_____

_____

_____

_____

_____

_____

DAY 2: YOU-SOLVE-IT MYSTERY | **WHERE IS APRIL?**

 Suggested Time: 15 minutes

 Memory Verse: But you must remain faithful to the things you have been taught. You know they are true, for you know you can trust those who taught you. —2 Timothy 3:14

 Teacher Tip: Punch it up by dressing up as Sandy the Superkid, telling the story and speaking in character, changing your voice and having fun with it.

Optional Costume: ☐ Colorful skirt and blouse, jewelry, feminine hairstyle, pink camera
Supplies: ☐ "CLUE!" sign or flashing light

Background:

Today, your children will hear a mystery story that they can solve themselves! Before reading this story, ask them to listen closely for clues and try to figure it out before you get to the end. **Bolded words** are slightly stressed because they help solve the mystery. For younger kids, you could hold up a "CLUE!" sign, or flash a light when a clue is revealed.

Story: Where Is April?

(If you choose to dress up as Sandy, have the kids shout, "Welcome, Sandy!" as you begin telling the story.)

When my friend April gives you her word, she keeps it. That's why I knew something was wrong when she didn't show. We made plans to meet at 10 a.m. at the hot dog stand on the **east side** of Duck Park. Duck Park is a theme park—you know, with roller coasters, Ferris wheels, games and lots of people walking around dressed as ducks. Because it's near Superkid Academy, we often go there for a weekend break.

I told April to go ahead without me because I needed extra time to get ready. I have a lot to do in the morning: hair, makeup, hair, fingernails, clothes, hair, perfume, jewelry…and did I mention my hair? So, anyway, April left for the park before me because she doesn't take as much "quality time" to get ready as I do.

By 9:45 a.m., I arrived at Duck Park. **I walked to the gigantic, orange Ferris wheel at the center of the amusement park. Then, I walked to our meeting place,** the east "Quacky Dogs" hot dog stand, to get in the shade. I didn't do anything else! So where was April?

As 10:15 approached, I was getting hotter and hotter and trying hard not to perspire. Perspiration isn't the best addition to my "look." Thankfully, **the sun was behind me on the way to our meeting spot**—otherwise I might have mascara smudged around my eyes. That's so gross.

Speaking of gross, it didn't take long for the stench of warm hot dogs to waft outside the little hut. I don't know why I don't like that smell. Hot dogs have always been a mystery to me. What are they made from anyway? I don't think I want to know. Really. But I've gotten used to it. **There's a hot dog stand on all four sides of Duck Park,** and before the day is through, the smell of "Quacky Dogs" becomes a regular part of the park's atmosphere. To occupy my time, I started reading the hot dog menu. "QUACKY DOG W/THE WORKS = 4 DUCK BILLS." I giggle.

Soon it's 10:30 a.m. One half-hour after we were supposed to meet. I wonder to myself if April went to the wrong hot dog stand. But, I know that's not the case. **She's** good with directions.

So, I stood there and prayed for a while that she'd be all right. I prayed, remembering that God's Word says angels have been put in charge of us, everywhere we go. Without question, God will protect His kids.* And, April is definitely a Superkid—there's no doubt about that!

I remembered back to when we first came to Superkid Academy. From day one, April didn't mind if everyone knew that Jesus is her Lord…and I'm happy to say she still doesn't.

She frequently reminds me of what it takes to be a Superkid. She says, "Sandy, don't forget who God has called you to be.** You're a Superkid! Jesus is your Lord. You tell others about Him, you honor and obey your parents, and you listen to and obey the Holy Spirit. You've got what it takes!" I was determined to remain faithful to the truth I'd been taught.***

As I remembered her words, I asked the Holy Spirit to show me the answer to this mystery because He always knows the solution. Where was April? Maybe it was time to alert Security. Standing by the "Quacky Dogs" stand, I prayed frankly (no pun intended), believing God would show me the answer. Not only did I want to find April, but there was someone in a big, fluffy duck costume heading my way, and I was hoping to avoid a clothes-wrinkling hug.

Suddenly, like a breath of fresh air, the Holy Spirit showed me the answer. He showed me right where April was! And you know what? She was right where He said she would be.

*Psalm 91; **Ephesians 4:1; ***2 Timothy 3:14

So, Superkids, have you solved the mystery? Can you think of where April might be? Does anyone know what some of the clues were? *(Allow time for the kids to take turns guessing. If no one gets the answer, suggest the clues to them again. Finally, reveal the answer by reading the Solution, and remind the kids how Sandy used today's memory verse in the story.)*

Solution:

The Holy Spirit showed me that April was right where she was supposed to be—at the "Quacky Dogs" stand on the east side of the park. I was the one in the wrong place. When I entered the park, I went to the Ferris wheel in the middle, and then I walked with the morning sun behind me. Because the sun always rises in the east, and I was walking away from it, I was going west. That's why I ended up at the west hot dog stand instead of the east one. Soon I found April safe and sound, though I was somewhat on edge. I had been crumpled by five unavoidable duck hugs on the way!

Notes: _____

_____

_____

_____

DAY 3: GIVING LESSON | FROM SEED TO BREAD

Suggested Time: 10 minutes

Offering Scripture: For God is the one who provides seed for the farmer and then bread to eat. In the same way, he will provide and increase your resources and then produce a great harvest of generosity in you. —2 Corinthians 9:10

Supplies: ■ Tiny seed (preferably wheat), ■ Bread (more fun if it looks like fresh-baked loaf of bread instead of sliced and packaged), ■ Pictures of the steps to making bread (Ex: harvesting wheat, kneading dough, etc.) (optional)

Lesson Instructions:

There are many steps a seed goes through in the process of finally becoming bread. *(This will be most fun if you show pictures of the steps, or bring up volunteers to act out the various steps.)*

I have a yummy loaf of bread here, and it was pretty easy for me to get. I just went to the grocery store and bought it with money. But does anyone have an idea of the things I would have to buy and how much I would have had to spend so I could make it myself—if I started from the very first step of planting the seeds?

What are some of the steps in taking this seed *(hold up the little wheat seed)* to making this loaf of bread? *(Hold up the finished loaf of bread.)*

From seed to flour:

- Plant seed in rich soil
- Fertilize and water it
- Pull out bad weeds
- When it is fully grown, cut the wheat with a scythe (sharp knife)
- Tie into bundles
- Thresh—beat the grain so it falls off the stalks
- Winnow—remove the wheat from the chaff
- Grind the wheat
- Sift out any remaining bad parts
- Now we have flour!

From flour to bread:

- Add ingredients: yeast, water, salt, cornstarch, honey/ sugar, milk, shortening and cornmeal

- Mix ingredients

- Refrigerate

- Knead, punch, fold, roll with hands

- Let it rest for an hour

- Bake for about an hour

- Now we have bread!

What a huge process! I would need seeds, a field, a lot of workers and even lots of other ingredients to take this grain of wheat and make it into bread. That would probably cost thousands of dollars to accomplish on my own.

Since I depend on the farmer, flour mill, bakery and grocery store to do all that work, all I have to do is take a few dollars to the grocery store and buy it already made.

Let's read 2 Corinthians 9:10. You can see, Superkids, God promised, in His Word, that we can depend on Him to take our seed and produce what we are believing for. He said He would minister and look over our harvest from the beginning, when it's just a seed, all the way through every process, until we have bread to eat! Isn't that awesome?

But, it gets even better! God is not only looking after our first seed, but also the seeds that come after. He said He would take us from having enough bread to feed ourselves, to enough bread to be generous and able to feed others, as well! What grocery store can promise you that?

REMEMBER: God is not just talking about your seed becoming bread. That was His example of how He watches over the seed you sow. That seed refers to ANYTHING you give to Him!

So, when you put money in the offering, it's just like the seed the farmer sows. YOU become the farmer. And then GOD watches over your seed until it becomes bread—or until it is FULLY GROWN. He INCREASES what you put in, until it grows up into what you are BELIEVING for! He is so good to us!

Notes: _____

_____

_____

_____

_____

_____

_____

_____

_____

DAY 4: ACADEMY LAB — MY COMPASS, MY CREED

Suggested Time: 10 minutes

Memory Verse: But you must remain faithful to the things you have been taught. You know they are true, for you know you can trust those who taught you. —2 Timothy 3:14

Supplies: ■ Compass, ■ Strong magnet (You can get this at a hardware store. A refrigerator magnet is too weak, so buy one with at least a 2-pound pull), ■ Needle, ■ Thin piece of paper, ■ Scissors, ■ Cup or CD to trace around to make your paper cutout, ■ Bowl (larger than your paper cutout) filled with water

Prior to Lesson:

Fill the bowl with water, and cut out your paper.

Lesson Instructions:

Hey, Superkids! Today, we're going to learn the importance of a compass. Does anyone know what a compass is, why it's important, or what it might be used for? A compass is an instrument for determining direction. It often has a balanced, magnetized needle that shows you where magnetic north is. This can be really important if you're lost or need to know what direction to go if you're somewhere you're not familiar with. You can't even use a map properly unless you know which direction is north. Once you know where north is, you can find south, east and west—and get to your destination!

Did you know the reason that a compass points north is because all magnets have two poles—a north pole and a south pole? You've probably noticed that when you try to put the opposite ends of two magnets together, it's really hard because they push away from each other. Well, the earth is also a huge magnet that can affect other magnets in the very same way. That's why the north end of a compass' magnetic needle is drawn to go the same way as the earth's magnetic field. Because the earth's magnetic north attracts the north ends of other magnets, the compass needle pulls to the north.[14]

I have a compass here with me, but did you know we can make our own compass to show us the right direction?

Today, we're going to make our own compass. First, we need to cut out a piece of paper. I've done that, so here is the paper, all ready to go! We're going to insert a needle into the center of the paper, but first, as we just learned, we'll have to magnetize it so the earth's magnetic north will be able to pull our needle in the right direction to show us which way is north. So, we're going to stroke the needle at least 20 times from eye to tip across this strong magnet so it will transfer its magnetism to our needle. We'll lift it away from the magnet between each stroke.

Why do we want to use a needle? Well, needles are made of steel, which contains a lot of iron, so it will pick up the magnetism from our magnet. The more times I stroke the needle across the magnet, the more the iron particles in the needle can pick up the magnetism and be pulled in the right direction of the earth's magnetic field.

Think about it! This magnet is like God's Word—the Superkid Creed. The more I allow it to direct my life, the more it can point me to the field (place) that God has for me.

Now, we're going to place the paper with the needle inserted into it, gently on the surface of this water so it floats. *(It's best if the bowl is placed on a still surface, not held.)*

We're going to wait a few seconds, and watch the eye of the needle pull around to point north, and tip point south. There it goes! Now, watch the needle be drawn to the north again after I spin the paper a little bit. The magnetized needle will always be pulled to point toward the north and south.

So, Superkids, let's learn from this magnet. The more time we spend in God's Word, the more He can take the parts of us that aren't going in the right direction, and transform us so that we will be going in the direction He has planned for our lives.

Every decision we make to follow the Superkid Creed is like stroking the magnet over the needle—we're allowing God to redirect our lives. When we make a firm decision to do something God's way, we're letting His (magnetic) pull become stronger than anything else. With each line of our Creed, we're giving over another piece of our lives to be redirected. So, even when circumstances try to push us into a bad direction, we always go back to point the way God wants us to—just like the needle remembers the direction given to it by the magnet. It goes back to pointing north-south. Stay faithful to your Creed, and don't let other things distract you. Let God's Word direct your particles in the right direction to live The Sweet Life—God's destination for your life!

---

14 "How Does a Compass Work?" Molika Ashford, *Live Science, Planet Earth,* July 28, 2010, 1:11pm EDT, http://www.livescience.com/32732-how-does-a-compass-work.html (4/7/16).

Notes: _____

_____

_____

_____

DAY 5: GAME TIME

TIC-TAC-TREAT

 Suggested Time: 10-15 minutes

 Memory Verse: But you must remain faithful to the things you have been taught. You know they are true, for you know you can trust those who taught you. —2 Timothy 3:14

Supplies: ■ 9 Lunchboxes (fun colors and designs), ■ 9 Lunch-style treats to place in each box (fruit pies, cupcakes, etc.), ■ Clipboard (for questions), ■ Questions from previous 6 weeks' teaching, ■ Sticky-backed hook and loop fastener (or tape) to place X's and O's on the lunchboxes, ■ 5 Large laminated X's and 5 large laminated O's, ■ Game-show music, ■ Glitzy costume (optional), ■ "Applause!" sign (optional)

Prior to Game:

This is a "game series" that corresponds with the teaching series (weeks 7-12). You can use the same supplies that you did in Week 7! This includes the same lunchboxes and laminated X's and O's. Place a treat in each lunchbox, and place the lunchboxes at the front of the room—with the X's and O's facing away from the Superkids.

Place review questions on the clipboard. *(Write your own, or use the ones provided.)*

Game Instructions:

Begin playing the game show music immediately. This game is all about presentation. To kick it up a notch, use a game-show assistant to turn the lunchboxes around (like a glamorous game-show assistant would, wearing a glitzy host costume and using dramatic hand gestures).

Hey, Superkids! Welcome to Tic-Tac-Treeeeeaaaat—the game where lunchboxes go from dull to delicious!

I'm going to choose 2 Superkids to answer our first question. If you know the answer, you must raise your hand. Whoever gets the right answer first, will get to pick whether he/she will be X's or O's and choose a lunchbox. But, I'll be the one to turn the lunchbox around. *(Read question No. 1. Call on the first player to raise his/her hand. Use this time to hype things up, like a game-show host.)*

Will it be an X or an O? Let's find out!

(After Player 1 has correctly answered a question and picked a box, ask a question of Player 2. If he/she is correct, a box may be chosen. If not, the play returns to Player 1, and so on, until someone has 3 X's and 3 O's, at which time, loudly declare: "We have a Tic-Tac-Treat!" Allow the winning Superkid to open the 3 winning lunchboxes, and take home the treats as their game prize.

(Note: This game is rather involved, so only 1 round is usually needed.)

Game Goal:

Whichever Superkid answers all questions correctly and has 3 X's or 3 O's, wins!

Final Word:

When we pay close attention to God's Word, there are lots of awesome "treats" waiting for us—even better than "Tic-Tac-Treats"!

Variation No. 1: Original Questions

Questions and answers have been provided, but if you would like to write your own questions, there is a question template provided.

Variation No. 2: Dress Up

Make it a game-show night complete with a host/assistant costumes—glitzy jackets, sunglasses, dress, etc.

Variation No. 3: Applause

Have someone hold up an applause sign at appropriate moments, like a TV game show.

Variation No. 4: Brown Paper Bags

Lunch-sized brown paper bags could be used instead of lunchboxes for your game. Your children can even decorate them with stickers before your game to build anticipation.

Variation No. 5: Family vs. Family

If you know of another family or have a co-op studying *Superkid Academy's Home Bible Study for Kids,* consider joining together—and facing off—for a fun evening or dinner and Tic-Tac-Treat. It's an exciting way to celebrate Bible study and godly friendships!

TIC-TAC-TREAT QUESTIONS:

(Review Taken From Weeks 7-12)

BIBLE LESSON:

#1   Q: Jesus' disciple Peter had a rocky start, but what changed his life drastically and strengthened him into who God called him to be?
     A: Being filled with the Holy Spirit/day of Pentecost

#2   Q: What are 2 things every Superkid should be quick to do?
     A: Listen and obey

#3   Q: How heavy was Goliath's armor?
     A: About 125 pounds (about the weight of a skinny teenager or David)

#4   Q: Fill in the blank: We live by _____, not by what we _____.
     A: Faith, see

#5   Q: Who did God send to Nineveh?
     A: Jonah

GIVING LESSON:

#6   Q: Commander Kellie used her faith for 3 things. What was one of the 3 things she believed for?
     A: A horse, a boat, a bicycle

#7   Q: What was the item Commander Kellie put on the refrigerator to help her remember to use her faith eyes?
     A: A specific picture of the item she was believing for

MEMORY VERSE:

#8   Q: What does Proverbs 4:7 NIV-84 say?
     A: "Wisdom is supreme; therefore get wisdom. Though it cost all you have, get understanding."

OBJECT LESSON:

#9   Q: Why is it important to know what kind of learner you are?
     A: To help you study and learn at school, home and ALSO with Bible verse memorization!

STORYBOOK THEATER:

#10 Q: Why did Encyclopedia Edie win the pageant?
     A: She correctly applied the wisdom she received.

TIC-TAC-TREAT (10 QUESTIONS TOTAL)

BIBLE LESSON: 5 QUESTIONS

#1 Q: _____

_____

A: _____

_____

#2 Q: _____

_____

A: _____

_____

#3 Q: _____

_____

A: _____

_____

#4 Q: _____

_____

A: _____

_____

#5 Q: _____

_____

A: _____

_____

Notes: _____

_____

_____

TIC-TAC-TREAT (10 QUESTIONS TOTAL)

GIVING LESSON: 2 QUESTIONS

#6 Q: _____

_____

A: _____

_____

#7 Q: _____

_____

A: _____

_____

MEMORY VERSE: 1 QUESTION

#8 Q: _____

_____

A: _____

_____

WILD CARD: 2 QUESTIONS

#9 Q: _____

_____

A: _____

_____

#10 Q: _____

_____

A: _____

_____

ACTIVITY PAGE

RUTH

Memory Verse: But you must remain faithful to the things you have been taught. You know they are true, for you know you can trust those who taught you. —2 Timothy 3:14

Name:_____

RUTH